Shadow Globalization, Ethnic Conflicts and New Wars

A political economy of intra-state war

Edited by Dietrich Jung

LONDON AND NEW YORK

First published 2003
by Routledge
2 Park Square, Milton Park, Abingdon, Oxon, OX14 4RN

Simultaneously published in the USA and Canada
by Routledge
270 Madison Ave, New York NY 10016

Routledge is an imprint of the Taylor & Francis Group

Transferred to Digital Printing 2005

© 2003 Dietrich Jung for selection and editorial matter; the contributors for individual chapters

Typeset in Sabon by Exe Valley Dataset Ltd, Exeter

British Library Cataloguing in Publication Data
A catalogue record for this book is available from the British Library

Library of Congress Cataloging in Publication Data
A catalog record for this book has been requested

ISBN 0–415–28203–9

Printed and bound by Antony Rowe Ltd, Eastbourne

Contents

PART III
Cases of war economies 117

Contributors

Jürgen Endres is Assistant Professor at the Institute of Oriental and Middle Eastern Studies, University of Leipzig.

Joakim Gundel is associated with the Danish Centre for Development Research and is an External Lecturer at the Centre for African Studies, University of Copenhagen.

Michael Robert Hickok is Associate Professor of Central Asian and Turkish Studies in the Department of Warfighting at the Air War College on Maxwell AFB, Alabama.

Dietrich Jung is Senior Research Fellow at Copenhagen Peace Research Institute (COPRI) and External Associate Professor in the Political Science Department of Aarhus University.

Michael Pugh is Reader in International Relations, Department of Politics and International Relations, University of Plymouth, UK and Director of the Plymouth International Studies Centre. He is also editor of the journal *International Peacekeeping*.

Klaus Schlichte is Director of the long-term research project The Micropolitics of Armed Groups that is conducted at the Social Science Department of Humboldt University in Berlin and funded by the *Volkswagen Foundation*.

Francesco Strazzari is a Ph.D. candidate in the Political Science Department of the European University Institute in Florence.

Hans T. van der Veen is Researcher at the Amsterdam Centre for Drug Research (CEDRO).

Series editor's preface

This collection of essays addresses an important gap in the literature on war and the state. By focusing on the political economy of a variety of contemporary intra-state wars, it is able to ask sharp questions of several widely held theoretical perspectives about the relationship between war and state-making. These include Kant's linkage of markets to social pacification, Tilly's war-driven model of how the modern state evolved, and Kaldor's idea about new wars. While not denying that these ideas have some force, the case studies in this volume show that other outcomes are both possible and in some circumstances likely. The dynamics of commerce, the impact of aid, and the structures of capitalism can just as easily feed mafias, warlords and civil wars as they can support peace and state development. One of the strengths of the book is that it raises questions about the very idea of "intra-state wars." By looking at their political economy, it becomes clear that these wars are intimately connected to the global economy, and that without that connection they would not happen in the way that they do. It is also that connection which provides the main leverage against Tilly's model of war driving the development of the modern state by forcing rulers and ruled into an ever wider and more negotiated relationship. A globalized economy provides a very different setting for state making than that in which most Western states developed, and one that is not necessarily, or even probably, supportive of domestic peace and political consolidation. In a global economy, the links between rulers and ruled that made war a driving force behind the development of the modern state no longer work. Any warlord able to control a resource with international market value can use the income to create and sustain military power without needing to consolidate a civil relationship with the citizenry. These ideas are traced in some detail through an impressive range of cases: the war on drugs, the mafia statelets emerging in the Balkans, the Kurds in Iraq, and the Lebanese and Somali civil wars.

The studies in this collection tie together several different debates: about war, about state making and development, and about international political economy. More than any amount of exhortation, they demonstrate the rewards to be reaped from tearing down the walls that separate security studies and international political economy (IPE). Peace researchers and strategists have now by and large overcome the oppositional stances that once made them almost unable to communicate or cooperate with each other. Security studies and IPE have yet to do so despite the mounting urgency of the evidence from the real world that neither can get to grips with their core problematiques without taking on board some of the insights and expertise of the other. If this book does nothing other than break a substantial hole in that wall, it will have been more than worthwhile. Its look at the dark side of globalization demonstrates both how political and military processes are closely tied to economic opportunities, and how impossible it is to separate economic activity, whether aid or commerce, from its politico-military consequences. But it offers more than just a pathbreaking exercise in the international political economy of security. Readers also get a set of self-contained and authoritative case studies that are based on substantial field experience and cover several of the focal points of international politics during recent decades. The kinds of insights generated by these studies provide many of the necessary starting points for understanding the post-September 11 world.

Barry Buzan

Acknowledgments

Meaningful academic research only succeeds as a collaborative effort. In particular a topic as complex as the political economy of current warfare calls for the cooperation and insight of a dedicated group of researchers. I am therefore first and foremost grateful to the authors of this book. They engaged in a rather long-lasting process of producing a book whose content indeed reflects the result of intensive discussion between them and the editor. To a certain extent, the evolution of this book can be traced back over a period of almost fifteen years to when I joined the "Working Group on Causes of War" (AKUF) at Hamburg University. Since then, war and conflict studies have developed into the main field of my research. Proceeding on this way, I was fortunate to make the acquaintance of the contributors of this volume, whom I met at different stages and while affiliated to different academic institutions such as Hamburg University, Bilkent University (Ankara), European University Institute (Florence) and Copenhagen Peace Research Institute (COPRI).

It was the last institution, COPRI, that provided the necessary framework to transform this long-standing relationship between the authors and myself into a book. First of all, some of the contributors were guest researchers at COPRI, thus giving me the opportunity of close collaboration with them on a day-to-day basis. Second, COPRI was the place where we had an author symposium in September 2000, which eventually set the stage for the materialization of this book. I am therefore in debt to Professor Håkan Wiberg, the former director of COPRI, who fully supported this project from its inception. Unfortunately, by the time this book appears on the market, COPRI will have ceased to exist. Due to political decisions, it will merge together with four other institutions to form the Danish Center of International Studies and Human Rights. At this point, it remains to be seen in an uncertain future whether the excellent scholarly atmosphere of COPRI will survive in the new institution.

I also owe an immense debt to the Carlsberg Foundation, which partly funded our author symposium in September 2000. Moreover, I would like to thank Routledge for producing this book. I am particularly grateful to its series editor, Professor Barry Buzan, whose valuable comments and editorial support contributed considerably to refining the manuscript of the book. Last but not least, I owe many thanks to Catherine Schwerin for her invaluable assistance in language editing.

Introduction

Towards global civil war?

Dietrich Jung

"This day has changed the world!" Numerous commentaries on the terrorist attacks in New York and Washington agreed that the collapse of the World Trade Center marked a turning point in world history. And indeed, the scenario of September 11, 2001 still sounds unlikely. Who would have guessed that NATO would invoke article five of its treaty after an attack that took place in the heart of the United States and that was conducted in kamikaze fashion using civil airliners? The strongest military alliance in history engaged in a war against an almost invisible enemy who was hiding in both the unapproachable mountains of Afghanistan and ordinary neighborhoods of Western cities. NATO saw itself drawn into a "war against terrorism," whose territorial, political, economic, cultural and social demarcation lines were completely blurred and in which the distinction between combatants and civilians was dissolved. With this war against the *al-Qaida* network, symbolized by the self-proclaimed avenger and religiously inspired ideologue Osama bin Laden, not only NATO but also Western societies as a whole suddenly became confronted with the terrifying reality of a boundless war. Gradually, the shock of the attacks gave way to the frightening awareness of being in the midst of an armed struggle in which the balance of conventional military forces ran the risk of being substituted by a balance of terror.

Since the Second World War, Europe and North America have been almost free of direct experiences of war. Despite the rather anachronistic terror movements in Spain and Northern Ireland and the bloody collapse of Yugoslavia, the main theater of warfare has been the so-called Third World. More than 90 percent of the 218 wars that were counted in the period between 1945 and 2001 took place in Africa, Asia, Latin America and the Middle East. The overwhelming majority of them were so-called ethnic and civil wars, which tend to last longer than classical inter-state wars and which are more difficult to end by political efforts and mediation of third parties.[1] In these intra-state wars, physical force has become a power resource of religiously, ethnically or ideologically mobilized militias and their "warlords," of various groups of organized crime, or of independently acting state security units following their own particular political and economic interests. In cases such as Afghanistan, Myanmar, Cambodia, Colombia, Lebanon, Liberia, Palestine, Somalia, or the former Yugoslavia, the population has been exposed to years of violent terror and destruction, whilst the majority in the Western world has experienced the growth of personal wealth and democratic liberties.

In spite of all globalizing forces, this bifurcation between democratic welfare and protracted warfare has suggested the emergence of a new global order divided in two worlds: on the one hand, into a zone of peace in which war has been ruled out as a means of conflict among democracies; on the other hand, into a zone of conflict in which political power is frequently contested by force and economic development does not make headway. The predominance of ethnic conflict and civil war in this zone led a number of scholars to claim the arrival of a kind of "new wars." September 11, 2001, however, has drastically unveiled the superficial character of this distinction between zones of war and peace. In the US-led war against terrorism, the two zones have been (re-)united and Western security forces have become embroiled in a kind of "global civil war."

Shedding some light on the economic logic of current warfare, this book suggests viewing the terror attacks against the USA as a historical culmination point rather than a turning point. In contrast to the image given by the above-mentioned debates, the political economy of contemporary wars shows that the zones of war and peace were already closely tied together. The factual absence of war among democracies, for example, does not mean that democracies do not fight wars at all. On the contrary, with the United States, Great Britain and France, three well-established democracies have been among those states that have been most engaged in warfare since 1945. Moreover, the case studies in this book – Iraq, Lebanon, Somalia and the former Yugoslavia – prove how structures of violence in the zone of conflict are clearly connected with international power relations. All cases underline that policy schemes of reconstruction and punishment, which are implemented by international powers in order to foster the establishment of market structures and democracy, can lead to the opposite of what they pretend. Mafia-style economies, warlordism and protracted internal warfare are often the unintended outcome of international interventions.

The political economy of intra-state wars reveals a complex interplay among local, regional and international forces. The studies compiled here can partly confirm the general contention that the age of globalization is characterized by a gradual erosion of state authority. However, while in the industrialized world this development can be associated with the liberal substitution of military strife by economic competition, this idea does not apply to the social reality in large parts of the world. On the contrary, outside the industrialized North, globalization has been accompanied in the emergence of violent war economies rather than pacified market structures. The revenues of these wars are derived from a variety of local resources, as well as from ties to formal and informal global markets. Moreover, humanitarian aid, foreign military assistance, diaspora donations and international political rents are playing an ever-increasing role in these war economies.

War entrepreneurs in the zone of conflict are at the same time local, national and global economic players, investing their financial assets in the zone of peace. The analytical distinction between formal and shadow economies thereby becomes blurred and offshore financial centers provide nodal points between war economies and liberal markets. The attacks of September 11 and the detection of the financial structures of *al-Qaida* were terrifying proof of the fact that this global mixture of peaceful trade and forceful economic appropriation of various kinds will not remain without political repercussions in the Western world. In this regard, not only the economic but also the political aspects of the war against terrorism are telling. With the internationalization of anti-terror law enforcement, the socio-political institutions of democratic states become intertwined with the authoritarian political strategies of their non-democratic allies. Thus, the necessary military cooperation in the global anti-terror coalition could entail both the gradual erosion of Western democratic institutions and further impediment to democratic state building in the Third World.

The shocking and outrageous experiences of New York and Washington should not deceive us: this undeclared global civil war has been looming for quite a while. The political economy of intra-state war shows that behind the stark contrast of images, the zones of war and peace have been much more integrated than we were willing to admit. Besides the visible forms of globalization, a kind of shadow globalization has taken place,[2] contradicting all-too naïve hopes for automatic global growth of democracy and welfare. Osama bin Laden symbolizes this shadow globalization in its extreme, and the attacks against the USA could be viewed as an indication that the economic and political interrelatedness of the two zones will also lead to a growing spillover of violence. September 11 was in this sense a culmination point that revealed the inseparable fate of an emerging world society. In order to avoid a global civil war, our ability to address this dark side of globalization after the first smoke of military campaigns has disappeared will be instrumental. There is a risk that this war against terrorism will develop into a war of attrition in which the initial political causes become hostage to a protracted spiral of violence. Lacking the explicit features of classical warfare, civil wars have a tendency to absorb all relevant social resources in a system of social reproduction that is dominated by physical force. Current intra-state wars rarely know winners or vanquished; they often end in mere social exhaustion. It is these lessons of recent civil wars that Western foreign policy-makers should take into account.

The structure of this book reflects both the conceptual and empirical interconnections between economy and politics in an age of globalization.

Moreover, it puts its focus on the interaction between states and shadow states, as well as formal and informal trades in the global political economy. Subdivided in three parts, the chapters lead from more general inquiries to particular case studies, at the same time maintaining a view that tries to bridge the global, regional and local divides. The two chapters in the first part of the book provide some theoretical and conceptual ideas necessary for the examination of changes in the global political order and their impacts on contemporary forms of collective violence. After my initial remarks on theorizing the paradox of a political economy of wars (Chapter 1), Klaus Schlichte (Chapter 2) takes up the classical question of the interrelation between warfare and state building. In assessing the effects of contemporary wars on state formation under three aspects – the administration of violence, forms of extraction, and the development of state mentalities – he comes to ambivalent findings. It largely depends on their historical timing, their global embeddedness, and the depth of social dynamics whether wars ultimately do make states or lead to something else.

In the second part of the book, the global perspective forms the framework in which the authors analyze the political economy of regional and local warfare. The first two studies examine how international policies of peacemaking and peace-enforcement are reflected in local realities. Analyzing the cases of Kosovo and Bosnia, Michael Pugh (Chapter 3) shows how the different purposes and interests of international and domestic parties find a common ground in the new political "protectorates" of south-east Europe. In a mixture of resistance and accommodation to internationally imposed conditions, local actors have been able to secure their wartime positions and to protect clientism within processes of privatization and deregulation. Michael Pugh comes to the conclusion that a strange coalition between war winners and external interveners has created a kind of anti-state, undermining the state's regulation of the economy. In a similar way, Michael Robert Hickok (Chapter 4) points at the ill-fated strategy of Washington and the United Nations to stir popular opposition by economic sanctions in order to overthrow the regime of Iraqi President Saddam Husain. He argues that this concept of economic punishment and its focus on short-term objectives has not only failed to achieve its intended goals, but has also set the stage for renewed intra-state conflict over reduced national resources in a post-Saddam Husain Iraq. In Chapter 5, Hans T. van der Veen studies the dynamics and outcomes of the global War on Drugs. In this ongoing struggle, political and economic interests of states and a multiplicity of non-state actors are involved. They have been shaping an "International Drug Complex" in which drug industries and law-enforcement practices interact in a systemic way and in which the production, trafficking and control of drugs contributes to the intractability and escalation of current inter- and intra-state conflicts.

The third part of the book contains three case studies intended to demonstrate the complexities of the political economy of current intra-state wars on the spot. In Chapter 6 on Lebanese militias as entrepreneurs, Jürgen Endres describes the evolution of a particular system of war economies in which waging war has become a condition for the highly profitable economic activities of Lebanese militias. Although not neglecting the crucial political issues behind the Lebanese war, the author stresses the importance of these specific war economies, characterized by both competition and cooperation, in sustaining the violent structures in Lebanon. In Chapter 7 about the "Balkan route," Francesco Strazzari focuses on the intertwining of ethnically defined institutions, mafia-style war economies and collusive patterns between different parties and their militias which have emerged throughout the bloody dismantling of the former Yugoslavia. In mapping out illicit economic flows and tracing power shifts in the region, he paints the complex and often bewildering picture of the important role that the changing geopolitics of the routes of criminal activities have played in war-making and state-making in the Balkans. Finally, in Chapter 8 Joakim Gundel demonstrates in the Somali example how foreign humanitarian assistance has become sucked into the deep political economy of violence. While significant results in terms of saving lives in Somalia have been achieved, this chapter points at the fact that the same assistance simultaneously contributed to the evolution and sustainability of the structure of warlordism. The author comes to the conclusion that in the context of conflict and extreme scarcity of resources, humanitarian aid represents a substantial resource, or spoil, that consequently can develop into the subject of violent competition.

In the concluding chapter, I briefly sum up the main arguments of the different contributions, putting them into the broader theoretical context of modern state formation. I will argue that the analysis of the economic aspects of current intra-state wars underlines the contention of an emerging new political economy, shaping and impeding the still ongoing formation of states. The conclusions will further pose the question whether this alternation of the relation between war-making and state-making is adequately captured by terms such as intra-state or new wars. More precisely, do the findings of this book confirm the alleged emergence of entirely new types of war? Generally speaking, the following chapters will suggest a change of perspective, stressing the global interconnectedness of local wars. From this perspective the causes and impacts of new wars are neither confined to a single zone of conflict, nor are they limited by the territorial demarcation lines of war-torn states. The events of September 11 confirmed that in a dramatic way. The lesson to learn from this change of perspective is that exclusionist concepts of national security are obsolete. Both the political economy of intra-state wars and the war against terror point to the fact that in the twenty-first century security policies have to be global.

Notes

1 The statistical material concerning current wars has been taken from the sources of the "Arbeitsgemeinschaft Kriegsursachenforschung," which is based at the Political Science Department of Hamburg University. Their research material is accessible at: www.akuf.de.

2 The term shadow globalization (*Schattenglobalisierung*) is taken from Peter Lock, "Zur politischen Ökonomie der Nachfrageseite in bewaffneten Konflikten," in A. Jennichen *et al.* (eds) *Rüstungstransfers und Menschenrechte*, Münster: LIT.

Part I

Theories of war-making and state-making under global constraints

1 A political economy of intra-state war

Confronting a paradox

Dietrich Jung

> Just as nature wisely separates peoples which the will of each state would like to unite under itself by cunning or force, and this even on grounds of the law of nations, so on the other hand she unites, by mutual self interest, peoples which the concept of cosmopolitan law would not have secured against violence and war. It is the commercial spirit that cannot coexist with war and, sooner or later, takes hold of every people. As namely, the power of money might well be the most dependable of all powers at the disposal of state power, states see themselves urged (hardly indeed just by springs of morality) to further the noble peace and to avert war by mediation wherever in the world it threatens to break out, as though they were standing in a permanent alliance for this purpose.
>
> (Immanuel Kant)[1]

More than two hundred years ago, Immanuel Kant identified in "commerce" a potential force to pacify the relations among states. He pointed at an intrinsic logic of commercial relations that eventually could render the means of force dysfunctional. Not in the application of cosmopolitan norms or the acquisition of a higher standard of morality, but rather in the economic rationality of commercial exchange did Kant localize the dynamic towards peaceful relationships. In line with this "economic" aspect of his perpetual peace, a liberal tradition has viewed the evolution of capitalist market economies as a development toward overcoming the propensity for resorting to military force in international relations. In analogy to the *homo œconomicus*, so the argument goes, states increasingly pursue their interests in a contractual manner, replacing forceful self-help by a system of shared norms and rules whose observance is in the mutual interest of all actors involved. Similar to the internal pacification of national societies, inter-state relations would tend to acquire the nature of market relations in which the acquisition of resources by force has been replaced by violence-free competition among economic actors.

Taking into account the origin of the very term of political economy in this liberal stream of thinking, the subtitle of our book – a political economy of intra-state war – seems to be paradoxical. If economy means the production, distribution and consumption of relevant material resources by the means of violence-free competition through market forces, a political economy of war is a *contradictio in objecto*. Yet, as Kant already indicated, the pacifying potential of trade does not unfold automatically and it is inseparably linked to specific political structures, in his version to a republican order. Karl Marx took up this intrinsic connection between economy and politics. Drawing on the works of early liberal thinkers such as John Stuart Mill and David Ricardo, he stressed in his famous *Critique of Political Economy* the ideological character that the liberal notion of economy contains. His critique aimed at the demystification of a capitalist market exchange free of force, and he pointed at the disguised power relations behind the only formally equal competitors of the market. In contrast to liberal thinkers, Marx stressed the factual inequality of capitalist market relations in which asymmetric and exploitative power relations prevail, guaranteed by the legal and coercive apparatus of the modern state.

With his critical look at the political economy of modern societies, Marx unveiled the role of physical force behind the establishment of liberal market relations. Yet this political economy of violence has decisively changed its face. While in traditional societies the application of direct physical force was a means of both assuming political power and making economic surplus, in modern capitalist societies economic profits no longer depend on the direct application of physical force. It is in this respect that even Marx confirmed that in capitalism there is an intrinsic tendency to establish "pacified" social relations. However, in his reading, this theoretically peaceful logic of capitalism is contradicted by its violence-prone historical evolution: "unheroic though bourgeois society is, it nevertheless needed heroism, sacrifice, terror, civil war, and national wars to bring it into being" (Marx 1852: 116).

In two respects, this project on the political economy of intra-state war took Marx's insights as its starting point. In the first place, this volume is intended to show that the global evolution of market forces does not necessarily bring about a simultaneous spread of pacified social relations. On the contrary, the establishment of market economies and democratic rule in Europe was accompanied by a series of wars, and historically peaceful social relations are a permanent task rather than an evolutionary end. Furthermore, current warfare proves that globalizing liberal market forces are quite compatible with regional and local structures of violence. In this regard, history has proven wrong the myth of a peaceful modernity. There is no linear relationship between the spread of capitalism and the pacification of social relations within and between states. In historical terms, modernization and violent conflicts are almost synonymous.[2] Second, this book nonetheless acknowledges that there is a principal potential of developed capitalism to pacify the inescapable struggle for scarce resources. The economic and political core institutions of modern societies – market economies, contracted and regulated labor relations, legal representative authorities, democratic procedures and the rule of law – provide an institutional arrangement in which the legitimate application of physical force is only a means of last resort.

Recent attempts to settle armed conflicts use this historically developed arrangement as a normative blueprint for the institutionalization of peace, welfare and democracy around the globe. "Liberal internationalism" as a single paradigm provides the guiding ideology behind various efforts of peace-building operations in which a multiplicity of international and transnational actors have been engaged. For this reason, peace-building has developed into an "enormous experiment in social engineering – an experiment that involves transplanting Western models of social, political, and economic organization into war-shattered states" (Paris 1997: 56). However, the studies in this book disclose the huge gap between liberal models and historical realities of global politics, and their authors point at the telling contradictions in which policies of peacemaking might get entangled. In order better to grasp this gap, this chapter discusses some theoretical concepts in the light of historical developments. The following section relates our research project to some theoretical and methodological debates in the fields of international relations and peace research. Given the importance of the concept of the modern state, the third section briefly recapitulates aspects of European state-building and its conceptualization as an ideal type. Against this ideal type of modern statehood, the fourth and fifth sections analyze some of the problems with which postcolonial state formation has to struggle and which are visible in phenomena such as mafia structures and warlordism. The chapter concludes with a final diagnosis of the "defective state."

Theoretical debates and methodological pitfalls

As already mentioned in the introduction to this book, the contradictory face of the contemporary global political economy is reflected in the field of International Relations in debates about the emergence of a new world order. Barry Buzan and Richard Little, for instance, stated that the current international order is divided in two worlds. On the one hand, there is a "zone of peace," a highly developed "postmodern security community of capitalist democracies" to which the old rules of realism no longer apply. On the other hand, there is the "zone of conflict," in which political power is frequently contested by force and the rules of power politics and self-help still prevail (Buzan and Little 1999: 101).

This two-worlds formula is an expression of the observation that since the demise of the Soviet Union an erosion of the classical grand theory of international relations has taken place. For decades the mainstream of the discipline has interpreted international politics against the model of the Westphalian order. Ending the Thirty Years War in 1648, the Peace of Westphalia laid the foundations for an international system whose core element was the territorially demarcated state. Externally isolated by mutual claims of absolute sovereignty, the modern state is internally based on its monopoly of physical force. In terms of systemic interaction, international relations were characterized by anarchy, the absence of a superior power other than the state. The structures of this anarchical international system resulted from the particular power relations among its units, and state behavior was explained with the help of abstract models such as security dilemma or balance of power.

Concerning the course of historical events, this classical picture of inter-national politics began to falter with developments that put its core unit – the modern nation-state – in question. The plethora of economic, political and cultural transformations that has been associated with globalization has found its academic reference in catchphrases such as the "end of territoriality" (Badie 1995; Ruggie 1993), the "retreat of the state" (Strange 1996), "the rise of the virtual state" (Rosecrance 1996), or "debordering the world of states" (Albert and Brock 2000). In this broad academic discussion, Kant's republican model is echoed by the debate around "democratic peace" (Brown *et al.* 1996; Williams 2001). With regard to the zone of peace, the proponents of Democratic Peace are claiming that war has been ruled out as a means of conflict among democracies. Instead, in the zone of conflict the occurrence of various forms of intra-state war led a number of scholars to claim to have observed the arrival of "new wars" or "postmodern conflicts" (Duffield 1998; Kaldor 1999; Laquer 1996). Within this framework, some studies also reveal a tendency on the part of great democratic powers to insulate some peripheral states rather than to integrate them into the global system.

It is one concern of this book to argue against the superficial character of an alleged clear-cut division between peace and war.[3] Contrary to the image given by academic debates, a global political economy of current warfare shows that the zones of peace and conflict are inseparably tied together. The factual absence of war among democracies, for example, does not mean that democracies do not fight wars. On the contrary, the United States, Great Britain and France, three well-established democracies, are among those states that have been most engaged in warfare since 1945 (cf. Gantzel and Schwinghammer 2000). Moreover, Michael Pugh (Chapter 3) and Michael Robert Hickok (Chapter 4) prove how structures of violence in the zone of conflict are inseparably tied to international power relations. Both authors underline that policy schemes of reconstruction and punishment that are implemented by democratically organized great international powers can cause the opposite of what they pretend to do. Thus, mafia-style economies and protracted internal warfare are often a result of international interventions which are actually claiming to foster the establishment of market structures and democracy. In this respect, it could even be stated that representatives of the zone of peace create for themselves their so-called "rogue state" adversaries in the zone of conflict.

The second major concern of this book is of a more theoretical and methodological nature. In recent years, not only new empirical patterns of world politics have caused cracks in the formerly firm pillars of international relations theory, but the gradually converging schools of neorealism and neoliberalism have also had to face the competition of a new powerful stream of theoretical reasoning. With the advent of a new world-order, a "sociological turn" has been contesting the theoretical domains of realism and liberal institutionalism (Guzzini 2000: 149). In replacing the "geopolitical gaze" (Tuathail 1996: 25) on international politics by the new catchword of identity, constructivist theories have made a major inroad in international relations (IR) theory. With their "idealist ontology," constructivists are seriously challenging traditional fixations of neorealist and neoliberal theory on viewing the structures of the international system as a mere distribution of capabilities and interests (Wendt 1999: 5). This trend toward addressing international affairs as matters of identity is clearly visible in the aforementioned academic debates. Whether we look at studies on the politics of transnational integration or at studies on ethno-national fragmentation, it seems to be identity that matters.

Particularly in the field of peace and conflict studies, both academic and public discourses have a tendency to overemphasize ideational aspects in explaining current warfare. Given the decades-long dominance of realist explanations of war, basing their analyses almost exclusively on the material capabilities and the respective interests of warring actors, the ideational turn certainly has its merits. In particular, aspects of ethno-national strife, such as the mobilization of public support and the legitimization of violence, demand approaches that include ideational factors in their understanding of the violent escalation of conflicts. It is in this sense that intra-state wars often feed on cultural differences that in the course of conflict tend to mutually enhance each other. However, there is also a danger. With their focus on ethnicity, a majority of recent studies run the risk of generally disregarding the material background of violent conflicts. Therefore, this examination of intra-state wars from the perspective of their political economy intends to stress that it is not only identity that matters, but that ethno-national conflicts reflect a complex historical interplay of material and ideational factors in the violence-prone process of global modernization.[4]

In order to grasp the complexity of current intra-state wars, we also must be aware of methodological difficulties caused by the uneasy relationship between the instruments and objects of our studies. Taking Kant's and Marx's theoretical assumptions seriously, we have to recognize that the internal logic of our analytical categories might not correspond to the historical realities of armed conflicts. To a certain extent our conceptual frameworks produce a manner of *in vitro* social relations, based on ideal types and clear distinctions between different levels of analysis. Historical developments, however, distort this *in vitro* condition in temporal and spatial respects. Thus, the conceptual logic is confronted with historical paradoxes. The simultaneous existence of interdependent zones of peace and conflict, or state formation and state decay, as well as of processes of cultural homogenization and fragmentation, are just some cases in point for these paradoxes with which our research efforts have to deal.

This problematic relationship between concepts and historical processes became increasingly apparent during the discussions among the authors of this book. The title itself could already lead to false conclusions. While indicating that the application of violent means is confined within state borders, the term "intra-state war" does not mean that those wars are merely internal affairs. To avoid this simplistic view, all the authors in their contributions had to transgress the classical division of levels of analysis such as international system, state, and individual. Jürgen Endres (Chapter 6) and Francesco Strazzari (Chapter 7), for instance, prove that, while militias in Lebanon or former Yugoslavia fight deadly conflicts on local grounds, they simultaneously appear as cooperative traders on the world market. Joakim Gundel (Chapter 8) shows in the Somali example that international aid organizations, which acquire and distribute resources in order to alleviate the plight of individuals in war-torn societies, at the same time turn into major resources of income for irregular armed forces. Thus, provisions to provide a minimum of social security contradict their purposes in sustaining military *in*-security. In Chapter 5 Hans van der Veen shows how individuals, societies and states become equally "addicted" to the structures of the drug economy, and how the production, distribution and consumption of drugs have entered a circular and mutually enforcing relationship with the international prohibition regime.

The general conceptual problematic mentioned above has been rephrased under its semantic aspects by Klaus Schlichte in Chapter 2 on state formation and war by his asking the question of how to talk about the state without using its language. Although current developments indicate a major shift in the way societies organize themselves politically, as reflected in the well-known discourse of the decline of the nation-state, analyzing these developments without using the conceptual lenses of an ideal type of state is barely possible. Regarding IR theory, for example, despite a rising awareness that states are empirically rather unlike- than like-units (Sørensen 2000), the state is nevertheless conceptualized according to the traditional model, i.e. as a unitary actor claiming sovereign political authority and pursuing its interests in a utility-maximizing way among other states. In a similar way, the state as a concept in political sociology still rests on Weber's definition of the legitimate use of physical force and its "twin monopoly" (Elias 1994), the monopoly of taxation. Thus the state remains at the center of conflict studies even when its empirical structures have come under heavy strains.

Not only in political but also in economic terms, the state as an ideal type still plays a decisive role as a means of conceptual differentiation. In this way, the concept of the "shadow state" is mirrored in that of the "shadow economy," or as Keen put it: "weak states are often reflected in weak economies" (Keen 2000: 28). While the concept of the shadow state hints at different forms of personal rule constructed behind the façade of *de jure* state sovereignty (Reno 2000: 45), shadow or informal economy is a label for unrecorded economic activities that lack institutional regulations and fall outside the purview of governments (Fleming *et al.* 2000: 387). In analyzing the political economy of current wars, the authors of this book had to deal with both categories in the one or the other way. Yet the studies assembled here also indicate that these clear-cut analytical distinctions tend to be characterized empirically by systemic interrelations. Therefore the general findings about the connections of shadow economies with formal economic transactions equally apply to the war economies that are analyzed in this book: "there is no clear-cut duality between a formal and an informal sector, but a series of complex interactions that establish distinct relationships between the economy and the state" (Castells and Portes 1989: 31).

Thus the state as a central level of analysis is drawn back into the conceptual considerations. While economists, politicians and academics loudly knell the death of the state, they do so while at the same time taking the features of modern statehood as their central conceptual reference in both analytical and normative terms. Ironically, globalization not only gave rise to the notion of the defective state, but it also spread the image of "state" around the globe.[5] Klaus Schlichte has drawn attention to the fact that the idea of the state as a particular form of social order is mentally well anchored in the world. Not only do leaders of militias, guerilla organizations or separatist groups often claim to be fighting for the establishment of a state proper, but notions of the state are also guiding the peacemaking efforts and democratization schemes of international and transnational actors. Their models of liberal political and legal procedures represent the congealed historical experience of the classical epoch of European state formation. Even the highest court of neoliberal restructuring, the International Monetary Fund (IMF), relies in its adjustment programs on the supervisory and regulatory functions of the state apparatus (cf. Lukauskas 1999; Önis and Aysan 2000). To a large degree, the whole debate about the end of territoriality and the decline of the state is deeply molded by the image of the state. For this reason, a brief re-examination of some crucial theoretical aspects of European state formation seems to be necessary, and the following theoretical remarks serve as a kind of implicit conceptual frame of reference for the studies in this book.

The ideal type: European state formation

Looking at classical IR theory, the state is defined as a unitary actor pursuing its interests against other states on rational cost benefit calculations (Gilpin 1981: 11–13). States form an international system in which political authority rests on territorially defined autonomy and "domestic political authorities are the only arbiters of legitimate behaviour" (Krasner 1995: 119). International relations are therefore characterized by anarchy, i.e. the absence of any overarching authority other than the state, and international politics is analyzed with the help of abstract models such as security dilemma, absolute and relative gains, game theory, or balance of power. From this IR perspective, the anarchic structure of the international system is the fundamental cause of war (Mandelbaum 1999: 26), and warfare results from the rationally calculated actions of a state or a group of states that expect economic and/or political benefits from taking action towards systemic change.[6]

In the light of the previous discussion, however, it is apparent that this state-centered system perspective does not really serve the explicative needs concerning the political economy of current intra-state wars. Admittedly, we can discern in the militia warfare in Bosnia, Lebanon or Somalia similar rationally calculated actions to those that realist theory claims for inter-state wars. Yet the fundamental problem in these intra-state wars is not the anarchy of the international system, but the very nature of the states in which these new wars take place. Evidently, the domestic social conditions of these societies at war move into the center of explanation. If Holsti's diagnosis is right that in current armed conflicts internal rule and state-hood are the major problems (Holsti 1998: 123), then the analysis of new wars and their interrelation with global developments needs both "system-level and unit-level theories in order to comprehend what is going on" (Buzan 1998: 226). In order to grasp both the internal logic and the complex interplay of local, regional and international factors in these intra-state wars, the conceptual tools of classical IR theory must be combined with some insights of the political sociology of the state.

In sociological theory, the state has been conceptualized from within as a particular political and social order. In contrast to IR theory, sovereignty is not the essential precondition for the theoretical framework, but the emergence of the modern, sovereign and territorial state marks the central question that political sociology intends to explain. According to Max Weber, the modern state is a political community "that (successfully) claims the monopoly of the legitimate use of physical force within a given territory" (Weber 1991: 78). Political power is based on legal authority with a formal order subject to change by legislation (Weber 1968a: 56). In spite of the fact that both theoretical approaches, IR theory and political sociology, share these key elements in defining a state, i.e. the monopoly of physical force and territoriality, processes of state formation are looked upon in different ways. Whereas IR theory is interested in state formation from an external, international system perspective, political sociology concentrates on internal mechanisms behind the monopolization of legitimate violence by the state as a political-territorial association (Weber 1968b: 904–905).

The key to understanding the European process of state formation lies in the circularity of control and extraction, in the interdependence between the state monopolies of physical force and taxation. It is upon this twin monopoly that the modern state developed as a social order of "legal authority." In Weber's terms, "legal [rational] authority is resting on a belief in the legality of enacted rules and the right of those elevated to authority under such rules to issue commands" (Weber 1968a: 215). Unlike traditional rule, which is based on personal authority and the obedience to age-old rules, legal systems of domination rest on an impersonal purpose and on the obedience to abstract norms. Accordingly, state formation means both the expropriation by the state of all autonomous actors who formerly controlled the means of physical force and the transformation from traditional political orders to legal rule, i.e. from the personal authority of rulers to legal political authority based on formal regulations. In the European example, the historical establishment of legal authority can be systematized according to four forms of statehood that have been shaped by the successive juridification of state–society relations:

First, the *absolutist state* signified the formation of the state monopolies of taxation and physical force, which, second, became legally anchored in political institutions and civil law in the *constitutional monarchies*. The emergence of the *democratic constitutional state* marked the third wave in which bourgeois revolutions brought about the "nationalization" of the two state monopolies, making them public institutions and thus breaking absolutist power. Finally, the formation of the *welfare state* tamed the autonomous dynamics that spring from the accumulative logic of the economic system and its generalized medium, money. It was not until the very end of this process lasting many centuries that representational forms of government, democratic procedures, and formal norms regulating the political and economic realms had been firmly established (Habermas 1986: 356ff.). Yet Norbert Elias reminds us that these processes of internal pacification and the establishment of democratic rule were not at all peaceful developments. He traced the origin of the state monopoly of physical force back to its opposite, the unrestricted and violent elimination contest in which any individual or small group struggles among many others for resources not yet monopolized (Elias 1994: 351). According to Elias, two phases of the monopoly mechanism can be distinguished:

> First, the phase of free competition or elimination contests, with a tendency for resources to be accumulated in fewer and fewer and finally in one pair of hands, the phase of monopoly formation; second, the phase in which control over the centralized and monopolized resources tends to pass from the hands of an individual to those of ever greater numbers, and finally to become a function of the interdependent human web as a whole, the phase in which a relatively 'private' monopoly becomes public.

> (Elias 1994: 354)

Putting IR and sociological perspectives, system and unit levels, together, state formation is a contradictory process in which the state appears as a cause for both war and peace. The internal pacification of social conflicts and the evolution of a "society of states" that is built on Westphalian principles such as territorial integrity, political sovereignty and non-interference were interrelated processes. Furthermore, conducting armed conflicts with neighboring states contributed to the emergence of distinct realms of state and civil society (Krause 1996: 326).[7] In Tilly's analysis, the "civilized" standards of both international law and the democratic state based on the rule of law were the late outcomes of an intensive bargaining process between war-makers and state-makers. This bargain reflected the particular historical context in which the circularity of the competencies of territorial control and economic extraction took its specific path. In this process, large nation-states were able to translate their national economic resources into success in international warfare (Tilly 1990: 160).

The dialectical relationship between civil claims of protection (security) and the states' need for extraction (taxation) tamed the violent forces of this accumulation process in two ways. Internally, the previously mentioned steps of juridification brought about liberal and pluralist state–society relations, whose normative provisions today serve as role models for the proponents of the paradigm of "liberal internationalism" promoting market economy and liberal democracy. Externally, the violent elimination contest of emerging states has been gradually transformed into economic competition between states as mutually accepted like-units that interact within the international framework of a "norm-governed society of states" (Brown 2000).

The problem: the postcolonial state

In Charles Tilly's view, the contradictions in European state formation were manifested in the "central paradox . . . that the pursuit of war and military capacity, after having created national states as a sort of by-product, led to a civilianization of government and domestic politics" (Tilly 1990: 206). Yet the theoretical devices of Marx, Weber, Elias and Tilly are abstractions from a historically very unique situation. During the nineteenth century, the territorially confined state assumed control over all three of what Elias called elementary social functions: the means of physical force, of material reproduction and of symbolic reproduction of society.[8] It was this historically particular empowerment of the state and the underlying compromise of its political, economic and intellectual elites that culminated in an equation of state and society. Whereas the international system characterized by anarchy and self-help reflects the war-waging experiences of European states, the notion of "like-units," states as unitary actors, expresses this conversion of control over economic, political and cultural power resources. Yet, contrary to this European model, most states have remained "highly unlike-units" (Sørensen 2000: 109).

Looking at the formation of postcolonial states, it can even be argued that the existing international order prevented the newly independent states from becoming like-units. In most parts of the globe, state building has been taking place under the normative and power-related constraints of the international system. The postcolonial state-makers were not able to fight those large-scale state-building wars in the same way as their European predecessors did. Dominated from its inception by the larger unit of the Western state system, non-European state formation has not operated by the same rules. In pursuing their interests, the political entrepreneurs of Africa, Asia, the Middle East or Latin America have had to conform their actions to the already existing norms and power relations of a hegemonic international system.

In analyzing Middle Eastern state formation, Carl Brown, for instance, discerned characteristic patterns of close interaction between the emerging Middle Eastern states and the international systems of states. The intense interrelationships between these unequal power systems led to a center–periphery struggle in which domestic and international politics became thoroughly blended and confused (Brown 1984: 72). While European powers found a convenient arena in which to fight out their rivalries with little risk, regional and local forces were able to instrumentalize great power politics to their own ends. The territorial demarcation of Middle Eastern states after the First World War reflects these compromises of interests among great international powers and assertions of regional non-state actors. Despite the fact that some of these regional actors could achieve formal statehood with the decolonization of the Middle East, this Middle Eastern experience can be read as a predecessor of the structural background against which the so-called new wars must be examined. In the same way as the militia leaders and warlords of current armed conflicts, Middle Eastern state-builders have been able to largely extract material needs from international resources. Bargaining processes between military rulers and civilian groups comparable to the European experience were thus essentially hampered. The security of the state and the security of its people have not yet been synchronized (cf. Krause 1996).

In many countries of the so-called zone of conflict, the political and economic elite has been less accountable to the "nation" than to international and transnational bodies, as well as to traditional communities such as the extended family, clans or tribes. This weak embeddedness of the postcolonial state in its own society equally applies to the emerging civil societies in the developing world. Instead of being engaged in a bargain with their respective state elites, civil society groups interact rather via international and transnational intermediaries. Thus current state-building processes lack the structural core feature of what brought about the democratic state in Europe. Tilly's analogy of war-making and state-making obviously does not apply to them. The new wars apparently contradict the European logic behind the competencies of territorial control and economic extraction and its translation into progressive steps of the juridification of state–society relations. Therefore, postcolonial state formation could hardly follow the European example, and visible steps of juridification have remained formal provisions that are counteracted by social and political practices. In extending and intensifying transnational aspects of political and economic integration, globalization seems to be further aggravating this situation of unfinished state-building.

The symptom: mafia structures and warlordism

The current blending of market economy with the forceful appropriation of economic means is best visible in structural settings that are generally labeled as "mafia-structures" or "warlordism." Although by no means new phenomena, mafias and warlords epitomize the confusion of the theoretically distinct realms of economy and politics. Today, as in the past, in traditional societies the term "warlord" refers to a mainly negative phenomenon, involving the use of military force on a certain territory in a narrow, exploitative and selfish way. What once distinguished the warlord from traditional leaders such as tribal chieftains, traditional notables, or landlords was the fact that he was not bound to the people under his domination by the reciprocal norms of traditional societies (Mackinlay 2000: 49). Yet, as Charles Tilly (1985) has shown, in the transition to modernity, the rackets of former warlords were able to develop into new forms of state-like political institutions, establishing a new kind of reciprocal relationship between military and civilian elites. In structural terms, this transitional power of warlordism is due to the fact that the major aspects of statehood – territoriality, the means of physical force, and the capacity of extraction – are at the warlords' disposal. In particular, the collapse of patrimonial empires saw the rise of warlordism and, based on this structural setting, some warlords later became dominant figures in the making of new states.[9]

The new warlords appear in situations comparable to the above-mentioned decline of empires, in which the political authority of postcolonial states has been eroded. Yet, contrary to their traditional predecessors, modern warlords act in a different context. Controlling local territories with their military power, they act both financially and politically in the international realm (Mackinlay 2000: 48). While the local conditions of insecurity serve them as a ground for economic extraction, global markets provide them with a secure environment for investment. The crucial linkage between protection and extraction is therefore severed, and parallel markets of violent expropriation and liberal accumulation coexist. In this sense, "the combinations of failing states, societies in transition, globalized markets, easy communications, improved transport technology and unprotected national resources have propagated new plunderers" (Mackinlay 2000: 60).

As in the case of warlords, mafiosi rely on a combination of physical force, territorial control, and extractive capacities. However, mafia structures profit from both the absence and the existence of state structures. In the absence of the state, the mafia provides protection and services to the population, whereas the prohibition of goods and economic transactions by the state opens to the mafia the field of private protection for illegal markets (Krasmann 1997: 203). Given this flexibility of mafia structures, it comes as no surprise that they are able to profit from both the spoils of war and the spoils of peace. This, the articles by Michael Pugh (Chapter 3) and Francesco Strazzari (Chapter 7) will clearly show. Furthermore, mafia structures are well suited to integrating war economies via illegal markets with the global economy. In this way, war zones and illegal markets form the areas in which the forceful means of war-related economic accumulation produce capital stocks for investments in the formal sectors of a peaceful global economy.

Generally speaking, mafia economies are market economies functioning outside of and against the state. Embedded in the overall context of a global market economy, the examples of Bosnia and Kosovo show how local political entrepreneurs have been able to make a profit from both the collapse of state control during the Balkan wars and the reconstruction of state structures by international actors. With the breakdown of the Yugoslav Federation, a variety of mafia-like actors emerged, mediating between market forces and a society in which social discord was universal and political authority precarious. In their attempts to rebuild peace, international organizations and Western states are compelled to cooperate with warlords and mafia chiefs who play an essential role in the maintenance of public order and the conducting of elections to political and administrative offices (cf. Arlacchi 1979: 57–65).

The diagnosis: the defective state

Against this background it becomes clear that the traditional position of international relations in viewing the world from the system level as a society of states, made up of territorially integrated and politically sovereign like-units, was a reification of a conceptually ideal type that was derived from the example of European nation-state formation. Applying the norms of the Westphalian system, decolonization has only established modern statehood as a form of external representation, i.e. as a formal territorial framework of international politics guaranteed by the world state system and by international law. While accepted as formally equal members of the society of states, most postcolonial states remained internally fragmented polities in which not the state but tribal, ethnic, local or religious groups have been the essential points of reference for shared identities and political loyalties. Robert Jackson put this experience of postcolonial state formation under the concept of "negative sovereignty," a formal legal entitlement with which "quasi-states" hide their lack of empirical statehood (Jackson 1990).

Viewed from the unit level, the formal foundation of postcolonial states was just one step in an ongoing process of global state formation. However, in sharp contrast to the European experience, in postcolonial state formation the rules of the international system did not emerge together with the state, but the Westphalian arrangement became a precondition for the internal sociology of postcolonial state building. In this context, Elias's monopoly mechanism has been turned upside down. In current intra-state wars, we do not observe an unrestricted elimination contest within formally established states, but rather an internationally restricted process of ongoing internal conflict. The "imported" modern state apparatus has not developed into the political representation of the nation (Badie 1992), but has become a contested object for the appropriation of resources by competing social groups (Wimmer 1997).

From this perspective, postcolonial states have been, from the beginning, defective states. In many of them a legitimate monopoly of physical force has not yet developed and the so-called new wars are therefore less an expression of state-decay than an indication that state-building processes have become increasingly derailed. If at all, the term *state decay* applies best to some states of the former socialist world. There, relatively firm monopolies of physical force had been established, yet the second phase of Elias's monopoly mechanism, i.e. that the monopoly becomes public, was still under way. The simultaneous introduction of grand schemes of political and economic liberalization has so far eroded the achievements of the first phase of the monopoly mechanism rather than brought about the liberal blessings of the second. Although the demise of the Soviet Union has led to fully-fledged wars only on its peripheries, Russia is nevertheless a good example of the partial erosion of the monopoly of physical force. In Russia, liberalization has been accompanied by the privatization of the means of physical force, thus elevating the use of force to a dominant economic factor.[10]

In conclusion, processes of state formation under the impact of globalization are seemingly not following the historical example that European state formation has given. The subsequent chapters of this book will highlight this general proposition by putting their focus on economic aspects of current intra-state wars. Without claiming to deal with the phenomena of current war economies in a comprehensive way, the authors will nevertheless underline that there is a new global political economy, shaping and impeding the ongoing formation of political entities. In order to maintain Kant's hope for perpetual peace, it is vital for academics, political decision-makers, and professionals who are pursuing policies of peace-making to reflect on this new global political economy and its interrelation with armed conflicts.

Notes

1 The quotation is taken from the first supplement of Kant's *Perpetual Peace*, cited according to the translation in Schwarz (1988: 102).
2 Regarding the violent aspects of modernity, Joas emphasizes that the modernization process has essentially been characterized by warfare and that the search for peace has to take into account the violent tendencies of modern society (Joas 1996: 23–26).
3 Just to make it clear, this is not the allegation of Buzan and Little, who even conclude that the nature of the interrelation between the zones of peace and conflict will be one of the great questions for the twenty-first century (Buzan and Little 1999: 101–102).
4 In focusing on the economic aspects of current wars, this book follows the trajectory of some pioneering work such as the books of Jean and Rufin (1996) or Berdal and Malone (2000). However, stressing economic aspects does not mean endorsing Paul Collier's contention that the "risk of rebellion" basically is conditioned by economic factors. In particular his conclusion that not political interests and objective grievances but economic characteristics cause civil war seems to be equally as exaggerated as the ethnicity argument (cf. Collier 2000).
5 Regarding this global success of the "nation-state model," see also Meyer *et al.* (1997).
6 For a typical example of this "rationalist explanation for war," see Fearon (1995).
7 About the interrelation between citizenship, conscription, mass democracy and representational institutions, see the "classical" article of Janowitz (1976).
8 For Elias's elementary functions, see Elias (1983). How his concepts can serve a broader theoretical framework, see Jung (2001).
9 Interesting examples of warlordism in the context of declining empires are the end of the Manju dynasty in China and the decline of the Ottoman Empire, see Jung (2000) and Jung with Piccoli (2001: 28–58).
10 Volkov (2000) differentiates between three specific types that represent this privatization of physical force in Russia. The new violent entrepreneurs of the country belong either to the state-related illegal type (members of state security units using force for the appropriation of material means), to the private legal type (private security providers), or to the private illegal type (organized crime). Based on a general lack of public security, these three types of violent entrepreneurs violently interact in highly competitive markets.

References

Albert, M. and Brock, L. (2000) "Debordering the World of States: New Spaces in International Relations," in M. Albert, L. Brock and K.D. Wolf (eds) *Civilizing World Politics. Society and Community Beyond the State*, Boston: Rowman and Littlefield.

Arlacchi, P. (1979) "The Mafioso: from Man of Honour to Entrepreneur," *New Left Review*, 118: 53–72.

Badie, B. (1992) *L'État importé. Essai sur l'occidentalisation de l'ordre politique*, Paris: Fayard.

—— (1995) *La fin des territoires*, Paris: Hachette.

Berdal, M. and Malone, D.M. (eds) (2000) *Greed and Grievance: Economic Agendas in Civil Wars*, Boulder: Lynne Rienner.

Brown, C. (2000) "The 'English School': International Theory and International Society," in M. Albert, L. Brock and K.D. Wolf (eds) *Civilizing World Politics. Society and Community Beyond the State*, Boston: Rowman and Littlefield.

Brown, C.L. (1984) *International Politics of the Middle East: Old Rules, Dangerous Game*, Princeton: Princeton University Press.

Brown, M.E., Lynn-Jones, S.M. and Miller, S.E. (eds) (1996) *Debating the Democratic Peace*, Cambridge, Mass.: MIT Press.

Buzan, B. (1998) "Conclusions: System versus Units in Theorizing about the Third World," in S.G. Neuman (ed.) *International Relations Theory and the Third World*, New York: St. Martin's Press.

Buzan, B. and Little, R. (1999) "Beyond Westphalia? Capitalism after the Fall," *British International Studies Association*: 89–104.

Castells, M. and Portes, A. (1989) "World Underneath: the Origins, Dynamics, and Effects of the Informal Economy," in A. Portes, M. Castells and L.A. Benton (eds) *Informal Economy: Studies in Advanced and Less Developed Countries*, Baltimore: Johns Hopkins University Press.

Collier, P. (2000) *Economic Causes of Civil Conflict and Their Implications for Policy*, New York: Development Research Group of the World Bank.

Duffield, M. (1998) "Post-Modern Conflict: Warlords, Post-Adjustment States and Private Protection," *Civil Wars*, 1 (1): 65–102.

Elias, N. (1983) "Über den Rückzug der Soziologen auf die Gegenwart," *Kölner Zeitschrift für Soziologie und Sozialpsychologie*, 35 (1): 29–40.

—— (1994) *The Civilizing Process. The History of Manners and State Formation and Civilization*, Oxford: Basil Blackwell.

Fearon, J.D. (1995) "Rationalist Explanations for War," *International Organization*, 49 (3): 379–414.

Flemming, M.H., Roman, J. and Farrell, G. (2000) "The Shadow Economy," *Journal of International Affairs*, 53 (2): 387–409.

Gantzel, K-J. and Schwinghammer, T. (2000) *Warfare since the Second World War*, New Brunswick: Transaction Publishers.

Gilpin, R. (1981) *War and Change in World Politics*, Cambridge: Cambridge University Press.

Guzzini, S. (2000) "A Reconstruction of Constructivism in International Relations," *European Journal of International Relations*, 6 (2): 147–182.

Habermas, J. (1986) *The Theory of Communicative Action: Lifeworld and System: A Critique of Functionalist Reason*, London: Polity Press.

Holsti, K.J. (1998) "International Relations Theory and Domestic War in the Third World: The Limits of Relevance," in S.G. Neuman (ed.) *International Relations Theory and the Third World*, New York: St. Martin's Press.

Jackson, R.H. (1990) *Quasi-States: Sovereignty, International Relations, and the Third World*, Cambridge: Cambridge University Press.

Janowitz, M. (1976) "Military Institutions and Citizenship in Western Societies," *Armed Forces and Society*, 2 (2): 185–204.

Jean, F. and Rufin, J-C. (eds) (1996) *Économie des guerres civiles*, Paris: Hachette.

Joas, H. (1996) "Die Modernität des Krieges. Die Modernisierungstheorie und das Problem der Gewalt," *Leviathan*, 24 (1): 13–27.

Jung, D. (2000) "Gewaltkonflikte und Moderne: Historisch-soziologische Methode und die Problemstellungen der Internationalen Beziehungen," in K. Schlichte and J. Siegelberg (eds) *Strukturwandel internationaler Beziehungen. Zum Verhältnis von Staat und internationalem System seit dem Westfälischen Frieden*, Leverkusen: Westdeutscher Verlag.

—— (2001) "The Political Sociology of World Society," *European Journal of International Relations*, 7 (4): 443–474.

Jung, D. with Piccoli, W. (2001) *Turkey at the Crossroads: Ottoman Legacies and a Greater Middle East*, London: Zed Books.

Kaldor, M. (1999) *New and Old Wars: Organized Violence in a Global Era*, Cambridge: Polity Press.

Keen, D. (2000) "Incentives and Disincentives for Violence," in M. Berdal and D.M. Malone (eds) *Greed and Grievance: Economic Agendas in Civil Wars*, Boulder: Lynne Rienner.

Krasmann, S. (1997) "Mafiose Gewalt. Mafioses Verhalten, unternehmerische Mafia und organisierte Kriminalität," in T. von Trotha (ed.) *Soziologie der Gewalt*, Kölner Zeitschrift für Soziologie und Sozialpsychologie, Sonderheft 37, Opladen.

Krasner, S.D. (1995) "Compromising Westphalia," *International Security*, 20 (3): 115–151.

Krause, K. (1996) "Insecurity and State Formation in the Global Military Order: The Middle Eastern Case," *European Journal of International Relations*, 2 (3): 319–354.

Laquer, W. (1996) "Postmodern Terrorism," *Foreign Affairs*, 75 (5): 24–36.

Lukauskas, A. (1999) "Managing Mobile Capital: Recent Scholarship on the Political Economy of International Finance," *Review of International Political Economy*, 6 (2): 262–287.

Mackinlay, J. (2000) "Defining Warlords," *International Peacekeeping*, 7 (1): 48–62.

Mandelbaum, M. (1999) "Is Major War Obsolete?," *Survival*, 40 (4): 20–38.

Marx, K. (1852) "The Eighteenth Brumaire of Louis Napoleon," in K. Marx and F. Engels (1972) *Gesammelte Werke (MEW), Band 8*, Berlin: Aufbau.

—— (1857–8[1974]) *Grundrisse der Kritik der politischen Ökonomie*, Berlin: Dietz Verlag.

Meyer, J.W., Boli, J., Thomas, G. and Ramirez, F. (1997) "World Society and the Nation State," *American Journal of Sociology*, 103 (1): 144–181.

Neuman, S.G. (ed.) (1998) *International Relations Theory and the Third World*, New York: St. Martin's Press.

Önis, Z. and Aysan, A.F. (2000) "Neoliberal Globalisation, the Nation-State and Financial Crises in the Semi-Periphery: a Comparative Analysis," *Third World Quarterly*, 21 (1): 119–139.

O'Tuathail, G.Ó (1996) *Critical Geopolitics: The Politics of Writing Global Space*, Minneapolis: University of Minnesota Press.

Paris, R. (1997) "Peacebuilding and the Limits of Liberal Internationalism," *International Security*, 22 (2): 54–89.

Portes, A., Castells, M. and Benton, L.A. (eds) (1989) *Informal Economy: Studies in Advanced and Less Developed Countries*, Baltimore: Johns Hopkins University Press.

Reno, W. (2000) "Shadow States and the Political Economy of Civil Wars," in M. Berdal and D.M. Malone (eds) (2000) *Greed and Grievance: Economic Agendas in Civil Wars*, Boulder: Lynne Rienner.

Rosecrance, R. (1996) "The Rise of the Virtual State," *Foreign Affairs*, 75(4): 45–61.

Ruggie, J.G. (1993) "Territoriality and Beyond: Problematizing Modernity in International Relations," *International Organization*, 47 (1): 139–174.

Schwarz, W. (1988) *Principles of Lawful Politics: An Annotated Translation of Immanuel Kant's Toward Eternal Peace*, Aalen: Scientia Verlag.

Sørensen, G. (2000) "States Are Not 'Like Units': Types of State and Forms of Anarchy in the Present International System," in M. Albert, L. Brock and K.D. Wolf (eds) *Civilizing World Politics. Society and Community Beyond the State*, Boston: Rowman and Littlefield.

Strange, S. (1996) *The Retreat of the State: The Diffusion of Power in the World Economy*, Cambridge: Cambridge University Press.

Tilly, C. (1985) "War Making and State Making as Organized Crime," in P. Evans, D. Rueschemeyer and T. Skocpol (eds), *Bringing the State Back In*, Cambridge: Cambridge University Press: 169–191.

—— (1990) *Coercion, Capital and European States, AD 900–1900*, Cambridge: Basil Blackwell.

Volkov, V. (2000) "Gewaltunternehmer im postkommunistischen Russland," *Leviathan*, 28 (2): 173–191.

Weber, M. (1968a) *Economy and Society. An Outline of Interpretive Sociology*, Volume I, New York: Bedminister Press.

—— (1968b) *Economy and Society. An Outline of Interpretive Sociology*, Volume II, New York: Bedminister Press.

—— (1991) *From Max Weber: Essays in Sociology*, London and New York: Routledge.

Wendt, A. (1999) *Social Theory of International Politics*, Cambridge: Cambridge University Press.

Williams, M. (2001) "The Discipline of the Democratic Peace: Kant, Liberalism and the Social Construction of Security Communities," *European Journal of International Relations*, 7 (4): 525–553.

Wimmer, A. (1997) "Who Owns the State? Understanding Ethnic Conflict in Post-Colonial Societies," *Nations and Nationalism*, 3 (4): 631–665.

2 State formation and the economy of intra-state wars

Klaus Schlichte

War-making and state-making: still a valid interrelation?

Contemporary civil wars have apparently lost any rationality, if not any political meaning. The cruelties committed in the course of war, the lack of political programs, and the endless proliferation of actors seem to hint at a growth of anomic violence. Some observers therefore argue that the development of warfare after the end of the Cold War displays only the irrationality of actors. Robert Kaplan's article on "the coming anarchy" in 1994 was as widely read and discussed in the US as that of his German counterpart, Hans Magnus Enzensberger, with its similar dark messages: "*Aussichten auf den Bürgerkrieg,*" in 1995. Both authors maintain a depoliticization of violence, an irrationality that renders it questionable whether a scientific explanation of current occurrences of wars is still possible.

Quite according to expectations, social scientists contradicted this view, for good and convincing reasons (cf. Kalyvas 2000). Despite the "atomization of goals" and the "radicalization of means" (Marchal 2000) that can be observed, contemporary wars have their underlying causes and complex interactions in the social and political spaces in which they take place. Therefore, this chapter starts with the assumption that actors of contemporary wars interact at least partly rationally. Its central question is whether the results of these interactions can be interpreted as an expression of a hidden logic, or, to put it in Norbert Elias's terms, as "unintended interlacements" (1977: 131): Is there a logic of state formation discernable in contemporary wars?

That there used to be a relationship between warfare and state-building in European history has become one of the most broadly acknowledged findings of the historically oriented social sciences. At least since Charles Tilly (1985) coined the phrase of "wars make states, and states make war," this insight has become general wisdom.[1] According to this view, the emergence and the institutional shape of European states are largely the result of their violent history. The core argument runs as follows: power-holders needed armed forces and material resources in order to foster their position against internal and external violent contenders. The installation of standing armies and of rigid extractive systems of taxation was thus mutually reinforcing preconditions for the maintenance of power positions. These efforts to erect the systems of extraction and of military capacities were at the basis of the emergence of the strong state in European history.[2]

There is a lot to be said about this subject. But this chapter will not contain any exhaustive discussion of its single elements or of historical knowledge related to the thesis. Its main question is rather directed towards its current validity: Is this relation between warfare and state-building still valid when it comes to contemporary wars and states?

In the following attempt to assemble some elements to answer this question, three points – two restrictions and one enlargement – seem to be necessary:

1   The considerations of this chapter will not deal with all aspects that actually needed to be taken into account. I will, for example, not deal with the effects of mere threats of warfare. Furthermore, there is no answer to the questions of whether the structure of the international system during the Cold War, the spread of the norm of mutual recognition of states, or the balance of powers have to a large extent prevented the – in other historical times – very common phenomenon of annexation of states.
2   As contemporary wars are mostly intra-state wars,[3] the considerations will only deal with those countries in which long enduring civil wars have been taking place in the last decade or so.[4]
3   The enlargement concerns the understanding of the term "economic." Contrary to the common usage, I employ the term for all kinds of activities and structures that concern the provision of goods and services, not just those covered by official macroeconomic statistics.

Some words about the term "state" might be appropriate though. Presupposing the vainness of looking for a generally accepted definition of the state, I will refer to an understanding of the state that takes it as a field of power shaped first by a general image of what a state ought to be and second by practices that are related to this image (Migdal and Schlichte 2002). In the *image* of the state that has been globalized in the course of what has become known as the "European expansion," the state is seen as a political organization, sovereign in its relation to other agencies concerning the administration of violence and the economic order and the establishment and enforcement of rules. This covers more or less the general self-understanding of state actors and the ideal of international organizations. However, most states are not what they would like to be. There is almost always a considerable gap between aspirations of state actors and actual forms. Any empirical investigation dealing with the state has to consider this remarkable difference.

Empirically, states differ enormously. Local traditions, the time and modes of integration into the modern world system, the specific blend of different political realms, such as in the experience of colonization – all this contributes to variations in the concrete forms in which single cases of state formation historically evolve. These variations can be observed in different *practices*, in the various ways states actually work. Thus, states differ from each other in more than one regard, in their inner working mechanisms, in their relation to other social and political agencies, and in the boundaries that delineate them – and this not only in a territorial sense.

With this distinction between the image of a state as a concomitant reference and the practices, the ways a state actually works, it shall be possible to assess and to describe the dynamics of contemporary state formation in a more appropriate way than this is possible with most current conceptions of state theories. These theories, which are themselves marked by the image of the state, attribute it with a functional core, namely an apparatus of coercion and control with a capacity of extraction and an ability to set and enforce rules. It is this functional core, however, that will serve as the structural background for this investigation. In three sections I try to assemble from the literature on contemporary wars some generalizations about the effects of "war economies" on states as they work. In this way, I try to assess how far contemporary wars lead to a greater convergence or dissociation between the image and the practices of states.

As will be shown, there are hardly any universal historical theses about the relationship between state-building and the inner economic order of intra-state wars. Apart from the specific structure of "an economy" in general, the relationship is determined by the pathways of integration in world markets and its "world historical timing." Thus, structures and opportunities decide about the possibilities and limits of war economies and their effects on those efforts to rebuild a state after a war. In contemporary contexts, I will argue, these possibilities are rather restricted. The economy of current intra-state wars creates structures that contradict the "traditional" logic of state-building in the Western experience. But this is, however, not the entire story: as can be seen regarding the extraction competence of the state, the control of the territory and regarding "state mentalities," there are also tendencies in the opposite direction. As a result of these contradicting tendencies, political forms that emerge from civil wars do not meet what is meant by the classical understanding of states.

Flows and registers: the state's competence of extraction

Contrary to the general impression, protracted warfare does not change everything in a society, nor in its political forms. As will be shown in this section, the kind of insertion in the global economy, for example, structures the "internal" economy before, during and also after the war. From an economic point of view, the pervasive informalization of the economy marks the main problem that intra-state wars cause for the post-war consolidation of states. Once established, state actors have huge problems to bring a war economy under control again, partly because rulers themselves rely on informal power resources. In this situation, the economy of international aid plays an important role as an "emergency exit" in the efforts of restoring political domination.

In intra-state wars, as has often been argued, state structures decay. Several reasons are behind this general tendency:

1   Under the conditions of warfare, state capacities focus on the organization and the fueling of the military machine, and the civilian functions of the state are neglected respectively.
2   In most intra-state wars the economy slows down as regular economic activities suffer under the conditions of insecurity. In particular flight, expulsion and the migration of substantial parts of the population lead to a decrease in economic activities.
3   Informal ways of economic production and distribution grow in importance. War times are times of shadow economy, times of informalization with the respective consequences for the state's cashbox.

Even in those states which had a rather high level of state organization in pre-war times, the informalization of the economy tends to be enormous. The bloody dismantling of former Yugoslavia is a good case in point. Hyperinflation, the loss of regular employment, and the rigidity of state regulations led or favored informal activities so that the population of the remainder of Yugoslavia in 1994 gained 50 percent of its income in the shadow economy (Reuter 1994: 491). These changes in the relation between the economy and the state do of course have their consequences for the forms of rule. Parallel structures of political authority develop and the holders of public offices also begin to rely on informal power sources. They "dub" the state and its official institutions by constructing a second network of power relations. In order to capture the meaning of these developments, William Reno (1995), for instance, has coined the term of "the shadow state"; Bayart *et al.* (1997) have been talking about the "criminalization" of the state.[5]

Yet when a war has ended and when some kind of internationally recognized political authority has been re-established, the question of the state's fiscal basis re-emerges – usually with a need to "officialize" fiscality. The emerging solutions show how much war economies alter state structures and in which regard. At this point, two economic facts come to the fore:

1   Even if wars last for many years or decades, many old economic structures have not ceased to exist. Wars change the face of an economy but they do not alter all of its structures. This applies particularly to the basic conditions of its insertion into the world economy. Export goods

are most likely still the same, and the economic position of a country within the international division of labor usually does not shift profoundly.

2   Intra-state wars cause a high degree of informalization of both the economy and politics.[6] This is a very problematic heritage for the re-establishment of statehood and severely hampers the legalization of new economic structures.

However, these problems of war economies concern not only the "normal" population but also the war-winners. On a "top-level" it might be relatively simple to go back to normal. In many cases, warlords create economic patterns that are not much different from pre-war structures. During the war in Liberia, for example, concessions for the export of timber and iron-ore were the most important sources of income for Charles Taylor's "National Patriotic Front of Liberia" (NPFL) (cf. Ellis 1999: 164–180). This rent and concession economy had already been the basis of the pre-war state. Through the international recognition of electoral results, which changed Taylor from a warlord into a head of state, the private, criminal economy of a warring faction was merely transformed into a state business. This resembled the form of state business that had formerly been in practice in Liberia from the beginning of the twentieth century.[7]

In the thousands of instances of less visible economic relations that develop during a war, the transformation is much harder to achieve. Economic opportunities have been appropriated by violent means and they might be defended by violence too. Attempts to "re-formalize" the economy – i.e. to bring it back under state control – might fuel tendencies to re-launch warfare. The transformation is also difficult as many of these relations spread across international boundaries. Thus, without territorial control extraction cannot be enforced, but without considerable extraction, territorial control cannot be achieved and maintained. Some examples prove this genuine circularity of the competencies of extraction and violence. The spread of the Liberian civil war into Sierra Leone and other neighboring states was typical in this regard. But also the intervention of Ugandan and Rwandan armed forces in the war in Congo (Zaire) can be seen as a continuation of such a trajectory: the appropriation of power resources by violent means. In these cases, the line between intra- and inter-state warfare becomes fluid, like any other boundary that delineates the state. Cambodia's post-war economy is just another example that shows how the re-establishment of state control of exports could not be achieved. The Khmer Rouge as well as Cambodian army officers were selling timber to foreign companies without paying any tribute to the central state (Möller 1998: 263). As a result of this circularity of extraction and territorial control, various forms of balances between informal arrangements and formal institutionalizations emerge. The basic problem for the transformation of a war economy, and therefore for sustainable peace-building, is to deal with economic opportunities that have been appropriated during the war. War economies create many losers, but also some winners. Should the rewards of peace not seem profitable, the winners are prone to use their means in order to continue war.

The post-war situation is further complicated through the "framing" of state actors by international agencies. The stalemate of extraction that results from informalization is the leverage for the introduction of those constellations that are euphemistically labeled "global governance," namely the interlacements of different agencies that circumvent, control and mix with the state on different levels. International "aid" for the reconstruction of war-torn societies comes in as the entire industry of "development" recommences after a war and delivers considerable flows of means. Yet this internationally steered rebuilding of states turns out to be a double-edged sword. On the one hand, this internationalization offers to some extent exits from warfare, as it allows a state budget to be run without putting too much pressure on the economy that could create resistance. On the other hand, the recourse to "aid" also sets essential constraints on the reconfiguration of state domination. Now rulers have to take external imperatives into account, and, of course, this internationalization of rule has its historical roots too, illustrated by the case of external debts. International political recognition means also the recognition of former obligations. Loans that have been taken on international markets need to be reimbursed, as well as obligations toward the international financial organizations.

Finally, the longer a war has lasted, the stronger is the "acclimatization" to the absence of the state. This raises psychological barriers and fosters coalitions of interest that hinder the reintroduction of state-imposed taxes, tolls and duties. It is also for this reason that post-war states slide deeper into international dependencies. The flows of aid allow the delicate affair of enlarging the tax base to be circumvented. The agencies and agents of aid induce a fiscal structure that can avoid immediate internal conflict. Those structures, obligations and alliances that were created before and during the war add to this. As a result, fiscal structures after an intra-state war are heavily shaped by international dependencies. In Mozambique, for example, grants and loans amounted to 75 percent of the post-war state's budget in 1994. As Michael Pugh (Chapter 3 in this book) shows, the post-war situations in Kosovo and Bosnia are no different in this regard. These cases display the same effect: once international dependencies are created they are difficult to overcome. In Uganda, where international donors attested huge successes in rebuilding state structures after the major war ended in 1986, 30 percent of the 1998 budget still consisted of external "grants and loans" (MFEP 1998). The extraction competence of the Ugandan state towards its "national" economy is mainly restricted to the taxation of international trade. Duties on petrol and vehicles and taxes on local products constitute the bulk of recurrent revenue. The much higher flows of labor remittances and incomes from the informal sector, however, escape the state's grip. Post-war states tend to have fiscal structures that are only loosely connected with their societies. It is anybody's guess whether the flow of international aid will be a first step to enabling a state to introduce a more "classical" fiscality or whether aid will develop into a stable system with its own logic and inner dynamic, rather preventing the reconstruction of the classical fiscal structures of extraction.

Capacities of control: the state and its competitors

States grow slowly. However clear and outspoken the image of a state might be, however pompous its rituals and scenic productions may appear, the actual practices in which a state really works do not need to correspond to this image. Practices change slowly, and their growth towards the globalized role-model image of the state is not inevitable. There are alternatives, even for the administration of violence. In this regard, intra-state wars are also seasons for the mushrooming of new forms for the deliverance of "public goods," and the efforts of state actors to integrate these forms into the framework of state control usually lead to ambiguous results.

In an intra-state war the administration of violence is no longer controlled by the state. Instead, the main organizations in charge of the domestic control of violence – police forces and the judiciary – are prone to dissolution. To them a general truth applies: intra-state wars have devastating effects on institutions because under the "preponderance of short-term thinking," investments in institutions do not pay (Genschel and Schlichte 1998). However, new forms of institution-building also take place during a war. There are developments that run counter to the general tendency of dissolution and decay. Therefore new forms for the control of violence also develop. There are numerous examples in the control of territories that make this clear.

In regions that are not directly affected by warfare, for instance, in many cases the state as an institution is nevertheless absent or unable to fulfill its functions. Yet the general problem of the control of the means of physical force needs to be solved. Typically, this is the hour of militias that pursue the aim of self-defense or develop their own policies in a war. The events in Somalia (cf. Menkhaus and Prendergast 1995) or Sierra Leone (cf. Abdullah and Muana 1998) are telling examples. The re-emergence of "traditional" forms of control of violence is another reaction to the decay of state institutions. In the years of anarchy that ruled in Uganda after Idi Amin came to power in the early 1970s, a system of "popular justice" developed. Culprits or suspects were judged and punished by local groups that gathered *ad hoc* and acted without written or formal rules. This "system" is of course extremely susceptible to arbitrary decisions and instrumentalizations for the private ends of local strongmen.

Another interesting example is the role of enclaves of modern capitalist production, or rather extraction, in war-torn societies. In these, private security corporations provide the necessary security environment for a profitable economic extraction. In this way, for instance, private companies have protected petrol sites in Algeria and Angola, or diamond mines in Sierra Leone while civil wars were in full swing. This, too, is nothing but the privatization of the means of physical force standing in a strange relationship with the essential tenet of the modern state.

These forms – militias as agents of self-defense, various institutions of "grassroots-justice," and the commercial privatization of security – need to be integrated in a state's system of violence control once a war is over and regular relations of public administration must be rebuilt. For a time, they might be seen as a "*décharge*" of the state (cf. Hibou 1999: 33–41), in the sense that the state outsources some of its tasks in order to alleviate the burden by granting more room to maneuver to intermediaries. But this, of course, enhances the danger that these intermediaries accumulate more and more power, and may later turn the relationship upside down. The state will be fragmented then, territorially or functionally.

A similar point can be made concerning the activities of non-governmental organizations (NGOs) and international organizations. In recent years, programs and measures of humanitarian aid, especially in the context of intra-state wars, have become one of the fastest growing sectors of official developmental aid – and of foreign policy in general. The relevance of humanitarian aid for the dynamics of, in, and after wars can hardly be overestimated. Meanwhile it is very well known and documented that despite good intentions, foreign aid may sustain wars instead of alleviating their effects.[8] The flow of resources through the sanctuaries of refugee camps or the demand for security of NGO personnel in war zones turn into economic opportunities for all kinds of protection rackets that fuel the war economy and thus sustain structures of violence beside the state-controlled monopoly of physical force. Equally important but largely overlooked are other long-term effects on the state's capacities of control. "Humanitarian corridors," for example, might turn into entry points for alliances that hinder the re-establishment of regular political authority. The interests of NGOs and those of war actors become intertwined very quickly. The result of these interlacements can grow into power alliances that make the political center more dependent on local power holders than it ever used to be.

In the course of intra-state wars, new political constellations arise in which the moral economy of the humanitarian unfolds.[9] This has important consequences for the possibilities of state rule. Large parts of those fields which, according to a classical understanding, belong to the domain of the state, are transferred into para-statal authority. Water supply, rural development, health and public education are some of those areas in which NGOs and international donors develop re-distributive functions, often in explicit competition with the state, which is thus no longer in a position to get the merits for delivering public goods. These developments normally originate in the situation of war, they grow stronger the longer the war endures, and they often petrify in the period of successful peace settlements.

Causes and effects of aid intervention can no longer be separated then: the lack of institutionalization and efficiency that is so characteristic of post-war states is the reason for the engagement of foreign actors, but their activities deprive the state of those gains in organization and legitimacy that it would achieve by developing its own capacities to deliver public goods. If this constellation applies equally to the function of security, as is the case when military intervention forces take over police functions as in Bosnia or Kosovo, the state eventually turns into a mirage. There is still an image of a state then, but practices of everyday life show a highly divergent picture. The division of labor between agencies of control that typically emerge in contemporary post-war situations is in striking contrast to the image of a world of unitary states that colorful maps let us think are real. Contrary to this image of a well-organized political landscape, rule and control have been increasingly internationalized, broken and assimilated with local power structures. There is no one political space dominated by the state, but an overlapping of different spaces of control, each of which is filled with commands, obedience and resistance.

Representations and rules: about the emergence of state mentalities

According to well-known classical state conceptions, loyal armed forces and functioning tax authorities form indispensable parts of any state. But a state needs more than that. A state must be able to introduce rules and to enforce them. As the broad literature on the subject of legitimacy suggests, this function of rule-setting and rule-enforcement presupposes that the state is anchored in the minds and thoughts of social actors. This does not imply that all the state's rules are obeyed and observed. There will always remain tension between legal regulations and private morals. However, the state needs to be accepted "as a part of the landscape" (Migdal 1997: 5) so that its requests are at least considered on the basis of being righteous or justified. This is what is meant by the term "state mentality," of which different kinds and degrees exist. They range from a very loose and skeptical attitude towards the state up to the kind of "state priests," as Karl Marx denounced jurists and lawyers (1968: 60). In any case, these mentalities cannot be reduced to mere output-oriented, instrumental attitudes by which organizational theories explain loyalty towards the state.

In intra-state wars, it is said, these kinds of state mentalities die out. Different experiences of violence split the population into different factions that pay tribute to other agencies, but not to an abstract state. The defeated develop a strong *ressentiment* against the new order, whereas the victorious consider the result of a war as their personal merit, so for them there is no need to share the gains for the sake of joint "statehood." It is the exception that the new state is seen as a solution by everybody. Intrastate wars destroy state allegiances because their costs are always enormous. There is not only impoverishment caused by inflation and military spending, but also the loss of relatives, and the hardship that with war enters all spheres of life might lead to a decrease in legitimacy that can grow into a "system crisis."

Given all that, states nevertheless do not simply vanish after civil wars. Despite the general impression of a decreasing importance of states, there have never been as many states as nowadays and there have never been so few voices calling for the abolishment of statehood. Neither corporate interests nor liberation movements want to live without a state. The former just want to restrict it, the latter just want their own. The project of the "statization of the world" (Reinhart 1999) was apparently successful: the idea of the state as a political form is mentally well anchored all over the world. And it is this image of the state that is nurtured by the rituals and actions of international politics as the form of interaction between states. States have seats and votes in international organizations, they mutually acknowledge each other, and they can even visit each other. The mist of the community of states has become that strong that it is almost beyond imagination that a state could vanish. Annexations do not occur,[10] the order of international boundaries is not discussed. Partition is the only way for states to vanish. The end of the Soviet Union and the decay of Yugoslavia are cases in point, not to mention the independence of Eritrea or the *de facto* secession of Somaliland.

International recognition could be one reason why states survive even long civil wars during which their entire infrastructure is dissolved. Liberia, Uganda, Lebanon – none of these states disappeared as an image, and, strangely, the image seemed strong enough to serve as a point of departure for the political reconstruction of these societies. Even in those states that are not much more than a mirage, the state as an image is present on coins and in national football teams, in passports and on license plates. Apparently, some decades of existence have been enough to anchor the state as an image so deeply that after a war there is little debate of rebuilding state-like authority. At least on the international level the persisting image of the state induces a certain kind of ascription of meaning even in the cases of the most hollow buildings of authority. In this regard, the fiefdom of the warlord Charles Taylor was the opposite of what Robert Jackson and Carl Rosberg (1987) described as the hollowness of the juridical statehood of African states.

Thus, it could seem as if in postwar settings state mentalities of international actors are pitted against non-state loyalties among the population. Accordingly, in international politics, the political task of rebuilding war-torn societies and states is conceived in this manner. A lot of peace-building efforts and programs of democratization aim at the introduction and support of those understandings of political rule that have this classical image of the state as its main reference. The international reputation of these states depends on the evaluation of their efforts in terms of "democratization" and the observance of human rights. Their international sovereignty is symbolized in their seats and votes in international organizations. Seen from outside, states appear as territorial organizations. Internationally, it is the "image" of the state that counts.

But in actual practices, things might look quite different. States may not be able to control the entire territory, their bureaucracies might be mere facades that do not play any role in the everyday life of the population. In most societies that were or are still affected by civil wars, the relative convergence of state images and practices has not yet been accomplished. Their sovereignty as an integral part of the image of a state might be faked. There are even examples of client states that were more or less made up by other powers in order to give the impression of independent statehood.[11] In all of these cases, the actual power of a state resides in quite different spheres than in the relation between the state and its "own" population. Political power is generated and fostered in political spaces that are not "national" ones.

Christopher Clapham has recently stated that the history of Ethiopia and Eritrea, so rich in warfare, has not led to a strengthening in state institutions simply because the costs of modern warfare have been so high that a peasant society could not bear these costs (Clapham 2000: 7). Not even the ideological effect one might have expected by the countless involvements in armed struggle has appeared, as the case indicates, when there are deeply separating lines within a society. Collective experiences, entrenched in the collective memory, can be much stronger than the effects of events that build an alleged "national fate."

Clapham hints at one interesting exception though, namely the "Eritrean People's Liberation Front" (EPLF). In its history of more than thirty years of armed struggle against the ambitions of different regimes in Addis Ababa, this movement has proved to be "one of the strongest insurgent movements of the modern era, not just in Africa but in the world" (2000: 9). It developed its strength, Clapham argues, because its neutral ideology could bridge the gap between inner oppositions and because a far-reaching network of exiled members generated considerable means in order to finance the war. Through this dense network and the intensive cultural life Eritreans developed in their "host" societies throughout the world, "Eritrea" had more than a virtual existence even before it became independent. This same "cement" then was the reason for the strong authoritarian centralism of the post-independence Eritrean state.

This case hints at a tendency that concerns the state as well as its challengers: the dislocation of political spaces. Other warring parties in other cases also live to a large extent on the support of exiled groups, for instance the Kurdistan Workers' Party (PKK) or the different political organizations of the Palestinians.[12] The "image" of a rebellious movement that is fighting and reproducing itself on a given territory is in contradiction to the practices of an organization that not only has modern logistics but is also accumulating support on different stages. The public sphere of Western media and the contributions of exiled groups are equally as important for its strength as the support of the local population in the actual war zones. The political space in which warring factions act is by no means restricted to a state's territory.[13]

These findings lead to reflections on the linkage between state mentalities and material flows. Is the flow of resources a necessary condition for the emergence of allegiances? Was Max Weber right in stating that, apart from the type of legitimacy, any state must "meet the material interests at least of its staff" (Weber 1985: 122)? In the light of the foregoing theses about the strange constellations between political authority and economy that are typical for postwar societies, there would be little reason to believe that allegiances to "a state" will develop.

The strength of the image of states, it could be summarized, rests largely on the orientation of international politics towards it. Actors in international politics need an addressee, they expect it to be a state and they imagine it according to the image of states. By contrast, local actors might think and act differently. They might have allegiances that are much stronger than their belief in the rights and the justification of a state. In some cases this kind of state mentality can develop in the course of a war, and there are cases where the respective state is not even "real" but more or less imagined by exiled groups. In other cases, the experiences of war rather deepen the frictions and fissures that run through a society and hinder the emergence of a state mentality as a prerequisite of legitimate rule. State mentalities are anything but a necessary result of intra-state wars.

Conclusions: forms of war and forms of states

The effects of contemporary wars on statehood are ambivalent. There is no single, unambiguous causal relation between states and wars. States are not simple war machines and warfare does not automatically lead to a strengthening or weakening of the state. Instead, the contradictions of war seemingly apply also to the state. In this sense, politics are just the continuation of war (Foucault 1999: 29). So it depends on concrete contexts whether the events and changes that occur during and after a war foster or weaken a form of political domination in which authority comes close to the "image" of the state.

In a plea for adapting the concepts of security studies to the reality of politics outside the Organization for Economic Cooperation and Development (OECD) world, for example, Keith Krause added further arguments as to why the process of the socialization of the state is not taking place ubiquitously. In the Middle East, he argues, the path dependency of authoritarian militarism and of international rent-seeking strategies allows the perpetuation of the separation between states and "their" societies. The relative independence of the rentier state from domestic actors leads to a situation in which the monopolization of the means of physical force has been achieved without simultaneously entailing the statization of minds (cf. Krause 1996). In the light of Krause's findings, some further general remarks concerning global historical timing can be made, however. They concern a point mentioned before, i.e. global historical timing. The analysis of the economy of contemporary wars and the focus on the proper dynamic of enduring violence should not deceive us about the conditions under which they take place. They are globally embedded, and this global embeddedness accounts for a variety of more general conditions of war economies and for the possible dynamics of states.

In European history, opportunities for state-building also depended on the possibilities of economic and social differentiation and chances of social mobility. In more than one sense, the history of state formation was also the history of capitalism. The state was of course itself an important vector of social mobility, but its formation was based on the emergence of social forces that counterbalanced the weight and the power of the state. And the emergence of these social forces was in turn a result of disruptive "modernization." The historical lesson is clear: it was only due to the pressure of powerful social forces that warfare led to pushes in democratization and enlargements of state functions. Warring Western states needed the support of all relevant social groups and therefore adapted distributive policies of inclusion and integration (cf. Eley 1995). There can be no civic-capitalist state without a bourgeoisie.[14] It is, however, questionable whether current global processes of differentiation and modernization will simply repeat the Western experience, i.e. whether it will come to analogous processes of *embourgeoisement* in other world regions. Current structures of the global economy might impede it, and other pathways into a capitalist modernity might lead to different political forms than classical statehood.

Most warring states in the early twenty-first century are integrated into the world economy on a very narrow basis. The bigger flows of resources are channeled through the state. Therefore in almost all of the cases the state has been the decisive site for the distribution of material benefits. That is why the incumbency of state offices is very often at the core of the conflict. The appropriation of all kinds of opportunities, offices, grants, aid and "projects" becomes the most important avenue for the accumulation of political power and economic wealth. In weakly institutionalized states such as those in Sub-Saharan Africa or South East Asia, the power balance on which the public order rests is one between patronage networks. This is also true in most contemporary war societies before and after the outbreak of violence. The basic disadvantage of these systems is, however, that they are not able to come to terms with the social dynamics that take place on their territory. Sooner or later, social imbalances emerge that cannot be solved with the restricted set of political instruments in these systems. Physical force then is one universal resource to achieve change when situations become unbearable.

The tensions that arise in these situations can easily escalate. In this regard, the stories of Lebanon, Uganda or Sierra Leone are quite similar. Paul Richards (1996) has sketched the following constellation of the latter case: marginalized young men for which a crumbling system of patronage could no longer offer any prospects have tried all kinds of ways to improve their personal situations. At some point, violent contest is one means, among others, in order to escape despair. The rebellion of these youngsters is "a blind jump in a dreamt modernity" (Marchal 2000: 174). Imagined rewards of this kind play a role in Algeria (cf. Martinez 1998), as they did in the motivation of those recruited for the Lebanese militias (cf. Beyhum 1999: 133). Social dynamics of this kind fuel wars and war economies, and this problematique is a major obstacle for any postwar settlement.

The political constellations that came into being in Bosnia, East Timor, Liberia or Kosovo seem to indicate what forms of political domination result from contemporary wars: a patchwork of appropriated competencies and vested interests, a mixture of local, international and "state" authorities that can hardly be called a coherent form of authority. One might wonder whether this kind of controlled anarchy will eventually lead to something that comes closer to what used to be called the state, particularly as the vested interests of foreign actors tend to prolong their activities eternally, and the behavior of local agents does not display visible tendencies towards state-like institutionalizations.

In the light of this comparison, it seems to be evident that the underlying social dynamics of contemporary violent conflicts are not the same as in the European past. The relation between political organization and mass violence is different. As has been alluded to in this chapter, actors in contemporary wars try to alleviate or improve their situations with strategies that were not at hand in other global times – or at least not in this combination. Clandestine or officially registered migration, the mutual help networks of diasporas, the variety of informal economy, the role of international aid organizations, and, last but not least, various forms of violent contest are part of these strategies and practices. Their emergence and development have, by the way, consequences for political forms that do not necessarily develop together with the occurrence of major armed conflicts (cf. Schlichte and Wilke 2000). In comparison to the profoundness of social and political change, war is still a "secondary phenomenon" (Porter 1994: 3).

It is not the classical territorial state, in control of its "national" economy and a community of citizens clinging to "constitutional patriotism," but the constant movement of fluid commitments and allegiances that form the structures of the global political space. The resulting forms will probably not be covered by the language of current state theory. Forms become more complex than the repertoire of conceptions political science has to offer. But this is not a new insight: the lemurs of science only emerge after dusk.

Notes

1 Max Weber as well as Otto Hintze and Norbert Elias had delivered main elements of this insight much earlier, and Tilly, of course, does not ignore their contributions. See e.g. Hintze (1906).
2 This is the vulgar version of the relationship. Charles Tilly (1992) differentiated it in an elaborated analysis, distinguishing different pathways of state building which can be traced back to differences in the accumulation and concentration of "coercion" and "capital."
3 For an overview of contemporary war development cf. the annual reports of the study group on causes of war at the University of Hamburg: http://www.akuf.de
4 The material on which these reflections are based is thus not representative for the entire reality of contemporary wars. The theses presented here are really hypothetical. The main basis for the following are Ellis (1999), Marchal and Messiant (1997), Schlichte (1996) and the contributions in Jean and Rufin (1996). In order to keep the text readable, not all references are made explicit.
5 The term "criminalization" is however problematic here, as it is actually the state that defines what is criminal. This hints at the general semantic problem in the study of the state: it is difficult to talk about it without using its language.
6 This informalization, however, can also take place without warlike events. Perhaps the most telling example is the case of labor remittances in Yemen that amounted to three times the GDP in the 1970s (Chaudry 1997: 244).
7 Former Liberian governments were charged with selling forced labor at the League of Nations in the 1920s or with selling huge plots of land to foreign companies, as in the case of the Firestone rubber plantation. On these war economies without wars cf. Young (1934) and Kraaij (1983).
8 Regarding this point, see Chapter 8 by Joakim Gundel on Somalia in this book.
9 Of which the emotions of the Western public are a constitutive part like the small crowd of moral engineers and intellectuals that together with eager politicians form the moral agenda of "urgent affairs" (cf. Pouligny 2000).
10 The only – disputable – exception in the times after the Second World War is the German Democratic Republic.
11 There is a multitude of policies in international relations that have led some authors to the conclusion that the idea and the talk of "sovereignty" is just hypocrisy (cf. Krasner 1999).
12 For the PKK see Paul White (2000); the history of Palestinian resistance is documented in Sayigh (1997).
13 The war between "liberation movements" and "states" is thus also a symbolic one. Besides the material economy of the war, there is a symbolic economy, closely related to the former. Successes in acquiring the better international reputation can easily lead to decisive material and strategic advantages.

14 But *embourgeoisement* is conflictive as such, as the global past has shown. This is because modernization means dislocation. The dissolution of traditional forms of social integration is part of it, like the decay of old patterns of reproduction and the individualization of property and income. The issue of land tenure in contemporary Africa is telling concerning the conflictivity of these processes. The history of Latin America is telling concerning the longevity of these conflictual constellations. And European history is telling as it shows that conflicts of modernization can only be contained in peaceful channels when a mode of distribution is installed that can satisfy most aspirations and organized interests.

References

Abdullah, I. and Muana, P. (1998) "The Revolutionary Front of Sierra Leone," in C. Clapham (ed.) *African Guerillas*, London: James Currey.

Bayart, J-F., Ellis, S. and Hibou, B. (1997) *La criminalisation de l'Etat en Afrique*, Bruxelles: Editions Complexes.

Beyhum, N. (1999) "Beyrouth, histoire de deux viles où tuer est une compulsion qui se répète," in J. Hannoyer (ed.) *Guerres civiles. Economies de la violence, dimension de la civilité*, Paris: Karthala.

Chaudry, K.A. (1997) *The Price of Wealth. Economies and Institutions in the Middle East*, Ithaca: Cornell University Press.

Clapham, C. (ed.) (1998): *African Guerillas*, London: James Currey.

—— (2000) *War and State Formation in Ethiopia and Eritrea*, paper presented at the colloque international "La guerre entre le local et le global: sociétés, Etats, systèmes," CERI, Paris, 29–30 May.

Eley, G. (1995) "War and the Twentieth-Century State," *Daedalus* 124 (2): 155–173.

Elias, N. (1977) "Zur Grundlegung einer Theorie sozialer Prozesse," *Zeitschrift für Soziologie*, 6 (2): 127–149.

Ellis, S. (1999) *The Mask of Anarchy. The Destruction of Liberia and the Religious Dimension of an African Civil War*, London: Hurst.

Enzensberger, H.M. (1995) *Aussichten auf den Bürgerkrieg*, Frankfurt a.M.: Suhrkamp.

Foucault, M. (1999) *In Verteidigung der Gesellschaft. Vorlesungen am Collège de France 1975–76*, Frankfurt a.M.: Suhrkamp, (first Paris 1996).

Genschel, P. and Schlichte, K. (1998) "When Wars Get Chronical," *Law and State*, 58: 107–123.

Hannoyer, J. (ed.) (1999) *Guerres civiles. Economies de la violence, dimension de la civilité*, Paris: Karthala.

Hibou, B. (1999) "De la privatisation des économies à la privatisation des Etats. Une analyse de la formation continue de l'Etat," in B. Hibou (ed.) *La privatisation des Etat*, Paris: Karthala.

Hintze, O. (1906) "Staatsverfassung und Heeresverfassung," in O. Hintze *Staat und Verfassung. Gesammelte Abhandlungen zur allgemeinen Verfassungsgeschichte*, ed. by Gerhard Oestreich, 3rd ed., Göttingen: Vandenhoeck & Ruprecht.

Jackson, R.H. and Rosberg, C.G. (1987) "Why Africa's Weak States Persist: The Empirical and the Juridical in Statehood," in A. Kohli (ed.) *The State and Development in the Third World*, Princeton: Princeton University Press.

Jean, F. and Rufin, J-C. (eds) (1996) *Economie des guerres civiles*, Paris: Pluriel.

Kalyvas, S.N. (2000) *"New" and "Old" Civil Wars: Is the Distinction Valid?*, paper presented at the colloque international "La guerre entre le local et le global: sociétés, Etats, systèmes," CERI, Paris, 29–30 May.

Kaplan, R.D. (1994) "The Coming Anarchy," *Atlantic Monthly*, February.

Kraaij, F.P.M. van der (1983) *The Open Door Policy of Liberia. An Economic History of Modern Liberia*, Bremen: Afrika-Archiv.

Krasner, S. (1999) *Sovereignty. Organized Hypocrisy*, Princeton: Princeton University Press.

Krause, K. (1996) "Insecurity and State Formation in the Global Military Order: The Middle Eastern Case," *European Journal of International Relations*, 2 (3): 319–354.

Marchal, R. (2000) "Atomisation des fins et radicalisme des moyens. De quelques conflits africains," ,*Critique Internationale*, 6: 159–175.

Marchal, R. and Messiant, C. (1997) *Les chemins de la guerre et de la paix. Fins de conflit en Afrique orientale et australe*, Paris: Karthala.

Martinez, L. (1998) *La guerre civile en Algérie*, Paris: Karthala.

Marx, K. (1968, 1842) "Kritik der Hegelschen Staatsphilosophie," in S. Landshut (ed.) (1968) *Karl Marx. Die Frühschriften*, Stuttgart: Kröner Verlag.

Menkhaus, K. and Prendergast, J. (1995) "The Stateless State," *Africa Report*, 40 (3): 22–25.

MFEP (Uganda Ministry for Finance, Economic Planning and Development) (1998) *Background to the Budget*, 1998/99 Kampala: Government Printing Office.

Migdal, J. (1997) "Why do so many states stay intact?," Seattle: mimeo.

Migdal, J. and Schlichte, K. (2002) "The State as a Process," in K. Schlichte (ed.) *The Dynamics of States*, London: Zed Books (forthcoming).

Möller, K. (1998) "Kambodscha nach UNCTAD: Das Versagen der Institutionen," in H.W. Krumwiede and P. Waldmann (eds) *Bürgerkriege: Folgen und Regulierungsmöglichkeiten*, Baden-Baden: Nomos.

Porter, B.D. (1994) *War and the Rise of the State. The Military Foundations of Modern Politics*, New York: Free Press.

Pouligny, B. (2000) *Les acteurs non-étatiques et la guerre: Reflexion à partir du cas des organisations non gouvernementales d'aide humanitaire*, paper presented at the colloque international "La guerre entre le local et le global: sociétés, Etats, systèmes," CERI, Paris, 29–30 May.

Reinhart, W. (ed.) (1999) *Verstaatlichung der Welt? Europäische Staatsmodelle und außereuropäische Machtprozesse*, München: Oldenbourg Verlag.

Reno, W. (1995) *Corruption and State Politics in Sierra Leone*, Cambridge: Cambridge University Press.

Reuter, J. (1994) "Die Wirtschaftskrise in der BR Jugoslawien. Reformen im Schatten von Krieg, Embargo und schleppender Transformation," *Südosteuropa*, 45 (8): 478–491.

Richards, P. (1996) *Fighting for the Rain Forest: War, Youth and Resources in Sierra Leone*, London: James Currey.

Sayigh, Y. (1997) *Armed Struggle and the Search for State: The Palestinian National Movement 1949–1993*, Oxford: Clarendon Press.

Schlichte, K. (1996) *Krieg und Vergesellschaftung in Afrika. Ein Beitrag zur Theorie des Krieges*, Münster and Hamburg: Lit Verlag.

—— (2000) "Staatsbildung und Staatszerfall in der 'Dritten Welt'," in J. Siegelberg and K. Schlichte (eds) *Strukturwandel internationaler Beziehungen. Zum Verhältnis von Staat und internationalem System seit dem Westfälischen Frieden*, Wiesbaden: Westdeutscher Verlag.

Schlichte, K. and Wilke, B. (2000) "Der Staat und einige seiner Zeitgenossen. Zur Zukunft des Regierens in der 'Dritten Welt'," *Zeitschrift für Internationale Beziehungen*, 7 (2): 359–384.

Tilly, C. (1985) "War Making and State Making as Organized Crime," in P.B. Evans, D. Rueschemeyer and T. Skocpol (eds) *Bringing the State Back In*, Cambridge: Cambridge University Press.

—— (1992) *Coercion, Capital, and European States, AD 990–1992*, rev. ed., Cambridge, Mass.: Blackwell.

Weber, M. (1985) *Wirtschaft und Gesellschaft. Grundriß der verstehenden Soziologie*, 5th ed., Tübingen: Mohr.

White, P. (2000) *Primitive Rebels or Revolutionary Modernizers? The Kurdish National Movement in Turkey*, London: Zed Books.

Young, J.C. (1934) *Liberia Rediscovered*, Garden City NY: Doubleday.

Part II

Policies of reconstruction and punishment

3 Protectorates and spoils of peace

Political economy in south-east Europe

Michael Pugh

Nobody thinks in terms of human beings. Governments don't. Why should we? They talk about "the people" and "the proletariat." I talk about "the suckers" and "the mugs" – it's the same thing. They have their five year plans, so have I.

(Harry Lime in *The Third Man*)

A critical perspective of protectorate political economies

The argument of this chapter is that while international agencies claim to be promoting economic liberalisation in the protectorates of south-east Europe, in practice they reinforce the dominance of clientist and corporatist political economies. In this respect there is cooperation as well as friction between international and domestic actors. The notion that "protectorates" operate in south-east Europe is not admitted by the states and international organisations involved in the region. But informed observers have argued that the only realistic goal of western policy in Kosovo would be an international protectorate that, as in Bosnia, would last indefinitely.[1] The inhabitants are deemed unable to determine their futures without paternalistic guidance and rules of governance determined from the outside. The rules reflect the values and norms of acceptable behaviour according to constructions by the powers that dominate the external institutions.

However, for local elites, the spoils of peace legitimised the war. In Kosovo, the Kosovo Liberation Army (KLA) became the *de facto* economic authority in the bulk of the country. In each of the Croat and Moslem areas of the Federation (*Federacija Bosne i Hercegovine*) and the Serb-controlled *Republika Srpska* (RS) of Bosnia and Herzegovina, the major political organisations that took Bosnia into war also controlled, and continue to control, the economies of ethno-geographical sectors. Movement has certainly occurred at political levels since the wars terminated and a period in which the external actors underwrote particular leaderships during and after the wars (Pugh 2000). In Kosovo, relative moderates took the posts of president and prime minister and formed a government in March 2002 after Ibrahim Rugova's Democratic League of Kosovo won the November 2001 election. In Bosnia the "Alliance for Change" coalition (based on the Social Democratic Party and the Bosniak Party for Bosnia) dented ethno-nationalist politics when it came to power in both Federation and state in February 2001.

Nevertheless, the external actors continue to confront "parallel" economies, with which they negotiate in order to implant neo-liberal policies. However, the neo-liberal precepts present opportunities for further wealth creation among the winners. In place of the pre-war statist order, the international agencies and local corporate interests manoeuvre to assert control and to negotiate areas of collaboration. From a critical theory perspective one can thus speak of "intermestic negotiation" – the term "intermestic" being defined as "the intermingling of domestic, regional and international factors that overlap or intersect and that can transcend traditional state-centric notions of sovereignty."[2]

In terms of sovereignty, Bosnia and Kosovo differ in a formal sense. Bosnia and Herzegovina (BiH) is constituted as a state with a seat in the United Nations, whereas Kosovo remains a province of the Republic of Yugoslavia. It had gained autonomy in the period 1968–1974 before this was reduced in 1988 and then revoked in 1990. But the two protectorates have three common characteristics:

1   External actors, such as the UN, the International Financial Institutions (IFIs) and the Organisation for Security and Cooperation in Europe (OSCE) have installed processes and institutions that were negotiated on the basis of settlements to stop violent conflict, rather than on the basis of internal political revolutions against authoritarianism and economic injustice. This has ensured a strong element of continuity from pre-war and wartime political economies.

2   State institutions function poorly in both cases. In Bosnia the central institutions are constantly thwarted at lower levels of governance. In Kosovo, the formal authority of Yugoslavia exercises no sway at all. The vacuum in governance is filled by struggles between local "ethnocracies" – those authoritarian political elites, controls and structures that parallel or overlap those imposed from outside.

3   In both protectorates, executive management lies with external actors: the Office of the Implementation Council's High Representative (OHR), the Missions of the OSCE, aid agencies and various IFIs. These are drawn into undemocratic micro-management to impose a vision of neo-liberal capitalism and democracy in which the forms are given greater emphasis than mediation for counter-hegemonic and accountable political leadership. The interests of external actors and those of the domestic elites coincide in the maintenance of entrepreneurialism and discrimination against state welfare (Cox 1998).

This chapter seeks to fill a gap in the literature on the political economy of intra-state wars. Since the pioneering investigations by François Jean and Jean-Christophe Rufin, several studies have traced the way that intra-state wars are financed in the absence of audited central taxation and disbursement.[3] However, there has been little published work on post-conflict political economies in contrast to work on "peace-building" in the areas of conflict resolution, social development, refugee returns, constitutional and electoral democracy, military security, policing and justice. Research sponsored by IFIs has a positivist and econometric approach to economic transformation that privileges global markets and undifferentiated consumerism as if this were a manifest destiny (Collier 1999). By contrast, Roland Paris (1997) and Gearoid O'Tuathail *et al.* (1998) have offered insights on the dysfunctional aspects of neo-liberalism and democratisation, and this chapter draws on aspects of their critiques. However, they do not fully acknowledge the extent of intermestic negotiation and manipulation in war-torn economies. This chapter contends that in a protectorate there is common ground between international and domestic parties as well as friction and resistance.

Critical theories that emphasise the place of the economy in society, instead of designing society as an adjunct of the market, offer an opportunity to see how manipulation of war-torn economies occurs (Inayatullah and Blaney 1999). Neo-liberal economic theories construct a spatial correlation between society, territory and economy – with a state or state-like authority acting as an intermediary between the global markets and the goals of citizens (Cameron and Palan 1999: 275). In the protectorates of south-east Europe, the intermediary is not so much "the state" as the war entrepreneurs and patrimonial elites interacting with international organs and external capitalist institutions. But in their efforts to extend the free market and privatise socially-owned assets, the external actors are caught between state building and contraction. Intervention stems from seeing "the other" as dysfunctional, war-wrecked statist economies, and from attempts to deal with the resistance of local war entrepreneurs to modify their "criminal," corporatist systems. The withdrawal impetus comes from representing integrative economies as those that "legitimise reductions in welfare spending and the privatisation of essential services" leading to differentiation between those able to participate in the neo-liberal project and the excluded poor, unemployed, inflexible and uncompetitive (Cameron and Palan 1999: 269–271). Similarly, the war entrepreneurs are caught between maintaining their clientist inefficiency and adapting to external conditionalities.

The analysis begins by tracing lineages of protectorate political economy in the pre-war and wartime aggrandisement of nationalists that carried over into the post-war settlements. Next, the overall goals and basic mechanisms of the "protectors" are discussed in the context of the development of parallel, anti-state, economies. The chapter then illustrates how economic cleansing and persistent clientism has been institutionalised in employment discrimination, and how the interaction of neo-liberalism and clientism is manifest in ethnic privatisation in Bosnia. The conclusion contends that neo-liberal prescriptions predicated on the free market are flawed in a context where local elites are subverting or capturing the restructuring. The protectorate political economies are unlikely to be restructured without an equivalent of statist provisions for employment, welfare and public services that will emancipate the populations from clientism and mafia welfare.

Lineages of clientist greed

The spoils of peace cannot be assessed adequately without reference to antecedents in the pre-war and wartime periods.

Pre-war period

First, it might be noted that statistical analyses of economic, social and political variables in states that erupt into conflict are inconclusive for the Yugoslav case. An analysis by a World Bank economist, Paul Collier, concludes that "the true cause of much civil war is not the loud discourse of grievance but the silent force of greed" (Collier 2000b: 101). Grievances, he argues, are manufactured by relatively wealthy rebels who acquire the means to prosecute war. The most likely countries to sustain war are those that not only have low national income but a high dependence on primary commodity exports because they present war elites with significant opportunities for revenue raising and profiteering. Collier's analysis assumes a rationale based on viability rather than motivation. He obliquely accepts that grievances can arise from economic decline, and this increases the risk of conflict (Collier 2000a). The relevance of his socio-economic variables to the Yugoslav case is open to dispute because the country was not a prominent example of absolute poverty in the international system and was not highly dependent on commodity exports (but on re-processing, tourism and remittances). More importantly, in pivoting his case around viability and in de-politicising the causes of conflict, Collier's thesis reifies the assumption that society can be designed around a competitive economy – provided greedy criminals are deprived of their niche in the competition.

Indeed other scholars contend that greed and grievance arose because of the drive to "subordinate the Balkan peoples to global capitalism" from the 1960s (Petras and Vieux 1996; Woodward 1995: ch. 3). In this respect, Carl-Ulrik Schierup's structuralist analysis is important for its contention that collapse began in the 1970s, when local communist and nationalist elites of Yugoslavia opted for fragmented integration into the capitalist system (Schierup 1993; Vucinich 1969). Although in Tito's period technocrats and managers were relatively free from political diktat and did not form a nomenklatura in the Soviet style, the "official economy" driving the orientation and pace of development failed to satisfy consumer demands. A private economy grew out of grey area activity. Small-holdings and service enterprises attempted to fill the gaps, and an informal economy operated among bureaucrats and within networks of loyalties to traditional kinship and patriarchs to cope with dysfunctions of the official economy (Korosić in Schierup 1990: 232). According to Schierup, profoundly authoritarian coalitions of local political elites and workers ensured fragmentation of the working class and ramified trends to corporatism and populist nationalist quests for regional autonomy (Schierup 1990: 244–256, and 1999). In Kosovo and the Moslem sectors of Bosnia this reinforced traditional patrimonialism, in which a small number of patriarchs dominated mayoralities (Skulić in Schierup 1990: 244; Sørensen 1999). In reaction to efforts in Belgrade to re-centralise the Federation's economic power in the 1980s, and efforts by the federal Prime Minister Ante Marković in 1989–90 to introduce market reforms to push integration forward, local nationalist elites intensified their carving out of economic empires. In effect, "structurally embedded economic warfare started years before the manifestly ethnically based political warfare" of the 1990s (Schierup 1993: 8). Schierup's analysis restores the structural parameters of political economy to a central position and opens the way for considering the fusion of politics and economy in both wartime and the relative peace of protectorates.

Wartime period

The violence in Bosnia and Kosovo presents a vivid picture of destruction, economic disruption and redistribution of assets. Communications break down, production and deliveries are attenuated, contractual obligations are worthless and trust is demolished. But modern conflicts also present new commercial opportunities for the exploitation of assets, investment, services, marketing and welfare. Indeed, as Jean and Rufin argue, war economies are not autarkies but penetrated by external goods and services furnished by diasporas, private security firms, aid workers and commodity markets (Jean and Rufin 1996: 13; Berdal and Keen 1997). True, entrepreneurs may conduct predatory operations – which loot, destroy and goad population movement to accompany or counterbalance military power. But they may also operate a more nuanced policy of criminalisation to sustain military campaigns through tribute, including the taxation of diasporas (a technique used by the KLA) (Rufin 1996: 36–42). Armed factions are remarkably adept at economic diversification and seeking optimum gains in the changing contexts of their struggle. Rather than being dismissed as regressive, these motivations may be considered functional and rational in conditions of poverty and economic decline. In a sense the phenomenon parallels "structural adjustment" policies that privilege private enterprise.

Xavier Bougarel demonstrates that in the Bosnia war, economic cleansing partnered ethnic cleansing and reinforced a parcelling up of territory (Bougarel 1996: 243). The nationalist communities began by replicating collapsed state structures, including major public industries such as Energoinvest (hydro construction), Sipad (forestry) and UNIS (metals and arms). In some cases socialist enterprises were commandeered to supply funds for the families of workers and combatants (former communists controlled the Zenica metal works for the benefit of the Bosniak SDA: Party of Democratic Action). Destruction and appropriation of abandoned assets contributed to a freefall in economic output so that by 1994 GNP was estimated at 25 per cent and industrial production at 10 per cent of pre-war levels. This led to more predatory activity and reliance on external subvention, including pay for soldiers from neighbouring states and the diversion and taxation of the humanitarian aid that an estimated 85 per cent of the population depended upon (Bougarel 1996: 244–247). Local militias, however, were supported by local taxes and voluntary contributions, and became part of an integrated subsistence economy. Even after the formation of the Bosnian–Croat federation, the Croatian "Herceg-Bosna authority" levied duties on goods destined for Moslem areas and took 30 per cent of the arms being supplied to the Bosnian government. Following the price distortion of civil goods and the establishment of enclaves, black markets flourished, and the protagonists cooperated regularly to control lucrative trafficking. Although the Croats blockaded Moslem territory in 1993–1994, racketeers in Banja Luka and Zenica established an exchange of key goods via Mt. Vlasić. Croat entrepreneurs also sent fuel to Serbs in exchange for weapons and the humane treatment of their kin in Central Bosnia (Puntarić 2001). The Sarajevo police chief accused a tri-ethnic mafia of deliberately prolonging the siege to profit from the black market (Bougarel 1996: 249). Disaggregation of communities from April 1993 to February 1994 marked the peak of predatory activity. But uneven economic distribution was a decisive factor in causing ruptures between profiteers and "regular" military units in each community and weakening morale in the Srpska and Bosniak armies. Contradictions inherent in prosecuting a war on the basis of criminal and predatory economies played a part in forcing the parties towards Dayton (Bougarel 1996: 255–261).

Post-war period

Features of wartime economies carry over into relative peace, as amply demonstrated in the Lebanon, where militias and political elites became "legitimate" reconstruction racketeers, dealers and directors taking advantage of the state's marginalisation and an ultra-liberal, unregulated economic environment in which public government has been paralysed (Picard 1996: 103). But in the case of Bosnia and Kosovo relative peace produced economies that blended pre-war and wartime clientism with market principles directly imposed by "protectors." The surviving features of pre-war and wartime political economy can be summarised as follows:

1 *Clientism*: personal and patrimonial links determine the distribution of assets and access to economic gains (e.g. the Čengić and Čelo Bosniak families).
2 *Corporatism*: a continuation of the vertically integrated control by political parties and patrimonies that link the welfare of supporters to economic empires based on hotels, casinos, construction and utility companies, and that tie small businesses to major banks (e.g. the Mostar-based empire of Bosnia's former Foreign Minister, Jadranka Prlić).
3 *Prebendary elites*: a primary concern of elites is to control rents and revenues for their own consumption (e.g. Ramiz Dzaferović, Director of the Federation Tax Administration was dismissed by the OHR not only for tax evasion but also for using his position to discriminate against the main political opposition).
4 *Nationalist politics*: formal politics are constructed around nationalist parties that are controlled by patrimonies and instil fear into voters about the threats to national unity. In protectorates they negotiate power with external agencies, and present a facade of legitimacy to the outside world (e.g. the crony of Alija Izetbegović and head of the *Elektroprivreda* energy company, Edhem Bičakčić, who was dismissed for corruption by the OHR in February 2001).

In brief, allegiances in the protectorates are dominated by a social clientism rather than a social contract, unmediated by constitutional accountability, legal norms and process. Wealth distribution and access to rights and opportunities are extremely uneven, and economic activity is privatised without accountability or provision for public infrastructure and welfare. Taxation is levied through imports of scarce essentials, and control over the extractive, service and distributive sectors (Le Billon 2000: 7). In place of former state-employed, urban middle-class technocrats who enjoyed privileges (many of whom fled the violence), war profiteers were often a new breed of gangster of rural origin.[4] Protectors of the local ethnic group, some of these underworld thugs adapted to conditions of relative peace and invested in post-war enterprises such as casinos, restaurants and banks. But the demise of some gangsters and the survival of pre-war entrepreneurs shows that this was not a wholesale revolution in the hierarchy of power. Fikret Abdić who, before the war, was charged with corruption over funds connected with running the *Agrokomerc* complex in Velika Kladuša, left for Zagreb when attacked by the Sarajevo-based Bosniak Army, but continued to pull strings in the Bihać region's reconstruction until tried in Croatia for war crimes in July 2001.[5] Moreover, the relationship between racketeers and politicians was not always cosy.

Scheming political bosses maintained a distance from the wartime thugs; the Bosniak Army tackled the Sarajevo gangs in 1992. But the smarter war racketeers who aligned themselves with politicians could guarantee post-Dayton respectability by funding nationalist parties.

Goals and mechanisms of the protectors

Neo-liberal and parallel economies

The new conditions in Bosnia and Kosovo are dominated by the presence of international agencies with executive power over development. As Mark Duffield argues, development policy is now far more discriminating about types of "other": developing some but allowing peripheral areas to be excluded (Duffield 1997, 2001).

Although much of south-east Europe is in dire straits socially and economically, it is widely assumed that the region falls into the first category, that indicators of economic and social development suggest that the area has the potential for conformity to west European requirements. Bosnia is joining the European Council and in 2002 applied for Partnership for Peace status in NATO. With German and US prompting, the EU and NATO have offered debt relief and other incentives to anchor the Balkans into the Euro-Atlantic structures at an anticipated cost of some 40 billion US dollars through the 1999 Balkans Stability Pact.[6] As with former trusteeships, the protectorates are not simply designed to save people from abhorrent histories, but to serve the interests of the protectors themselves. Various goals include the return of refugees, the integration of south-east Europe into the sphere of western European capitalism, and the extension of NATO's influence in the region. Indeed, Kosovo has been dubbed "NATO's Republic" (Ali 2000; Booth 1999; Wiberg 1999).

Key neo-liberal components of the Stability Pact are economic privatisation and deregulation. Neo-liberalism can be considered as a discourse of norms comprising: the ideal of a non-interventionist state (to facilitate the norm of free exchange); the reification of trade liberalisation and anti-protectionism; and the discounting of political and social dynamics except in so far as the components are recognisable economic units (Hibou 1998). It is a discourse that has evolved since 1997 to reinvent the role of central state power in conducting economic reforms. The unintended consequences of neoliberal intervention thus include the reinforcement of corrupt elites, the siphoning of privatised public assets into private pockets and the privatisation of government. Moreover, although the protectorates might be characterised as sinks for credits and reconstruction funds, direct economic assistance to the Balkan region as a whole, mostly in the form of loans which increase foreign debt burdens, is too limited to enable these countries to provide more than degrading incomes for their peoples. But it is a testimony to the existence of an elite with expensive tastes that "status retailers," such as United Colors of Benetton and Versace, have opened for business in Sarajevo where unemployment is about 40 per cent.

Nevertheless, international actors have to consider how far to go in confiscating or eliminating the economic power of war entrepreneurs, and in the transfer of legitimate economic activity to new owners. Against this, they have to balance the benefits of cooption by offering war entrepreneurs a stake in a pattern of economic activity under market rules.

Confiscation and co-option

Confiscation, elimination and transfer pose an intrusive challenge to the economic control and ownership patterns of war entrepreneurs. This requires large-scale (and honest) policing by the external actors, and materially they are not in a position to achieve this. Generally the protectorates have acquiesced in, or assisted, the process of expropriation that has already occurred among the local actors. In a region where social ownership was common, the external actors may devise mechanisms for transferring ownership to a broad base of investors, to workers or "approved" commercial interests.

Broadly speaking, Bosnia has witnessed co-option within boundary re-drawing whereas Kosovo has seen wholesale expropriation and transfer. An example of the latter has been the forcible confiscation and closure of the polluted Trepca mining complex of Mitrovica, with the expropriation of Serb employment and income.[7] In Bosnia the external actors were assisted by the movements of population and by the separate entity and cantonal territorial arrangements of Dayton that led to asset and ownership transfers in many areas. Here, the inheritance of state assets by the main political groupings has enabled them to resist foreign investment by levying formal and informal premiums. It is not so much a case of foreign carpetbaggers replacing home-grown mafia as the prospect of coexistence in which the population is squeezed from two directions (Wright 2000). Some people may have been able to sustain their previous standard of living, but a great many more have been sunk in poverty, especially the elderly, the unemployed, middle-class technocrats and those in social and educational services. In an economic situation that was officially described as "dire" six years after Dayton,[8] an estimated 46 per cent in the Federation and 75 per cent in RS were living in poverty, and one authoritative source considered that most people were getting poorer (ICG 2001: 6).

Co-option is less demanding in terms of policing. But it suppresses ethical considerations because war profiteers are effectively rewarded on account of the risk they present to peace. This communicates the lesson that, to a point, the more of a popular "nuisance" a rebel is, the greater this person's value to a peace process. Who might and who might not be legitimated in this way is largely a matter of political construction by external actors. A popular nuisance may be designated a scapegoat or demonised (as Radovan Karadžić has been). Alternatively, those who have committed atrocities may be legitimised in order to isolate bigger fish. In Cambodia, Ieng Sary, a prominent Khmer Rouge leader, was given conces- sions in logging and gems, as well as immunity, in reward for his defection (Keen 1998: 56). However, co-option also risks presenting conflict entre- preneurs with platforms from which to continue the struggle, as occurred in Sierra Leone, where the Revolutionary United Front leader, Foday Sankoh, was made "Minister for Jewellery" after the 1999 Lomé peace agreement. The lack of consistency in applying post-war justice creates political space for protecting local agents of wider strategic economic and political interests and merely requires some effort of self-reinvention and adaptation by locals when aid is conditional on conformity to the free market and privatisation.

Co-option also involves conditionality: making grants or loans condi- tional on full implementation of the Dayton agreement, for example. The United States withdrew financial support for privatisation to exert leverage on its pace and direction.[9] But studies have shown that conditionality does not work because aid has limited influence in the dynamics of local political struggles (Uvin 1999). Joanna Macrae argues that the EU's "Energy for Democracy" (ostensibly a humanitarian programme, though rejected as such by the European Commission's Humanitarian Office because of its political selectivity) has not empowered oppositions because the state acquired supplies from Russia and China, the amounts were small, it was implemented by international firms rather than local institutions, and its selectivity was politically counter-productive (Macrae 2000).

Parallel economies

Economic units in the protectorates (households, businesses, administra- tions), can be said to interact with four kinds of economy: the *official/ white*, the *clientist/nationalist*, the *"survival"/grey*, and the *mafia/black* economies.

1   The *official/white economy* is characterised by its regulation and penetration by international protectors. It provides a management framework for external actors and, in Bosnia, for government depart- ments. Thus, for example, although taxation and fiscal policies are devolved to the entities, monetary policy is controlled by external executives through the Central Bank (essentially a Currency Board). Executive powers over the official economy serve to create the condi- tions necessary for foreign penetration to make legitimate headway in the protectionist and clientist division of spoils.

2   The *clientist/nationalist economy* forms the core of the spoils of peace: the war gains inherited from dismantling former Yugoslavia (not necessarily of course with any major change of management, though

inevitably purified of contesting loyalties). This has been the arena where political and economic power are most closely in step. In the banking sector, for example, the major nationalist parties divided the spoils of the old Yugoslav Payments Bureaux (PBs) created in the 1950s for social book-keeping and monopoly control over financial transactions. Both pre- and post-war they were extremely inefficient, costly to use, error-prone, a nightmare for international investors to deal with, completely unaccountable, and so lacking in confidentiality that wealthy clients were targeted by organised crime. Each hegemonic nationalist party created its own successor to the Republic PB because it gave them access to funds and control over money flows. Politically the PBs became very powerful. The Bosniak PB funded the election campaigns of Alia Izetbegović and Haris Silajdzić, for example.[10] As a huge obstacle to the free movement of capital and thus to integration into the global economy, the PBs became top of the hit list for the external donors and IFIs. Abolished for commercial reasons, their functions were taken over by the banking sector. Commercial banks have been no less linked to nationalist factions. The Bank of BiH has close links to the SDA.[11] The Hercegovacka Banka in Mostar – raided by the Stabilisation Force (SFOR) in April 2001 – on suspicion of money laundering was closely linked to the Croat Defence Council and a faction of "Generals" led by Ante Jelavić, including directors of the Mostar Aluminium Company, Pension Fund and Monitor Construction Company (ICG 2001). Moreover, nationalist parties control the financial police of each canton, enabling them to target groups for auditing on the eve of elections.

3   The *"survival"/grey economy* is only partly subject to records and accounting. It enables the majority of the population to get by in a situation where half the adult population is formally unemployed. It subsists on windfalls through personal diaspora contacts and humanitarian agency aid, and through barter, undeclared earnings, and tax avoidance. The survival economy is facilitated by a high proportion of cash transactions.

4   The *mafia/black economy* is outside regulation and beyond accountability. It is partly sustained by the taxation of diasporas and huge sums raised in foreign countries for which there are no proper accounts.[12] In order to exact high returns from smuggling and other operations, it relies on the existence, or deliberate creation, of scarcity and on the absence of social welfare.

Regarding the relation between mafia and market economies two points are crucial. First, mafia structures are virtual communities with a special kind of existence in the imagination that for the most part has a disempowering impact, though there is a great likelihood of people being beneficiaries without realising it. It reduces responsibility, in the sense that the mafia are cited as a *deus ex machina* to explain economic conditions and instil fear of a pervasive power. The black economy works by hidden authority. Corrupt figures who are arrested and face charges are rarely prosecuted by the clientist justice system.[13]

Second, smuggling, moonlighting and so on, are usually constructed as deviations from an ideal standard of market behaviour and a menace to the neo-liberal agenda because they are beyond the control of the IFIs. The grey and black economies are labelled as criminal. But they clearly perform a service in a welfare vacuum: providing means of escape, sustenance, employment and the prospect of personal enrichment. In some communities the mafia economy takes a sophisticated form of parallel governance. The Colombian Revolutionary Armed Forces (FARC) adopted "a minimum wage for coca leaf pickers, a minimum price that must be paid to farmers and a social security system which, amongst other things, provides pensions for retired guerrillas" (Suárez 2000). However, in the black welfare systems of south-east Europe, employees typically forgo formal contracts which regulate employer–employee relations and the system undermines delivery of social protection because the government is deprived of tax income. In Bosnia, retail distribution of cigarettes, chocolate, soap and other commodities is partly in the hands of kerbside sellers who survive on wholesale supplies of dubious origin. World Bank microcredit incentives in Bosnia, pitched at small enterprises and valued at €250–1,000 per project, are insufficient to run a business and only make a sure return if used to feed the black economy in the buying and re-selling of goods.[14]

We should also note, however, that black economies are integral to regulated capitalism. Undeclared work is a prominent feature of societies where welfare provision is inadequate. Corruption may cost the Bosnia government 500 million US dollars annually in lost revenue (equivalent to the budget deficit),[15] but as a percentage of GDP, the estimated black economies in western Europe range from 3 to 7 per cent for Denmark and Sweden to 29–35 per cent for Greece.[16] Indeed, in his investigation into a missing one billion US dollars of public funds in Bosnia in December 1999, US Ambassador Frowick used this argument to play down allegations of corruption.[17]

Strictly speaking the above economies are not parallel and competitive, since they overlap and any one economic unit may be tapping into several forms of activity. In general, international collaboration occurs at the junction between the official and clientist economies. Thus, as will be shown, the formal process of privatisation is subject to capture by the nationalist party system. Corrupt elites thrive in a political vacuum or a compliant political framework. Their niche may be guaranteed by a clientist relationship with politicians of a particular ethnic group. But, unlike the nationalist politicians, the mafias parody the ideals of multi-ethnicity that have been vaunted by international protectors. The mafias trade with any ethnic group to protect and further their empires. To illustrate the survival of corporatism, clientism and the close linkage between political and economic control, we now turn to the case of economic exclusion through labour management in Bosnia.

Politics of privatisation and exclusion

Economic exclusion: workplace discrimination in Bosnia and Herzegovina

Discrimination had already begun in former Yugoslavia as a corollary of economic decline, became a norm during the war, and persisted after the conflict. An investigation by OSCE Human Rights Officers in February–March 1999 found discrimination to be widespread (OSCE 1999). To speak of it as a "labour market" is false because the assumptions of market rationalism are manipulated in order to maintain a closed, protected political system that rewards loyalty and penalises workers who are perceived as threats. Next to the recovery of property, unemployment and the opportunities this creates for discrimination was one of the main concerns of people in Bosnia and of Serbs in Kosovo.[18] Unemployment remained high, at between 40 and 50 per cent (including those on waiting lists) in September 2001, compared to about 15 per cent in 1990.[19] Yet demonstrations and strikes have been rife (340 in 2000) in spite of the risks to workers and the queues of replacements (ICG 2001: 6–7).

The drop in formal economic activity during the war (from the closure or destruction of plants and managers and employees fleeing from frontline areas) provided an alibi for employment discrimination. In conditions of low economic output, high investment risk, restructuring for the market and dysfunctional administrations, employers can still disguise discrimination. Technical obstructions are placed in the way of employment, such as the inability of former workers to retrieve their record of employment or workbook from another entity. Since the workbook is a means of obtaining social security and other rights, inability to recover it is a huge disadvantage. In the absence of positive prohibitions against discrimination in the wartime decrees and in the absence of a new consolidated state law, sackings continued to have deleterious effects on the employment situation. The grounds for discrimination have been more varied since the war, though the majority of cases continue to be related to ethnicity. In this respect the foundation of resistance to outside influence is located in the clientism of the pre-war industrial economy of Yugoslavia.

First, the wartime decrees continue to be respected, and appeals continue to clog the courts. There was a disproportionate effect on those who were persecuted for their identity, penalised indirectly because they could no longer attend a workplace through deportation, flight or fear. In May 1992 Serbs in Bugojno and Donji Vakuf were identified as siding with the "aggressors" and sacked (OSCE 1999: 4). Wartime decrees in the

Republic of Bosnia-Herzegovina and Herceg-Bosna in 1992 led to many being laid off. The former allowed workers to be sacked after twenty days' unjustified absence or if they were defined as aggressors. The latter provided for dismissals for three days' absence without leave and participating in "enemy activities" or "rebellion," as in the case of Livno and Tomislavgrad, where all non-Croats were sacked between July and October 1993. Prominent cases in the Federation in 1997–1998 include the Croat-owned Livno Bus Company and the Mostar Aluminium plant. The education sector has also been a nationalist target for dismissals (OSCE 1999: 11).

Second, workers are penalised for breaking solidarity with the hegemonic nationalist party. Croats in Odzak who backed opposition parties to the Croat Democratic Union (HDZ) were dismissed, and the local President of the Industrial Association, who argued for pre-war workers to be allowed to return to their jobs, was shot. Supporters of Abdić in Bihać and Velika Kladuša were dismissed by SDA managers (OSCE 1999). The close relationship between politics and economic control is illustrated by purges in RS. When the hardline Serb Democratic Party (SDS) won elections in mid-1996, more than a hundred Socialist Party supporters and others were removed from their positions, notoriously at the Kozaraprevoz firm. When the party of Biljana Plavsić won in 1997, SDS members were fired.[20]

Third, trade unionism is also seen as a threat to ethnic manipulation in some areas, even where unions have been ethnically purged. The integration of politics and economic control enables ruling political elites to control workers as well as other economic assets. Trade unions bargain with government officials and are also close to the nationalist parties. Independent unions are discouraged. In Croat areas of the Federation a decree of the Croat Defence Council (HVO) in 1992 prohibited social and civil organisations from former Yugoslavia. Here, "yellow unions" comprise employers and the HDZ officials, and Croat employees have not participated in Federation union meetings (Picod 1999).

Fourth, women are vulnerable to discrimination in the RS and Croat areas of the Federation because priority is given to the families of combatants killed in action, disabled veterans and other ex-combatants (OSCE 1999: 10).

It is a measure of the dislocation of social welfare and employment that "waiting lists" of registered dismissed persons were considered to provide protection against absolute unemployment because those registered were often paid a small sum, at least for a time. In an economy for which labour was as much a social security net as a factor in production, the laying off of "surplus" on to waiting lists (i.e. waiting for war circumstances to end) was as much a political as an economic imperative. The waiting lists were disproportionately filled with minorities who were usually not properly informed and could take no steps to secure redress. The "lists" were meant to be the first resort of employers when re-engaging staff, but minorities are not usually reinstated even though others of the same ethnic group as the employing institution are. The lists continued to be used, illegally, as in the case of non-SDA supporters of the Agrokomerc company, who were placed on the list in 1997 (OSCE 1999: 11).

The structuring of political nationalism incorporates a weak institutional framework for labour relations and a biased judicial system that makes it difficult to secure redress. Social and labour provisions are entity competencies, and in employment issues the state hardly functions. Moreover, within each entity the responsibility for labour is split between government and municipal or cantonal levels. In the Federation there is a Ministry for Social Affairs, Refugees and Displaced Persons which also deals with labour issues, and an equivalent ministry in every canton. Responsibility for labour policy and its implementation is uncharted and virtually a dead letter. Labour laws do not make adequate provision for implementing the anti-discrimination provisions that do grace the constitutions and statutes of the entities. The Labour Inspectorates have powerful formal authority to inspect employers' decisions, but the protection they afford to workers is negligible. Each entity and the Croat areas of the Federation have separate inspectorates, and these are part of the ethnocratic clientism, closely linked to the nationalist parties and to the employers through the enterprise boards appointed by the government or municipality/canton (Picod 1999). The prevalence of abuse and clientism in the legal system also adds to "an atmosphere of impunity." Courts are long-winded and findings in favour of plaintiffs are not implemented (as in the Kozaraprevoz case in RS).

Moreover, it cannot easily be proved that the ethnic, gender or political orientation of those discriminated against is deliberate rather than coincidental. In effect, market rhetoric is employed by nationalist groups to resist the imposition of market principles. But the IFIs appear less concerned to protect employment rights or even to secure the market principle of hiring according to competence, than to reduce entitlements, privatise and "downsize" the labour force in old industries (IMF 2000; Tuzla Citizens Forum 1999). Article 143 of the October 1999 Law on Work meant that 53,993 workers who had been registered on the "waiting lists" lost their job claims at the end of 2000 without an unemployment insurance system in place.[21]

The combined impact of nationalist and international manoeuvring, then, has been to swell the ranks of the economically excluded. Far more critical to the neo-liberal agenda than safeguarding employment has been the push for privatisation. Indeed, collaboration in dismantling social ownership in favour of national and international rentiers has dominated the negotiations over economic change. The policy of privatisation takes precedence over all else. Thus employment creation comes well down the list of criteria for lending by USAID (behind "quick start," exploitation of local raw materials, export potential and exclusion of war criminals).

USAID teams have required borrowers to take their advice or are otherwise deliberately bankrupted.[22]

Ethnic privatisation

According to a UK White Paper on Kosovo: "[t]here is no alternative [to privatisation]; state or socially owned enterprises simply do not work well enough to provide the growth, the new jobs, and the new investment Kosovo needs if it is to meet the aspirations of its people" (in ICG 2000: 37). Privatisation has been top of the international agenda in Bosnia, too. Its implementation demonstrates the extent to which local elites have adapted neo-liberalism to ethnic nationalism. International actors have made a determined drive to redistribute securities, assets and investment opportunities that were formerly in social ownership or under worker or party management. There has not been quite the same opportunity in Bosnia to actually seize assets by force, as in the Trepca industrial complex in Kosovo, but the effort has been sustained through the manipulation of legislation vested in the OHR and conditionalities imposed by IFIs. In the spring of 1997 USAID and other lenders denied credit to inherited state-owned enterprises. In 2000, the OHR, Wolfgang Petritsch, amended the Federation Law on Funds Management Companies and Investment Funds on the grounds that: "Privatisation is a central part of the economic reform that BiH must undergo to bring prosperity and stability to the region."[23]

State enterprise accounted for most of the pre-war production in BiH, as in the rest of former Yugoslavia. The post-war privatisation drive was initially seen as a threat to the division of spoils by the nationalist parties, which did their best to delay its introduction. By the end of 1998 only 26 of an estimated 1,600 companies in RS and 258 of more than 1,600 companies subject to privatisation in the Federation had prepared privatisation plans.[24] For the external IFIs, however, privatisation and the market were non-negotiable conditions of integration that would facilitate foreign investment and market penetration. For example, the widespread public distrust of the private banking sector after a series of frauds and collapses meant that the Central Bank sought foreign bankers to compete in and develop the banking sector, controlling loan policy, investment and credit. In 2001 they controlled 40 per cent of the Federation's bank assets (ICG 2001: 22).

"Ethnic privatisation," the term used by Professor Žarko Papić, was the compromise that the parallel nationalist economies absorbed in order to take advantage of development and aid funds. After a phase of resistance to privatisation from 1996 to 1998, the nationalist parties sought to control both the process and the asset holding.[25] The ownership and management of enterprises were determined by the nationalist parties. Telecommunications (including broadcasting) and energy (electricity and gas) were divided on ethno-party lines to provide major sources of revenue for the nationalist parties and their parallel structures.[26]

The favoured model in Croat parts of the Federation was "co-capitalis-ation," invented by Franjo Tudjman in Croatia proper for distribution of government and socially-owned assets. It was first introduced into Mostar and other Croat councils, and then copied in Bosniak areas. The process involved the creation of shadow boards for taking over enterprises prior to privatisation, often consisting of the same people who controlled the post-war division of spoils. The management would then write contracts making it impossible to privatise the firm unless the existing director had con-tinuity. Former state enterprises are commonly allowed to run down, the assets stripped, and the property sold to the shadow board at rock bottom price. War damages have been falsified in order to claim that investment has been spent on repairs. The enterprises are expected to make contributions to the dominant local nationalist party.[27]

Ethno-privatisation should matter to overseas investors. A nationalist rather than profit-maximising ownership is likely to incur opportunity costs in lost efficiency, and the informal or illegal taxation adds significantly to development costs. But the normative assumptions of the external actors and the interests of domestic elites coincide in extracting profit from public goods and in fostering opportunities from privatisation and discrimination against social ownership. This seems more fundamental than divergences between clientist and neo-liberal strategies for managing investment, shares and profits. For example, the HDZ took over manage-ment of Aluminij Mostar in 1996 and had the enterprise valued at 84 million US dollars, a fraction of its pre-war value of 620 million US dollars, though the plant had suffered little war damage and its exports in the first year of revival reached 85 million US dollars. The management privatised the company through a co-capitalisation process, with shares almost exclusively allocated to Croats. At the same time, Daimler Chrysler of Germany planned to "rescue" the company, and the OHR appointed a team of independent auditors. The auditors acknowledged that illegalities had occurred but "for political and practical reasons" recommended that the ownership structure should remain undisturbed. The UK Ambassador observed that the ownership structure was illegal and the company scanda-lously managed. "Alliance for Change" politicians refused to recognise the audit and demanded that the OHR restore the company to the state, but Petritsch demurred on the grounds that he could only offer counsel.[28]

Conclusion: dilemmas of neo-liberalism

Re-structuring has produced a capitalist nomenklatura that orders the economy for the benefit of patrimonies and party structures, collaborating with international actors where it sees benefits. Entrepreneurs in the protectorates have thus successfully transferred the clientist system into the post-conflict political economies. Resistance and then negotiation with the conditionality imposed by "protectors" has ensured that they have secured a healthy position to protect clientism within the processes of privatisation and deregulation. Various pressures have gathered against them. Elites in Bosnia, for example, have had to adapt to a diminution of economic support from patrons outside, whether Moslem, Croat or Serb. An inability to deliver economic growth and social services appears to have encouraged voting for non-nationalist groups (Cobble and Pugh 2001). The EU is committed to a new kind of contractual relationship with south-east Europe, holding out the prospect of EU membership and new standards of governance. A Consultative Task Force has been created to help Bosnia meet the technical conditions of an association agreement that could entail the dismantling of corporatist structures. The war elites exert influence over the forces of law and order and judicial systems and are seemingly immune from prosecution. Moreover, the sector that could have provided the focus for generating a divorce between economic and political institutions, a reformist middle class and technocracy, is too sparse for mediating social development and building state-like institutions for perhaps another fifteen years (Peirce and Stubbs 2000). For the foreseeable future, economic empires will be maintained by massaging old patrimonial, corporatist, clientist and nationalist structures, values and attitudes.

This has led some observers to call for greater international trusteeship rather than less. For example, independent "think-tanks," such as the International Crisis Group (ICG) and European Stability Initiative (ESI), have recommended smashing the clientist power structures to facilitate integration into the Euro-economy (ICG 1999; ESI 2000). The ESI considers that external agencies *have* succeeded in some areas, in creating a Central Bank for example. More intrusive manipulation, through the OHR's authority, the IFIs' conditionality and selective budgetary support from the major donors, is proposed in order to break up existing structures.

But such solutions would require full-blown trusteeship that ignores an inherent contradiction in the promotion of deregulation and democracy through an unaccountable, dirigiste and authoritarian executive that enables war entrepreneurs to evade responsibility. It overlooks the extent to which neo-liberalism might foster social divisions and, through deregulation, facilitate black and grey economic activities. Besides, it is unlikely that the external agencies are willing to commit themselves to this level of authoritarian intrusion for an indefinite period.

Alternatively, the IFIs have launched measures designed to mitigate the harmful impacts of economic liberalisation – notably the substitution of "shock therapy" and "structural adjustment" programmes by "poverty reduction strategies." Although raw neo-liberalism has been softened, developmentalists show that this has not changed the macro-economic conditionalities or provided additional and adequate means to sustain public social services, employment and local productive capacity. Reformism has had little overall effect on reducing poverty, and is "blind to the crucial role of basic social services" (Thomas 2000: 93–109; Willett 2001: 35–45). In

May 2000, the World Bank's country assistance strategy for Bosnia included strengthening the social safety net. The Bank approved a 14.6 million US dollars credit, repayable over thirty-five years, for educational development and welfare policies for the most vulnerable.[29] But this represents only about a third of the sum committed merely to managing the privatization process.

Apart from their recent wars and ethnic cleansing, the protectorates in south-east Europe display similarities with the disruptive transformations of post-socialist economies in central and eastern Europe. But unlike central and eastern Europe they have been subject to direct governance by externals who were in a position to build on collectivist traditions operating on the political economy. External policies might have nurtured protection of local production and sufficiency in a mixed economy with an emphasis on self-sustaining cooperative ventures, the public aspects of infrastructure reform and social services, including attention to improved and regular pay for public sector workers. Commensurate with alternative strategies for local economic self-reliance elaborated since the mid-1990s,[30] investment in public/cooperative ownership and welfare would be appropriate alternatives to corporate control of social assets. The current balance in negotiation does not deliver economic or social justice to the majority of the populations. Indeed, the political economies of the protectorates are unlikely to sustain human needs without some analogue of collective provision for employment, welfare and public services to protect the populations from clientism, mafia welfare and neo-liberal priorities.

Acknowledgement

An abbreviated version of some of this chapter's content appeared in *Global Governance*, 8 (4), autumn 2002.

Notes

1 John Gray [Professor of European Thought, London School of Economics], "Our newest protectorate," *The Guardian*, 27 April 1999.
2 Thanks are due to Alan Bullion who first used the term (1995: 161).
3 See Berdal and Malone (2000), Collier (1999, 2000a), Cooper (2001), Duffield (1998, 2001), ICRC (2000), Jean and Rufin (1996), Kaldor (1999), Macrae and Leader (2000).
4 They included the Geči and Jashari clans in Kosovo, the Croat 'Tuta' in Mostar, the Bosniak Naser Orić in Srebrenica, the Serbs Grujić in Zvornik and Milan Lukić in Višegrad, and the Bosniak Čelo in Sarajevo. The Bosniak, Jusuf 'Juka' Prazina, threw in his lot with the Croats, then fled to Belgium where he was assassinated in 1993. See Mueller (2000: 34).
5 "Islamska Zajednica u Velikoj Kladuši," *Dani*, 6 August 1999: 26–27.
6 Martin Walker, "Balkan nations could join EU," *The Guardian*, 9 April 1999. The sum includes loans that will have to be repaid.
7 UNMIK web site, 14 August 2000 (www.un.org).

8 OHR press release, "High Representative and PIC [Peace Implementation Council] Steering Board call on Alliance Government," 13 September 2001.

9 BiH TV News, 22 December 1999, OHR E-mail service.

10 USAID, *Payments Bureaus in Bosnia and Herzegovina: Obstacles to Development and a Strategy for Orderly Transition*, Final Draft, Economic Reconstruction Office, Sarajevo, 15 February 1999, pp. 90, 101; International Advisory Group, *Functional Analysis and Strategic Implementation Plan: Transformation of the Payment Bureaus in Bosnia and Herzegovina*, Sarajevo, July 1999.

11 "Abeceda korupcije," *Dani* (Sarajevo), 27 August 1999: 16–21.

12 The "Saudi Arabian Appeal" occupies a large, handsome building at 10 Maršala Tita, a prime site in Sarajevo.

13 Instances of corruption are legion, and in 1999 several Tuzla canton ministers were charged with embezzlement and other offences. But the Mayor of Sanski Most appears to have broken all records for the range and number of corruption charges. Interview with OSCE office, Tuzla, 27 September 1999.

14 Interview with Azra Hasanbegović, President, *Udruženje Žena BiH*, Mostar, 20 September 1999.

15 Peter van Walsum, OHR Economics Division, in *UN Envoy says Officials Involved in Corruption*, UN Wire, 17 August 2000 (http://www.unfoundation. org). The RS Customs Service uncovered a smuggling operation when it investigated the GMD-Hercegovina company of Trebinje for tax avoidance of €160,000. Open Broadcast Network (henceforth OBN), 8 and 19 January 2000, OHR E-mail service.

16 European Commission Report cited by Martin Walker, "EU 'victim of growing black economy",' *The Guardian*, 6 April 1998.

17 See Xavier Bougarel, "Ten-Year Chapter of Errors: Mixed Motives in the Balkans", *Le Monde diplomatique*, September 1990; "Kako I gdje je skršena milijarda," *Dani* (Sarajevo), 20 August 1999: 18–19; "Otkriti i napasti temelje kriminala I korupcije," *Osloboddenje*, (Sarajevo), 18 September 1999; R. Jeffrey Smith, "In Bosnia, Free Enterprise Has Gotten Way Out of Hand," *International Herald Tribune*, 27 December 1999.

18 Federation Ombudsman, Annual Report on the Situation of Human Rights in BiH, Sarajevo, March 1997, cited in Picod (1999).

19 Central Bank of BiH, "Economic Indicators," *Statistical Bulletin*, No. 3, January–September 2001, Sarajevo, p. 8.

20 Interview with Agnes Picod, Human Rights Officer, OHR, Sarajevo, 30 September 1999; OSCE (1999: 19).

21 OBN, 1 May 2000, OHR E-mail service.

22 Interview with Dr Mike E. Sarhan, Director Economic Restructuring Office, USAID, Sarajevo, 16 September 1999.

23 OHR press release, Sarajevo, 18 August 2000, OHR E-mail service. See also, *Privatization News*, Agency for Privatisation in the Federation of BiH, Sarajevo, various issues.

24 Obstacles to privatisation are revealed in "Private Sector Development," progress report of the Private Sector Development Task Force Secretariat, Sarajevo, September 1999.

25 Interview with Professor Žarko Papić, Independent Bureau for Humanitarian Issues, Sarajevo, 30 September 1999; "Ethička privatizacija: neograničene mogućosti prevare," *Dani*, 6 August 1999: 20–21.

26 For example, the SDA controls utilities such as the PTT, Elektroprivreda, and Energoinvest, *Dani*, 6 August 1999: 16–19; European Stability Initiative, "Reshaping International Priorities in Bosnia and Hercegovina," part 1, "Bosnian Power Structures," Berlin, 14 October 1999; "Taking on the Commanding Heights," Berlin and Brussels, 3 May 2000.

27 A major quarrel occurred in Croatia when the beneficiary of a hotel in Split failed to make a large enough contribution to the HDZ. Interview with James Lyon, ICG, Sarajevo, 29 September 1999.

28 UK Ambassador Graham Hand in "Privatizacija Aluminija je potpuno kriminalna," *Dani* (Sarajevo), 24 August 2001; "German Daimler Chrysler wants to Purchase Aluminij Mostar," *Jutarnji List* (Zagreb), 28 August 2001; "Political War over the Mostar-based 'Aluminij'," *Večernji List* (Zagreb), 31 August 2001; "The Suspicious Privatization of 'Aluminij'," *Nacional* (Zagreb), 6 September 2001.

29 UN wire, "Bosnia-Herzegovina: World Bank Announces Assistance Strategy," www.unfoundation.org (25 May 2000).

30 See, e.g. The Earth Charter Intiative, "The Earth Charter," Costa Rica, March 2000, para.10c (available at: www.earthcharter.org/draft/charter.htm).

References

Ali, T. (ed.) (2000) *Masters of the Universe? Nato's Balkan Crusade*, London: Verso.

Berdal, M. and Keen, D. (1997) "Violence and Economic Agendas in Civil Wars: Some Implications for Outside Intervention," *Millennium*, 26 (3): 795–818.

Berdal, M. and Malone, D. (eds) (2000) *Greed and Grievance: Economic Agendas in Civil Wars*, Boulder: Lynne Rienner.

Booth, K. (1999) "NATO's Republic: Warnings from Kosovo," *Civil Wars*, 2 (3): 89–95.

Bougarel, X. (1996) "L'economie du conflit Bosniaque: entre predation et production," in F. Jean and J-C. Rufin (eds) *Economie des Guerres Civiles*, Paris: Hachette.

Bullion, A. (1995) *India, Sri Lanka and Tamil Crisis 1976–1994: An International Perspective*, London: Pinter.

Cameron, A. and Palan, R. (1999) "The Imagined Economy: Mapping Transformations in the Contemporary State," *Millennium*, 28 (2): 267–288.

Cobble, M. and Pugh, M. (2001) "Non-Nationalist Voting in Bosnian Municipal Elections: Implications for Democracy and Peacebuilding," *Journal of Peace Research*, 38 (1): 27–47.

Collier, P. (1999) "On the Economic Consequences of Civil War," *Oxford Economic Papers*, 51 (1): 168–183.

—— (2000a) "Economic Causes of Civil Conflict and Their Implications for Policy," World Bank, http://www.globalpolicy.org/security/issues/diamond/wb. htm

—— (2000b) "Doing Well out of War: an Economic Perspective," in M. Berdal and D. Malone (eds) *Greed and Grievance: Economic Agendas in Civil Wars*, Boulder: Lynne Rienner.

Cooper, N. (2001) "Conflict Goods: The Challenges for Peacekeeping and Conflict Prevention," *International Peacekeeping*, 8 (3): 21–38.

Cox, M. (1998) *Strategic Approaches to International Intervention in Bosnia and Herzegovina*, paper given at Third International Security Forum, Zurich, 19–21 October.

Duffield, M. (1997) "NGO Relief in War Zones: Towards an Analysis of the New Aid Paradigm," *Third World Quarterly*, 18 (3): 527–542.

—— (1998) "Post-Modern Conflict: Warlords, Post-Adjustment States and Private Protection," *Journal of Civil Wars*, 1 (1): 65–102.

—— (2001) *Global Governance and the New Wars: The Merging of Development and Security*, London: Zed Books.

ESI (European Stability Initiative) (2000) *Taking on the Commanding Heights*, Berlin and Brussels, discussion paper, 3 May.

Hibou, B. (1998) *The Political Economy of the World Bank's Discourse: From Economic Catechism to Missionary Deeds (and Misdeeds)*, Les études du CERI (39), Paris.

ICG (International Crisis Group) (1999) *Is Dayton Failing? Bosnia Four Years After the Peace Agreement*, Sarajevo, 29 October.

—— (2000) "Kosovo Report Card," *Report no. 100*, Pristina/Brussels, 28 August.

—— (2001) "Bosnia's Precarious Economy: Still Not Open for Business," *Report no. 115*, Sarajevo/Brussels, 7 August.

ICRC (International Committee of the Red Cross) (2000) *Forum: War Money and Survival*, Geneva: ICRC.

IMF (International Monetary Fund) (2000) *Bosnia and Herzegovina: Selected Issues and Statistical Appendix*, Washington DC, 26 June.

Inayatullah, N. and Blaney, D. (1999) "Towards an Ethnological IPE: Karl Polayni's Double Critique of Capitalism," *Millennium*, 28 (2): 311–340.

Jean, F. and Rufin, J-C. (eds) (1996) *Economie des guerres civiles*, Paris: Hachette.

Kaldor, M. (1999) *New and Old Wars: Organized Violence in a Global Era*, Cambridge: Polity Press.

Keen, D. (1998) "The Economic Functions of Violence in Civil Wars," *Adelphi Papers*, 320, Oxford: Oxford University Press.

—— (2001) "War and Peace: What's the Difference?," in Adebajo Adeyke (ed.) *Conflict Management in the New Millennium*, London: Frank Cass.

Korosić, M. (1988) *Jugoslavenska kriza*, Zagreb: Naprijed.

Le Billon, P. (2000) *The Political Economy of War: What Relief Agencies Need to Know*, HPN Paper 33, London: Overseas Development Institute.

Macrae, J. (2000) "Oil . . . and Water: Political and Humanitarian Intervention in the Serbian Energy Sector," *Relief and Rehabilitation Newsletter*, 16: 26–28.

Macrae, J. and Leader, N. (2000) *Shifting Sands; The Search for "Coherence" Between Political and Humanitarian Responses to Complex Political Emergencies*, Humanitarian Practice Group Report no. 7, London: Overseas Development Institute.

Mueller, J. (2000) *The Banality of "Ethnic War": Yugoslavia and Rwanda*, paper given at American Political Science Assocation conference, Washington DC, 31 August–3 September 2000.

OSCE (1999) *Employment Discrimination in Bosnia and Herzegovina*, OSCE Mission to BiH Human Rights Department, Sarajevo, June 1999.

O'Tuathail, G., Herod, A. and Roberts, S. (1998) "Negotiating Unruly Problematics," in A. Herod, G. O'Tuathail and S. Roberts (eds) *Unruly World? Globalization, Governance and Geography*, London: Routledge.

Paris, R. (1997) "Peacebuilding and the Limits of Liberal Internationalism," *International Security*, 22 (2): 54–89.

Peirce, P. and Stubbs, P. (2000) "Peacebuilding, Hegemony and Integrated Social Development," in Michael Pugh (ed.) *Regeneration of War-torn Societies*, Basingstoke: Macmillan.

Petras, J. and Vieux, S. (1996) "Bosnia and the Revival of US Hegemony," *New Left Review*, 218: 3–25.

Picard, E. (1996) "Liban: la matrice historique," in F. Jean and J-C. Rufin (eds) *Economie des Guerres Civiles*, Paris: Hachette.

Picod, A. (1999) *Discrimination in Employment*, background paper, OHR, Sarajevo, January 1999.

Pugh, M. (2000) Protectorate Democracy in South-east Europe, working paper 10 Copenhagen: COPRI.

Puntarić, M. (2001) "Three Herzegovinian Kings of Oil," *Slobodna Dalmacija*, Split, 21 September (OHR trans).

Rufin, J-C (1996) "Les economies de guerre dans les conflits internes," in F. Jean and J-C. Rufin (eds), *Economie des Guerres Civiles*, Paris: Hachette.

Schierup, C-U. (1990) *Migration, Socialism and the International Division of Labour*, Aldershot: Avebury.

—— (1993) "Prelude to the Inferno. Economic Disintegration and Political Fragmentation of Socialist Yugoslavia," *Migration*, 5: 5–40.

—— (1999) "The Spectre of Balkanism," in C-U. Schierup (ed.) *Scramble for the Balkans*, London: Macmillan: 36–39.

Suárez, A.R. (2000) "Parasites and Predators: Guerillas and the Insurrection Economy of Colombia," *Journal of International Economic Affairs*, 53 (2): 577–601.

Sørensen, J.S. (1999) "The Threatening Precedent: Kosovo and the Remaking of Crisis," *MERGE* paper on Transcultural Studies 2/99, Umeå/Norrköping.

Thomas, C. (2000) *Global Governance, Development and Human Security*, London: Pluto.

Tuzla Citizens Forum (1999) *The Right to Work: Social Aspects of Privatisation*, round table report, Bijeljina, 16 September.

Uvin, P. (1999) *The Influence of Aid in Situation of Violent Conflict*, report of the Informal Task Group on Conflict, Peace and Development Cooperation, Development Assistance Committee, Paris: OECD, September .

Vucinich, W.S. (1969) "Nationalism and Communism," in W.S. Vucinich (ed.) *Contemporary Yugoslavia: Twenty Years of Socialist Experiment*, Berkeley and Los Angeles: University of California Press.

Wiberg, H. (1999) *Background and Phases of the Kosovo Conflict: NATO Goal Attainment*, paper presented at "The Lessons of Kosovo," COPRI conference, 13 September, Copenhagen.

Willett, S. (2001) "Insecurity Conflict and the New Global Disorder," Institute of Development Studies Bulletin, 32 (2): 35–45.

Woodward, S. (1995) *The Balkan Tragedy: Chaos and Dissolution after the Cold War*, Washington DC: Brookings Institution.

Wright, P. (2000) *Sanctions and Yugoslavia: from Stalin to NATO*, paper at conference on "The Yugoslav Crisis," University of Bradford, 24–26 March.

4 Suspended reality

Historical perspectives on the political economy of northern Iraq

Michael Robert Hickok

Introduction: embargo politics

The 1991 defeat of Iraqi forces following their invasion of Kuwait by the American-led coalition prompted a series of political and economic changes in Iraq that have yet to be fully resolved. Baghdad was able to use the remains of its security forces to put down political resistance in the northern and southern provinces by the summer of 1991 but has yet to reintegrate these portions of the country as part of the post-war reconstruction. The northern Kurdish provinces in particular have been the site of regular international intervention, competition between various Kurdish political factions, and a consistent attempt by Baghdad to manipulate events, most directly in an armed attack in September of 1996. Despite negotiations between the United Nations and Iraq to ease the economic sanctions and restore basic living conditions, the political exploitation of internal economic policies has set the stage for future conflict.

Alexander Joffe argued recently that "the most immediate issue concerning Iraq today, as it has been for nearly a decade, is how to rid the country of Saddam Husain and the odious Ba'th regime" (Joffe 2000: 33). To achieve this end, he advocated convening an international conference to design a truth and reconciliation commission, spreading criminal indictments beyond Saddam Husain and his immediate advisors, organizing study groups to examine the dismantling of Iraqi security organizations, and finally communicating these plans to the people of Iraq. The equating of the Iraqi experience with the approach to post-apartheid South Africa highlights the tenuous assumptions underlying much of the debate on Iraq following the formal end of Gulf War hostilities.

In the immediate aftermath of the war, the Bush administration believed that a disgruntled military leadership would turn on Saddam Husain, replacing him but otherwise leaving the country relatively intact. When faced instead with Saddam Husain's consolidation of control over the government and the people in 1991, the Bush administration chose to follow an indirect method of persuasion through continued economic sanctions backed by intermittent military strikes. A US State Department official publicly noted that although Saddam Husain had previously enjoyed the support of Iraq's middle class, it "will have to be bought off after this war but there's less money to do it with now." He went on to argue that "to rule a prosperous Iraq, Saddam Husain needed a happy army, but the army was happy when it had toys."[1] Economic sanctions designed to increase the level of popular discomfort were meant to realize a change in regime where outright military defeat had failed. In other words, the economic sanctions were created with a simplistic political goal in mind, giving little thought to the longer-term impact on the economic system in Iraq.

One of the difficulties of using economic sanctions to achieve an absolute political objective – the removal of Saddam Husain's government – is that it allowed the Iraqi leader to control the intermediate measures of its effectiveness. Surveys of the damage done by the sanctions generally focused on the destruction of the health care system, the chronic malnourishment, the increase in child mortality, and the collapse of the education system (Zunes 1998: 101–103). Washington has attempted to defend the policy by reminding the international community that it is the Iraqi government that decides where to invest its limited national resources and that the suffering represents Saddam Husain's callousness and not American indifference to the fate of the Iraqi people. Long-time observers of the Middle East were well aware prior to the Gulf War that Saddam Husain and his ruling elite did not care much for the people of Iraq, in particular those in the Kurdish north and the Shiite south. However, the purpose of the sanctions was not to kindle in the president's heart a sense of responsibility for the welfare of his people but to spark the fire of revolution in an oppressed population. This approach also underscored the failure to understand the interaction and broader historical context of the political and economic trends in Iraq, downplaying the difficulties of rebuilding the country regardless of regime orientation.

America's simplified formula for a post-war Iraq can be characterized by three clearly recognizable courses of action that have also shaped the international community's behavior in Iraq over the last decade:

1 Washington continued to demonize Saddam Husain publicly while trying to force his removal as president through indirect means.
2 The United Nations acting under pressure from the United States retained economic sanctions and weapons inspections while seeking to lessen the humanitarian impact on the population as a whole.
3 By means of both the campaign to remove Saddam Husain and the program to diminish the suffering linked to the sanctions, it was intended to achieve the rebuilding of the economy and the formation of a more democratic state. This rested on the implicit belief that a post-Saddam Husain, post-sanctions Iraq could divert restored oil revenues to this purpose.

Using the situation in northern Iraq – where the United Nations and the Western military alliance has had the greatest freedom to act – this chapter will attempt to argue that the analysis of the political economy in Iraq was distorted after the Gulf War and has actually raised the likelihood of further regional conflict. The argumentation will be developed in four steps. First, the country assessments of the post-war situation in Iraq made in 1991 concentrated on the immediate circumstances and masked endemic structural problems in the economy. Second, the analytical work done on the economy in the northern Kurdish provinces has accentuated the political rivalries by positing the need for continued integration in an Iraqi state with the current sovereign boundaries. Third, the attempt by the international community to create a self-sustaining economy in northern Iraq in the 1992–2000 period ignored the main political objectives of the Western alliance and the underlying dynamics of the regional markets. When combined, these policy trends have established an artificial situation in northern Iraq that is unsustainable regardless of whether Saddam Husain and the sanctions disappear or of the eventual flow of oil. They have increased the incentives for competition instead of cooperation.

The morning after the bombs

The internal situation in Iraq in the aftermath of the war did not really draw attention until efforts by the Baghdad government to restore control over the Kurdish north and the largely Shiite south led to refugee flows crossing into neighboring states. The commanders of the coalition forces had turned away from the military implications of Saddam Husain's internal security campaigns but were forced into responding with activities like "Operation Provide Comfort" to meet the humanitarian crisis of displaced populations. The confusion about the condition and future of Iraq in the spring and summer of 1991 prompted a series of early assessments.

In July, the UN released the report of Sadruddin Aga Khan – the Secretary-General's Executive Delegate for the UN Inter-Agency Humanitarian Programme for Iraq, Kuwait, and the Iraq/Iran and Iraq/Turkey border areas – who had led a mission to visit the country from 29 June to 13 July 1991. His group examined Operation Provide Comfort's activities to relocate and provide basic services to the Kurdish refugees in the north and surveyed the damage done to the Iraqi economy during the war. The report's summary concluded the obvious that Iraq "continued to face an enormous challenge in its attempt to recover from the ravages of the war."[2] The focus of the report, however, suggested that the impact of the economic and financial sanctions imposed on Iraq was "very substantial" on both its economy and the living conditions at a time when allegedly the last food reserves were being exhausted. The UN went so far as to place a special alert on 19 July 1991 to donors to meet immediate food needs in Iraq. Sadruddin Aga Khan argued in the report that the collapse of the health system, transportation network, sanitation infrastructure, and energy grid was leading to a humanitarian crisis of unprecedented proportions, placing most of the responsibility on damage incurred during the war while making some reference to the difficulties caused by the Baghdad government. Members of the mission told reporters that "Iraq should be allowed to sell oil to buy food and medicine and to restore sewage systems destroyed by bombing in the war . . . Iraq is seen needing 6.85 billion US dollars in the next years to prevent this disaster."[3] These official statements were given human faces by press reports from damaged cities throughout the country. For example, Mary McCory – citing official Iraqi sources – ran a series of stories, claiming that "the West and the US have done nothing to prevent massive die offs [*sic*] of Iraqi children."[4]

In contrast, there were reports that Iraqi leaders were exaggerating the immediate humanitarian problems to manipulate international sympathy. Descriptions of Baghdad's use of untraceable fiscal reserves to finance rebuilding projects and to purchase food on the international markets began to surface in the winter of 1991.[5] Foreign journalists toured Baghdad with mixed impressions. Two Soviet reporters contrasted the consumer situation prior to the war with the situation in spring 1991. They concluded that while inefficient and badly stocked state stores and offices had taken over much of the economy from private stores, which had previously sold goods stolen from Kuwait, daily life continued uninterrupted.[6] Later studies suggested that the threat of imminent social collapse resulted from hysteria over the unproven linkage between the shortages in food, power, and public services and their effect on the life of the Iraqi people. For example, one scholar has argued that in 1991 "Iraqi women personally and physically replaced, through their household labor and management, the entire high-tech infrastructure and non-domestic economy of wartime and post-war Iraq" (Cainkar 1993: 16). These descriptions of Iraqi adaptation to the economic restrictions and of efforts to rebuild the damage from the war bolstered American arguments that continued economic sanctions would remain necessary to force a behavioral change in the political regime. The willingness to accept that the situation in Iraq was not as bad as was being reported by the UN and others gained strength as Saddam Husain's military continued operations against opposition movements in the north and the south.

The curious element to competing descriptions about Iraq's looming collapse or about Saddam Husain's economic reserves and the resilience of the Iraqi people was the willingness of observers to accept the validity of largely circumstantial evidence. This became most obvious in the debates in New York over the UN resolution to permit Iraq to sell oil to raise money for humanitarian needs. The official UN position during the deliberation rested primarily on the conclusions set out in Sadruddin Aga Khan's report. The UN had initially advocated allowing Iraq to sell more than the 1.6 billion US dollars' worth of oil over six months, to which the

UN finally agreed in the belief that Iraq's domestic crisis was significantly greater than was widely understood.[7] In support of this position, France and China were pressing for an outright lifting of the sanctions. A Chinese Foreign Ministry official in March 1991 publicly advocated an end to Iraq's economic isolation, saying that "a cease-fire of the Gulf war is achieved and the innocent Iraqi people are having serious difficulties in daily life."[8]

Skeptics argued that any revenues generated by the sale of Iraqi oil should be used first to pay war reparations. On an issue raised initially by British officials, the American representatives at the UN also were insisting that oil profits subsidize the relief operations in northern Iraq, which were expected to cost 500 million US dollars over six months.[9] Washington at the outset wanted over 50 percent of the oil income to be set aside for repaying Kuwait, suggesting that the alleged suffering of the Iraqi people was at best a secondary concern. The Iraqi diplomats did not help matters when they protested that Iraq had the sovereign right to dispose of its resources in the matter deemed most necessary by the government. Their position implied that Baghdad also did not believe that the economic and humanitarian situation throughout the country was the primary concern for a rebuilding program.

Unable to confirm the true extent of the crisis in Iraq, the UN demonstrated with this resolution that sanctions policies would be shaped less by economic and humanitarian considerations than by political goals as articulated primarily in Washington. In theory, oil revenues would be sent directly to the UN, which would first pay down war reparations with a third of the money. Second, the funds themselves were to be held in an escrow account which Iraq could access for credit to purchase specific humanitarian goods as approved by a special UN oversight board. Without going into the details of the UN sanctions regime, this paternalistic oversight of the oil revenues set the stage for the current situation where the UN directly manages the percentage of the funds earmarked for northern Iraq while allowing Saddam Husain's government control over the disposition of resources in the rest of the country. In 1991, the debate remained largely academic as Baghdad's refusal to accept the terms of the resolution postponed the country's return to the official oil markets for several years. The bottom line remained, however, that the humanitarian relief policies, like the economic sanctions regime, came to serve the political objective of putting pressure on Saddam Husain's government and not to ameliorate the living conditions of the Iraqi people, for which there was no real consensus in the first place.

There was a certain degree of irony in this course of events. A series of lesser-known studies at the UN and in Washington on Iraqi activities leading to the invasion of Kuwait was beginning to make a case for an economic crisis in Iraq that predated the Gulf War. The implicit conclusion in many of these reports was that, although the damage incurred during the war was significant, the historic and systemic economic problems in the country overshadowed these more obvious conditions. The authors cautioned that relief activities designed to address the refugee situation might have the adverse and unintended impact of making eventual reconstruction more difficult.

In March 1991, UN Under-Secretary General Martti Ahtisaari led a mission to Iraq to assess the humanitarian needs in Kuwait and Iraq in the immediate post-crisis environment. It was his mission's conclusion that the Iraqi people faced an "imminent catastrophe, which could include epidemic and famine, if massive life-supporting needs are not rapidly met" (Ahtisaari 1991). This early survey formed the basis for the more detailed work done by the second UN mission in July. But in an often quoted, initial impression of the country, Ahtisaari noted:

> The recent conflict has wrought near-apocalyptic results upon the economic infrastructure of what had been, until January 1991, a rather highly urbanized and mechanized society. Now, most means of modern life support have been destroyed or rendered tenuous. Iraq has, for some time to come, been relegated to a pre-industrial age, but with all the disabilities of a post-industrial dependency on an intensive use of energy and technology.
>
> (Ahtisaari 1991: S/22366, Paragraph A)

Although he claimed that his mandate limited him to an assessment of the requirements for urgent humanitarian assistance, Ahtisaari added to his initial impression of the situation that the obstacles to rebuilding Iraq's economy were huge and appeared in part to have preceded the conflict. Looking at the shattered infrastructure, his team wrote that much of the public works and transportation net had already been in a state of decline prior to their destruction by the allied bombs.

In a staff report to the US Senate Committee on Foreign Relations, similar conclusions were being raised about the historical context for the current situation, in particular in the northern provinces. The committee had tasked Peter W. Galbraith to prepare a study on the civil war in Iraq and the prospects for the rise of political opposition in the face of Saddam Husain's campaigns to restore central control. Much of the report focused on the northern Kurdish provinces where alliance military forces were cooperating with the UN to solve the refugee crisis on the Turkish border and return the Kurdish villagers to their homes. In the process of chronicling the horrors committed by the Iraqi military during its campaign to retake control of northern Iraq in March 1991, Galbraith indicated that much of the damage being reported by American Special Forces officers and by UN officials as they traveled through the Kurdish areas actually dated back to the mid-1980s when Baghdad had attacked Kurdish insurgency forces then supporting Iran during the Iran–Iraq war. According to the Senate committee report, much of the destruction in northern Iraq – described in the UN mission's July report as resulting from post-Gulf War fighting between the Iraqi military and the Kurdish opposition forces – had been inflicted years previously and was indicative of long-standing Iraqi economic policies in relation to its northern provinces (Gailbraith 1991: 11–13).

Jonathan Randal, who covered Operation Provide Comfort for the *Washington Post*, made the same argument in his study of America's Kurdish policy (Randal 1997). The humanitarian crisis in northern Iraq in 1991 represented the culmination of long-running political and economic trends that, although accentuated by the Gulf War, were not fundamentally the result of the damage suffered during the aftermath of Iraq's loss. Historically, the main economic activity in these Kurdish provinces had been grain production and herding. Baghdad's counter-insurgency campaigns in the 1970s and 1980s relocated much of the rural population into urban slums or into centralized villages, making it difficult to continue traditional modes of agricultural and pastoral production in the one area of Iraq that gets enough rainfall to forgo the problems of irrigation.

In addition to the security concerns, Saddam Husain's government also adopted a trade policy that changed the country's system of domestic production. Despite receiving the largest share of investment in development planning, the agricultural sector had declined in importance in the three decades prior to the Gulf War (Al-Roubaie 1990: 85–86). Iraq adopted economic policies to use currency earned from oil exports to import food and consumer goods. For political reasons, it was unlikely that Baghdad would welcome international efforts to restore agricultural production in the northern Kurdish provinces thereby creating a potential dependency on a segment of the Iraqi population with clear anti-Saddam Husain leanings. Moreover, economists were arguing prior to the Gulf War that the government's trade policy had created a situation where the impact of increased production in certain economic sectors including agriculture would only "produce a limited effect on the rest of the economy" (Al-Roubaie 1990: 89). For example, cereal production at the end of 1989 had dropped to 52 percent of its level at the beginning of the decade. For political and economic reasons, there was doubt about the efficacy of changing the regime's behavior by holding "the bread basket of Iraq" – as the north was described in Western discussions – hostage to Saddam Husain's future cooperation. Baghdad had created much of the economic devastation long before the Western alliance came along and had only limited interests in seeing things remedied. In fact, Iraq's response to the Western military intervention during Operation Provide Comfort was to impose its own economic embargo on those areas of northern Iraq where Baghdad had limited or no authority.

From Saddam Husain's perspective, the economic situation in northern Iraq was minor in comparison to the larger structural problems facing the country's economy. It had started to occur to outside observers that in addition to whatever irrational and megalomaniac motivations existed for Saddam Husain's decision to invade Kuwait in 1990, there were also some basic economic realities involved. A decade of destruction caused by the Iran–Iraq war led to the convergence of three economic problems in 1989:

1   There had been a continual decline in oil revenues, which were the sole significant source of export for Iraq and subsidized the importation of food and consumer goods.
2   Iraq had borrowed heavily for the first time during the war years, ending in an estimated 86 billion US dollars in debt to the West, the Soviet bloc, and to other Arab countries.
3   Baghdad attempted to attract foreign investors by privatizing and deregulating state industries. Although the long-term effects of this policy change were derailed by the war, the immediate effects in 1989 and 1990 were an increase in consumer prices, system-wide inflation, and unemployment, lowering the living standards of millions of Iraqis.

As the economist Abbas Alnasrawi argued:

> While political historians and other analysts will debate the motives, the causes, and the objectives of the invasion there is little doubt that the crisis which engulfed the Iraqi economy played a decisive if not the decisive determining factor in the decision to invade, occupy and annex Kuwait . . . by 1990 the economy had reached a dead end from which there was no prospect for recovery. It was in this context that the Iraqi government decided to invade Kuwait and annex it. Had the annexation of Kuwait succeeded, the prospects for the recovery of the economy and its growth would have vastly improved.
>
> (Alnasrawi 1992: 343–344)

Alnasrawi went on to note that were Iraq to have regained control over its oil exports in 1991 at the pre-war levels of production, it would still have taken the equivalent of a decade of revenues to replace the infrastructure lost during the war. This would not account for the money necessary to import food and consumer goods as required under past Iraqi trade policy. In fact, he concluded that "regardless of how the Iraqi government conducts its economic policy in the post-war period its options are very few and very narrow . . . it will be decades before the country can regain the economic initiative it once had" (Alnasrawi 1992: 353).

Unlike Western policy-makers, Iraq's leaders understood the economic problems that had led them in part to their war in Kuwait. Baghdad did not believe that a restoration of oil revenues – in return for cooperation with Western demands for arms inspections and regime change – would significantly alter the prospects for long-term recovery despite relieving some short-term discomforts. Kurdish opposition leaders shared Baghdad's views. Much of the attempt to establish an independent Kurdistan in early 1991 reflected the culmination of nationalist aspirations and decades of struggle against Baathist repression. But it also demonstrated that the main Kurdish leaders, Masud Barzani and Jalal Talabani, did not believe that the northern provinces could be restored as long as their economy was tied to Iraq's recovery (Khadduri and Ghareeb 1997: 207–211). Both leaders assumed that Saddam Husain had forfeited the future of Iraq through his ill-conceived wars with Iran and then with the West. Kurdish leaders listened patiently to the UN and to Western officials about the needs to rebuild the economic infrastructure in northern Iraq to provide a model and symbol for the rest of the Iraqi population should it choose to overthrow Saddam Husain.

The tension between Kurdish aspirations and Western economic assistance offers some insight into the political hostility that has persisted throughout the 1990s and suggests why Kurdish political leaders have pursued continued relations with Baghdad in the face of Western opposition. Yet the internal attempts by Kurds to rebuild their villages and local economy reproduced older modes of production and regional market relations that predated Iraqi independence in the 1950s, suggesting that historical patterns of regional behavior are perhaps more relevant in order to understand northern Iraq than sanctions theory.

Bringing the past forward

Historians of the Ottoman period have begun to reconstruct the history of the regional economy in northern Iraq, placing it within the larger context of Ottoman trading policy and within the development and modernization theories of the nineteenth and early twentieth centuries. These recent efforts revised the accepted understanding of the economic relationship between rural producers and the surrounding cities. They also suggested a way of understanding the difficulties that post-colonial Iraq had in integrating the northern provinces into the market relationships already extant between Baghdad and Basra. Finally, a review of the British technical surveys made in the 1950s suggested that 1991 was not the first time people had begun to explore the problem of "rebuilding Iraq." The linkages between these historical studies and the economic policy options explored during the 1990s place the choices in a wider perspective.

According to Ottoman tax records and cadastral surveys from the sixteenth and seventeenth centuries, approximately 35 percent of the population in what is now broadly northern Iraq, including the city of Mosul, lived in the countryside, with the remaining population split between smaller market towns and a few large trading cities (Khoury 1997: 25–28). In times of war or poor harvests this ratio fluctuated, but in general the population dispersion remained relatively constant. Because of uncertain political conditions in this border province, almost two-thirds of the rural population were devoted to semi-nomadic pastoral economic activities with the rest participating in agricultural cultivation on land geographically nearby larger villages or towns. This was unusual for Ottoman lands where conditions were ideal for larger farms distributed throughout the province. Moreover, the Ottoman records suggest that the interaction among pastoralists, villagers and urban merchants was relatively limited and that the main contact occurred through the administration of taxes by local officials.

Though overly simplified, the picture of the traditional economy that emerges from the Ottoman records indicates an economy structured around regional trading patterns with limited need for outside contact with either the imperial center in Istanbul or the provincial capitals like Baghdad. Herders raised sheep and traded their goods in village markets in exchange for local produce and locally manufactured goods. Village traders took the animals and animal products to cities like Mosul to be exchanged for manufactured items and limited luxuries. Mosul, along with Irbil, Kirkuk, Zakho, and Amadiyya, "catered to the regional and local trade in pastoral goods such as leather, wool, and meat, and agricultural products such as grain and fruit" (Khoury 1997: 34–35). The region did only restricted trade in imported luxury goods and its main connection with bigger regional trading centers such as Baghdad, Basra, and Aleppo was as a transit point for bulk items like cotton and silk, which were taxed at a lower rate than luxury items. Within this system, the regional players developed sophisticated relations and the government's main role grew around taxation and regulation of economic transactions.

The state of affairs appears to have remained relatively constant until the mid-nineteenth century. Traditionally, the view of the region's reaction to the introduction of European economic forces spurred by the industrial revolution has fallen into two broad lines of analysis. First, it was assumed that the Ottoman economy was hopelessly backward and incapable of sustaining a level of production necessary to meet the basic local needs. This paternalist and Orientalist analysis argued that because the farmers, manufacturers, and merchants of northern Iraq were not trying to market their goods abroad their economy was underdeveloped. In this view, European penetration of the markets in northern Iraq integrated the region into the world economy for the first time. As Khoury and others discovered in their survey of the Ottoman records for the previous centuries, the economy of northern Iraq was not underdeveloped. It was simply not oriented toward export markets.

The second theoretical framework for understanding the impact of world trade on the region in the nineteenth century accepts the possibility that the region had a viable economy prior to European intervention. But this school contends that Ottoman merchants in the large trading cities attempted to reorganize the regional economy to compete directly with

European merchants (Reilly 1992: 3–8). The result was an eventual failure due to competitive disadvantages with the consequent destruction of the traditional regional economy and market relations. In either case, both development and modernization theories leave a picture of northern Iraq's economy in the nineteenth and early twentieth centuries that is disrupted and in search of a means of integrating into economic relations across a broader geographic and political base. It is a vision of northern Iraq that insists that historically the region remained economically unviable without trading relations to outside international markets.

However, other scholars have argued that the basis of our understanding of the region's economy is prejudiced by the availability of data on international trade in contrast to information on local market relations.

> While recognizing the long-term adaptations of this economy to new contacts with Europe, it is essential to recognize that European trade remained only a small part of Mosul's economic activity. Local and regional trade has been much more difficult for researchers to quantify because of the limitations of most of our sources. But, as Hala Fattah pointed out, regardless of whether this local trade was documented, it nevertheless existed . . . prosperity remained tied to exploitation of its own hinterland and exchange with its neighboring provinces . . . most trade was not for long-distance export and most commerce did not involve Europe.
>
> (Shields 1991: 32–33)[10]

These observations have modern relevance when extended to the current analysis of trade in northern Iraq. Much of international attention has focused on the smuggling of petroleum, narcotics, and weapons through Iraq into surrounding states and into European markets. In the same manner, reporting has also concentrated on the establishment of small factories – cement, leatherworks, and food processing – under the auspices of the international relief efforts whose theoretical markets would exist outside the region. Although well publicized, none of these activities are likely to contribute to the eventual development of a self-sustaining economy in Iraq. They are easy to see and to control, however.

The situation in the post-Gulf War Iraq is in many ways similar to the problem faced in the 1950s when Iraq finally gained its full sovereignty. The British technical surveys done at the request of the Iraqi government offer some insight into the government's attempt to move from the region-ally isolated economies of the Ottoman period into a more integrated national economy. Several recommendations in these reports stand out and are relevant to the current situation.

The reports described northern Iraq as an upland plain in a rain-fed zone stretching from northern Mosul to Sulimaniya. In this plain, extensive cultivation of wheat and barley formed the basis for agriculture. North and north-east of the plain were mountains where raising cattle, sheep and goats was the foundation of economic activities, supplemented by the localized cultivation of tobbaco, timber, and fruit. The British experts discovered that except for small handicraft there was limited native industry in the region. Mosul, despite being Iraq's second largest city, remained a commercial center for the transit of export trade to Syria and Lebanon. The only significant difference from the description of the economic life of the region in the 1950s from the Ottoman records in the sixteenth century was the emergence of Kirkuk as the center of Iraqi oil production. Despite the stories of economic breakdown in the post-Ottoman decades, the British teams were left to survey a regional economy that resembled the historic norm. Their challenge was to make recommendations about fusing it into Iraq as a whole.

First, "as long as the oil revenues continue to be assigned to the [Development] Board, no serious difficulties in financing the contemplated development programs should be encountered" (EDI-Report 1952: 74). However, the report continued by saying that these revenues need to be centrally controlled and allocated specifically to industrial expansion. Because of unpredictable fluctuations in oil prices, any attempt to meet government service costs or subsidize public welfare programs from these sources would not only make financing industrial development less secure, but would create unwanted political pressures on the allocation of oil revenues. Another technical report supported these conclusions and added that oil revenues should not be used to subsidize the importation of food or consumer goods that would compete with local production (Qubain 1963: 167–168). The basic conclusion regarding the Iraq oil industry in the 1950s was that it offered the government a source of financing for economic development but that in and of itself oil would not be sufficient to rebuild Iraq and construct a viable economy. The danger for future Iraqi governments, from the perspective of the British experts, was the temptation to use the oil revenue to subsidize the status quo without establishing the infrastructure for industrial diversification. The Bank Mission report concluded "the future would hold little prospect for relief if the only remedy available were a more equitable division of income" (EDI-Report 1952: 96).

The second main recommendation from the British reports attacked this exact problem. "Improved levels of national income can be obtained only by fuller utilization of domestic economic resources. As Iraq's two great resources are agricultural and chemical [in addition to petroleum reserves], development cannot proceed on the basis of local markets alone" (Qubain 1963: 169). This point was reiterated in the conclusions of the Bank Mission report: "The development of an agricultural extension service and the introduction of measures for the gradual improvement of livestock are of highest importance. The temptation to put off such activities because they show no early visible or quick returns can be a strong and continuing one" (EDI-Report 1952: 86). All the reports indicated that the focus of these efforts should come first in the northern provinces, where annual rainfall would allow the development of intensive cultivation without the initial costs of building irrigation systems. Increased oil revenues could then be used to develop the central and southern provinces spreading out along the Tigris and Euphrates river valleys, eventually meeting all of Iraq's internal agricultural needs and then gradually expanding to export to regional markets in the Middle East and Europe. It was argued that Iraq lacked the necessary resources and technical skills to create an indigenous manufacturing capability, but that agriculture in combination with export revenues from the sale of natural resources would provide a stable base for sustained economic development. Specifically, the technical experts agreed that industrial expansion should complement agriculture.

As previously mentioned, Baghdad, after years of internal political instability, adopted a trade and development policy by the 1970s that in effect ignored these recommendations while at the same time increased the country's vulnerability to the kinds of oil price fluctuations that worried the British advisors. More important, the 1950 reports listed the obstacles to economic development which could be used almost verbatim for hurdle to the UN assistance programs in northern Iraq today:

1   The level of expenditure was likely to fall short of the available finances. In other words, the financial resources exceed the number of meaningful economic development projects largely due to constraints in the Iraqi administration and in basic infrastructure.
2   Participation of the public administration was key to a centrally organized development program. Government officials could no longer afford to play distanced regulatory and taxation roles in the economy. Improved administrative skills would be required for supervising and coordinating the integration of multiple projects.
3   A vast increase in the technical staff employed by the government was critical for the success of the reconstruction. Though large projects would likely require the participation of foreign experts and outside technical assistance, the majority of small local projects fell on the shoulders of local engineers and specialists.
4   A supply of skilled labor beyond technical expertise was also required to see these projects through to completion. The British advisors were concerned that shortages in skilled labor would encourage Baghdad to divert workers from agricultural activities.
5   As the development projects grew, the importance of foreign imports would increase. Iraq did not have the industrial base to supply sophisticated equipment through domestic manufacturing. Any disruption in foreign imports would have adverse effects on the pace of economic development.

6   Competing domestic and international interests, along with tension among political, social, and economic objectives, had already created problems, for the Iraqi government in prioritizing its development planning. For example, concerns about the political reliability of Kurds in the north had undermined foreign efforts to direct agricultural projects into that region.

All these concerns proved relevant in the decades between 1950 and 1990 and foreshadowed the difficulties in establishing a working economic reconstruction program in northern Iraq after the Gulf War. Restructuring the economic flows that reshape the political landscape proved a difficult task in historical periods when the central government in Baghdad was relatively weak. Saddam Husain's ability to consolidate his power in 1991 complicated all subsequent attempts by internal opposition and by outside agencies to influence the creation of economic policies in the 1990s.

Sustaining the crisis years, 1992–2000

Though relief efforts in 1991 appeared to have staved off the humanitarian catastrophe prophesied by the UN reports, little efforts were made to improve the economic situation in northern Iraq during the spring and summer of 1992. UN officials concentrated on getting Baghdad to accept the terms of the resolution to allow the limited sale of oil in exchange for humanitarian aid. The UN had reason to believe that the promises of aid donations for Iraq were likely to fall short of the projected requirements. In the northern provinces, Kurdish leaders and Iraqi opposition politicians vied for power in local elections. Competing candidates made promises to the Kurdish population about their relative ability to distribute foreign aid. Iraqi military forces maintained their position along the line of control established by Operation Provide Comfort and enforced Baghdad's economic blockade. Little attempt was made by any of the parties to create the basis for a self-sustaining rebuilding program.

The first significant disruption in the situation came in July 1992 when the UN and international aid agencies began to withdraw workers from northern Iraq in response to alleged attacks by Iraq-sponsored activists.[11] The loss of foreign technical experts in the summer had a serious impact on the future of international aid in northern Iraq. This shift prompted the UN and other agencies to delegate responsibility for distributing aid to local government officials – inadvertently providing the newly elected politicians with access to funds and goods to make true their campaign promises – as well as hiring local workers to fill the technical and skilled labor positions previously staffed by foreigners. The short-term staffing shortage also clouded the assessment being made of local requirements. During these summer months the relief agencies had more funding than they had well-developed projects. Moreover by placing the blame on Iraqi security forces for the attacks, the international community strengthened American arguments for maintaining a hard line on the economic sanctions regime, thereby in a roundabout way preventing the UN from gaining access to additional resources to provide humanitarian aid.

In general, the summer and fall of 1992 slipped by without any real change in the economic situation in northern Iraq. Local leaders were positioning themselves to take advantage of the smuggling opportunities created by the sanctions while also seeking to assert influence over the distribution of aid. The international community remained concerned with the security threat and reduced its presence on the ground while publicly arguing for the necessity of increased commitments to helping the Iraqi people. The contradictions in all these positions came to a head in the winter.

Over 200 million US dollars in aid had been promised the people of northern Iraq in 1992 but by November only a small percentage of that had arrived due to the political and security problems during the summer. UN officials claimed, despite a continued Western military and relief presence in northern Iraq since April 1991, that the Kurds faced a humanitarian disaster greater than that of the previous year. Officials on the ground in northern Iraq admitted that the hastily planned relief efforts to deliver kerosene and food might not succeed in meeting the region's needs. A UN officer confessed "we are way behind and we have grossly underestimated what the Kurds need. Even if we had enough to hand out, which we do not, I do not think we could get it in time."[12]

Yet in March 1992, Melinda Kimble, Deputy Assistant Secretary for International Development and Technical Specialized Agency Affairs, testified to a Congressional House Select Committee on Hunger that the international efforts to ease the suffering of the Iraqi people were proceeding as planned. She claimed that the UN projected that in 1992 exports of food to Iraq were expected to meet 76 percent of the country's pre-war food imports.[13] Specifically, she reported that by spring 1992 the United States alone had spent approximately 500 million US dollars on Operation Provide Comfort in northern Iraq, raised another 100 million US dollars in aid to be distributed through the UN and private relief agencies, and had delivered 63,000 metric tons of food. Local Kurdish leaders were less positive about the effects of the aid, accusing that of the 90 million US dollars planned by the UN for its emergency winter program only 20 million US dollars was actually raised and a quarter of that was spent on overhead costs in Geneva.[14] The UN kerosene deliveries were not distributed locally until March 1993, but luckily the winter weather turned out to be mild despite pessimistic forecasts made in November. The discrepancy between the reporting on the size of international aid to northern Iraq and the "unexpected" nature of the humanitarian crisis that developed at the end of the year raised concerns about the organization and the oversight of relief activities in the north. Congressional critics in America demanded that the administration gain greater control over economic rebuilding efforts in northern Iraq.

In fact, reports began to leak out in early 1993 that the West wanted to free itself from direct responsibility in the Kurdish areas. Flying in the face of the 1950s advice on creating a viable economy in northern Iraq, the planning for a restored economy banked heavily on the export of oil.

> The US and its allies are planning to make the Kurdish region carved out of northern Iraq economically self-sufficient. The cost is estimated at $1 billion over the next five years and may include "a little rule bending to skirt the UN restrictions against Iraq," but since the UN restrictions were only intended to restrain Iraq, the EC and US can ignore the restrictions at will. The de facto state created under the northern No Fly Zone includes 3.5 million Kurds. The mini state lost its only source of income in 1992 when Turkey cut off the diesel fuel trade between Iraq and Turkey on which it levied taxes. The key to Kurdish economic development is uncapping several oil wells and bringing a small oil refinery on line.[15]

In the meantime, the programs underway in the north to rebuild the economy seemed uncoordinated and lacking in prioritization.

One observer contrasted efforts by UN agencies, pointing to UNICEF activities to provide soap for children with head lice against the UN Development Program's failure to initiate any projects to relocate people back to the villages in an effort to restore the agrarian economy.[16] By early spring, UN officials were projecting budget requirements of over 450 million US dollars for its action plan in Iraq but less then 2 million US dollars had been raised by mid-summer. Furthermore, the leaders of the nominal Kurdish government in the north were doing no better in their labors to stabilize the economic situation. The promises of future oil revenues were less significant than the reported 50,000 US dollars per day in "taxes" that the different factions within the Kurdish government were getting from smuggled oil and gas crossing the border into Turkey across the bridge at Habur. Yet this cash flow was not being used to encourage an expansion of local agriculture. The possibility of an abundant grain harvest in northern Iraq was evident by late spring. The Kurdish government wanted to buy the grain to distribute to the population but was unwilling to use its own cash to buy from the farmers. Instead the Kurdish leaders appealed to the UN to raise the estimated 50 million US dollars needed to buy the grain at harvest but donors had only agreed to pledge 7 million US dollars. Many Kurdish farmers decided to sell their harvest to representatives of the Baghdad government for distribution in the south rather than make no profit on their labors.[17]

The willingness of international donors to use resources to dole out soap but to restrain from pumping cash into the local economy to buy food supplies locally hit many indigenous observers as an indication that the international agencies had no real interest in rebuilding the economy. This sense of helplessness grew as they realized that their own elected officials shared to some degree in these sentiments. In addition, the release of an academic study on Iraq's economic prospects undermined the hope that international efforts to divert expected oil revenues into development programs would make improvements in the living standards in northern Iraq. Abbas Alnasrawi argued publicly that:

> Regardless of whether Iraq is free to sell its oil or not, its prospects for economic recovery are remote because of the inevitable huge gap between its potential foreign exchange earnings and its foreign exchange requirements. Oil revenue is not expected to reach prewar levels for some time to come; its new status as a major debtor country will severely narrow its options; and the war claims it will have to pay will overburden the economy in the future.
>
> (Alnasrawi 1994: 167)

In short, officials from both the government in Baghdad and the provisional Kurdish government had little incentive to negotiate terms for long-term rebuilding programs with the international community. These officials all looked toward maximizing their percentage from each individual deal and then transferring these funds abroad when possible. At a local level, entrepreneurship could not flourish as long as the rewards for participating in the local economy were not secure. Both privately and publicly the basis for participation in the economy in northern Iraq became centered on the ability to position oneself politically to extract revenues from external trade that transited the region. Indigenous agriculture and basic manufacturing became confined to the immediate areas. In many ways, the situation had regressed to a micro-economy similar to the conditions described in the fifteenth-century Ottoman records.

Chalabi, the national leader of the Iraqi political opposition, publicly admitted to the reduced expectations about the reconstruction of his country's economy in a letter to the government in Kuwait in July 1994.[18] He argued that the renewed debate about the UN resolution to let Baghdad sell 1.6 billion US dollars' worth of oil every six months was immaterial because the revenues failed to reach the people of Iraq in a meaningful manner after being filtered through international agencies. In direct contradiction to the British advisors of the 1950s, Chalabi suggested a system be created so that each Iraqi citizen receive a direct payment from a UN account as their share of the nation's resources. He indicated that if Kuwait in particular and the international community in general was really concerned about the fate of the Iraqi people and the future prospects of the country's economy, then the distribution of international aid and the debate over modifying the Iraqi sanctions regime would be handled very differently. This cynical view about the international community's motives gained credence when it was reported that French and Russian companies had opened negotiations with Baghdad for future oil concessions regardless of whether Saddam Husain remained in power.[19] By early 1995, UN officials were also indicating publicly that the sanctions could last for decades.[20] Behind the press stories on malnutrition and poor health care, Kurds in northern Iraq began to position themselves to manipulate the limited extant market activities – smuggling, pastoralism, small-scale agriculture, extortion of international aid workers – for immediate gain without any consideration of the long-term impact on rebuilding the region's economic infrastructure. By mid-1995, for example, Masud Barzani, whose forces controlled the border crossing with Turkey, was no longer sharing the 50,000 US dollars per day in taxes derived from petroleum smuggling with his fellow Kurdish leaders, despite a 1992 agreement.

The results of this internal competition came to crisis in 1996. After brokering a deal with Baghdad for military support, Barzani directed his Kurdish Democratic Party militia members in September to take the main urban areas in northern Iraq and the hydro-electric generation facilities in an attempt to provide unified control over all of northern Iraq (cf. Gunter 1996). Although Barzani's efforts failed, the September campaign and the American retaliation with military strikes against Iraqi air defense targets brought to an end a series of fundamental changes in the political economy in the post-war northern provinces. In May, Saddam Husain had finally agreed to UN Resolution 986, which allowed Iraq to sell limited amounts of oil in exchange for food and medicine. Moreover, the terms of the resolution guaranteed an estimated 150 million US dollars every three months for UN relief programs in northern Iraq, creating a significant incentive for gaining sole political control over the region. In addition to helping Barzani's forces through direct military support, Baghdad dropped the internal embargo on the Kurdish provinces. Whatever the political consequences of making a deal with Saddam Husain might have been, Barzani positioned himself as the Kurdish leader responsible for restoring economic contact with the rest of Iraq. Finally, the open conflict between Barzani and those Kurdish forces loyal to Jalal Talabani – along with the ambiguous role played by the Iraqi military in the fighting – created enough pressure for Washington to end Operation Provide Comfort and withdraw all Western ground forces out of northern Iraq.

The unintended consequence of ending Operation Provide Comfort for the hopes of economic rebuilding in the northern territory was the evacuation of Kurdish workers who had been employed by the UN relief organizations. The only significant pool of trained workers who were not directly associated with one of the major Kurdish political factions or with the Baghdad government fled the country at the end of 1996. If the earlier UN draw down of foreign experts in 1992 and 1993 had slowed the development program, the loss of the Kurdish technicians and Western-trained aid workers crippled what efforts had continued into 1996. The 1950s British warnings about the need for securing stable foreign assistance and assuring a trained workforce proved prophetic as 1996 came to a close.

The UN had acknowledged the non-economic implications of the sanctions policy in Iraq. In a report released publicly in 1996, UNICEF officials noted that "the poor economic conditions in the country has had its [*sic*] adversities on the social sector where social characteristics and behavior are undergoing a total change in a society once known for its virtual attributes ... this situation is unlikely to witness immediate improvement even if the economic and trade sanctions are lifted or eased" (Davidson 1996: section 2). Observers also discovered that the oil infrastructure in Iraq was no longer able to handle the limited export amounts as allowed by the UN. By the end of 1998 for example, Baghdad was receiving only a quarter of the revenues to which it was entitled.[21] Some analysts in the West came to the conclusion that the level of economic disruption in Iraq as a whole was not enough to create the level of social crisis and political pain – imagined at the beginning by American planners – necessary to provoke a regime change. However, the resultant stagnation of the local economy was sufficient to generate persistent and lasting health problems, social deviance, and humanitarian emergencies.[22]

In the northern provinces, the situation has evolved into a UN-managed welfare state. Many Kurds will admit that the UN administrators run the region. A village headman told reporters that "different UN agencies laid the road to the village, handed out building materials for houses, put up a school and house for the teacher, vaccinated the children, and cleared the nearby minefield."[23] Reportedly the UN was using over half of its funding to distribute food and medicine directly to the population while the other half was being dispersed through the local government agencies as control between Barzani and Talabani. The most visible use of this second tranche of funding was the construction of a new sports stadium in Erbil and the paving of the road to Turkey to facilitate smuggling. Though the changes in Iraq between 1996 and 2000 eased the immediate humanitarian crises, they have done little to create the economic base to provide employment or to encourage local investment for the longer term. Most of the industrial projects paraded before international observers as evidence for the success of economic restructuring in Kurdistan – the Khalan–Rezan road project, dairy cow breeding in Ainkawa, the Ajga irrigation project, Hareer tinning factory, and Hawler textile factory – all date from the 1997–1998 period and have fallen on difficult times since the initial investment by aid organizations. The same is true for the income generating projects that had been established in the early 1990s, many of which were suspended in 1994 when it became clear they were not self-sustaining.[24]

Conclusion: prospects of regime change

In reviewing the success or failure of international policies aimed at modifying Baghdad's behavior, Amatzia Baram has argued that "since August 1990 life in Iraq has been on hold" (Baram 2000: 219). According to his survey, it is clear that standards of living in Iraq as a whole have declined but the lack of reliable data makes it difficult to gauge the level of humanitarian suffering and has allowed Saddam Husain to use misery to generate nationalist resentment toward Western powers, neighboring states, and Iraqi minorities which have benefited to some degree from international protection.

The Western political objectives for northern Iraq have been a microcosm of the broader policy agenda for the country at large. American and UN officials sought to reduce and then to remove Saddam Husain's influence. Under pressure from Washington, the international community tried to maintain a sanctions regime to create a level of economic discomfort which was not life threatening and did not impede long-term restoration. From various motives, all sides tried to re-establish Iraqi oil production in the belief that oil revenues would underpin the country's eventual rebirth. The first step, as Alexander Joffe, argued at the beginning of this chapter, was just to "rid the country of Saddam Husain" (2000: 33).

These policies, I would argue, have been failures at all levels. The unwillingness to look at historical precedents for the regional market economy coupled with a disregard for the British efforts in the 1950s to create a self-sustaining economy four decades earlier have left the current hard work for naught. The efforts in northern Iraq have created an artificially independent rentier state reliant on oil revenues, international aid, and pseudo-taxation of smuggled goods. A decade later, removing Saddam Husain has returned to the cutting edge of American foreign policy, but the failure to establish an economically viable opposition state in the north is undermining Washington's efforts to push for direct efforts at regime change.

As Vice President Dick Cheney discovered in his March 2002 tour of the region to generate support for a coalition to overthrow Saddam's regime, Iraq's neighbors as well as America's clients in northern Iraq all benefit economically from the current state of affairs (Kitfield 2002). The extant situation provides the context for both internal and regional political and economic relations albeit in a somewhat fragile state. All agree that the removal of Saddam Husain would be a better solution but most fear that Washington lacks the conviction and resources to rebuild Iraq after the war is over. A fight over the spoils of a prostrate Iraq appeals to none. America's Kurdish allies, the likely nucleus of an anti-Saddam ground force, worry that with his government gone and the sanctions lifted Washington would also see no need for continued development aid. Congressman Brad Sherman reinforced these views during a recent House

Committee on International Relations meeting on Iraq policy, noting that post-Saddam he did not "know whether we need humanitarian aid for Iraq because, frankly, that is a country capable of producing oil revenues enough to make it a relatively well-off country."[25] These views reflect the short-term focus of Washington's strategy with little thought to the enduring problem of correcting at least two decades of economic mismanagement.

More troubling, the international community fails to consider that the current situation in Afghanistan where factions vie for influence in the post-Taliban landscape is likely to be similar and even more of a problem in a post-Saddam Iraq. Most people in Iraq see Washington as only slightly less evil than Baghdad when measured by the impact on their daily life. It is unlikely that Iraqis would welcome an American-sponsored stabilization force into Iraq, making the possibility of a civil war even greater given the resources available to the victors.

Notes

1 D. Waller, "Bush's Rude Surprise," *Newsweek*, 22 April 1991.
2 "Region Faces Enormous Challenge in Recovering from Gulf War," *UN Chronicle*, 28 (4), December 1991: 21.
3 Tom Foley, "UN Urges Lifting Sanctions, Says Iraq Faces Catastrophe," *People's Weekly World*, 20 July 1991.
4 Mary McCory, "Justice Is an Uncommon Dish in Iraq," *Arizona Daily Star*, 7 November 1991.
5 "Sanctions Against Iraq Futile? Government Has Secret Cushion of Funds for Projects, Says UN," *Tucson Citizen*, 10 December 1991.
6 V. Litovkin and Yevgeny Bai, "Life Goes On in Blockaded Baghdad," *World Press Review*, January 1991: 30–33.
7 Paul Lewis, "U.N. Permits Iraq Limited Oil Sales for Civilian Needs," *New York Times*, 20 September 1991.
8 "News in Brief," *Beijing Review*, 1–7 April 1991.
9 Elain Sciolino, "U.S. Wants Iraq to Finance Kurdish Relief Operations," *New York Times*, 2 May 1991.
10 See also Shields (1993, 1996 and 2000).
11 See for example Chris Hedges, "Baghdad Said to Sponsor Attacks on Aid Missions," *New York Times*, 29 July 1991, or "Rethinking Iraq," *Wall Street Journal*, 22 July 1991.
12 Chris Hedges, "Blockaded Iraqi Kurds Face Fearsome Winter," *New York Times*, 27 November 1992.
13 "Humanitarian Situation in Iraq," *U.S. State Department Dispatch*, 3 (12), 23 March 1992: 223–225.
14 Joost R. Hiltermann, "For Kurds – Hope and Hard Times," *Nation*, 256 (24), 21 June 1993.
15 "West Hopes to End Kurdish Dependency," *Seattle Post-Intelligencer*, 26 February 1993.
16 Joost R. Hiltermann, "For Kurds – Hope and Hard Times," *Nation*, 256 (24), 21 June 1993.

17 Chistopher Dickey and Russell Watson, "The Kurds are Suffering," *Newsweek*, 122 (1).
18 As quoted in "Iraq's Starvation Will Not Bring Peace or Democracy," *Manchester Guardian Weekly*, 24 July 1994.
19 James Tanner, "Iraq is Negotiating With Other Nations About a Possible Return to the Oil Markets," *Wall Street Journal*, 11 October 1994.
20 As quoted in an interview with Rolf Ekeus in "Embargo on Iraq May Last 15–20 Years More," in *MacNeil-Lehrer Newshour*, 13 April 1995.
21 Laura Silber, "Iraq Oil: Sales Well Below Target," *Financial Times*, 19 August 2000, and "Parts Shortfall Forces 10% Cut in Iraq Oil Deals," *Financial Times*, 5 September 2000.
22 See for example Center for Economic and Social Rights, *Unsanctioned Suffering: A Human Rights Assessment of United Nations Sanctions on Iraq*, New York: CESR Publishing, 1998.
23 As quoted in "The UN's Own Little Kurdish State," *Economist*, 20 February 1999.
24 See new reports at: www.krg.org.
25 Testamony during the House Committee on International Relations: Subcommittee on the Middle East and South Asia Holds Hearing on the U.S. Policy Toward Iraq, Washington, DC, 4 October 2001.

References

Ahtisaari, M. (1991) "II. Summary of Findings and Recommendations in Regard to Iraq: (a) General Remarks, part 1 of 2," in *Report of Mr. Martti Ahtisaari Concerning His Visit to Iraq*, New York: United Nations Press.
Alnasrawi, A. (1992) "Iraq: Economic Consequences of the 1991 Gulf War and Future Outlook", *Third World Quarterly*, 13 (2): 335–353.
—— (1994) *The Economy of Iraq: Oil, Wars, Destruction of Development and Prospects, 1950–2010*, Westport: Greenwood Press.
Al-Roubaie, A. (1990) "Structural Changes and Iraq's Structure of Production," *Arab Studies Quarterly*, 12 (3/4): 83–102.
Baram, A. (2000) "The Effect of Iraqi Sanctions: Statistical Pitfalls and Responsibility," *Middle East Journal*, 54 (2): 194–224.
Cainkar, L. (1993) "The Gulf War, Sanctions and the Lives of Iraqi Women," *Arab Studies Quarterly*, 15 (2): 15–52.
Davidson, E. (1996) *Economic Sanctions Against the Iraqi People: Consequences and Legal Findings*, Reykavik: UNICEF.
EDI-Report (1952) *The Economic Development of Iraq: Report of a Mission organized by the International Bank for the Reconstruction and Development at the request of the Government of Iraq*, Baltimore: Johns Hopkins Press.
Galbraith, P.W. (1991) "II. The Humanitarian Crisis in the North: (b) The Destruction of Kurdish Villages," in *Civil War in Iraq: A Staff Report to the Committee on Foreign Relations*, Washington: United States Senate, 1 May.
Gunter, M. (1996) "Civil War in Iraqi Kurdistan: The KDP–PUK Conflict," *Middle East Journal*, 50 (2): 225–242.
Joffe, A.H. (2000) "After Saddam is Gone," *Middle East Quarterly*, VII (3): 33–42.
Khadduri, M. and Ghareeb, E. (1997) *War in the Gulf, 1990–91: The Iraq–Kuwait Conflict and Its Implications*, New York: Oxford University Press.

Khoury, D.R. (1997) *State and Provincial Society in the Ottoman Empire: Mosul, 1540–1834*, Cambridge: Cambridge University Press.

Kitfield, J. (2002) "The Little War With Iraq," *National Journal* 34 (9): 606–610.

Qubain, F.I. (1963) *The Reconstruction of Iraq: 1950–1957*, New York: Praeger.

Randal, J.C. (1997) *After Such Knowledge What Forgiveness? My Encounters With Kurdistan*, New York: Farrar, Straus and Giroux.

Reilly, J.A. (1992) "Damascus Merchants and Trade in the Transition to Capitalism," *Canadian Journal of History*, 27 (1): 2–28.

Shields, S.D. (1991) "Regional Trade and 19th-century Mosul: Revising the Role of Europe in The Middle East Economy," *International Journal of Middle Eastern Studies*, 23 (1): 19–37.

—— (1993) "Take-off into Self-sustained Peripheralization: Foreign Trade, Regional Trade and Middle Eastern Historians," *Turkish Studies Association Bulletin*, 18 (1): 1–23.

—— (1996) "Sheep, Nomads and Merchants in Nineteenth-Century Mosul," *Journal of Social History*, 25 (4): 773–789.

—— (2000) *Mosul before Iraq: Like Bees Making Five-sided Cells*, New York: State University of New York Press.

Zunes, S. (1998) "Confrontation with Iraq: A Bankrupt U.S. Policy," *Middle East Policy*, VI (1): 87–108.

5 The War on Drugs in the creation of the new world (dis)order

Hans T. van der Veen

> Order and disorder remain in opposition, all the time, everywhere. The tilt between the two is eternally precarious and temporary, and is manipulated by conditions that cannot always be contained. Countries will always experience the relentless competition between the two; it cannot be escaped. Order breeds disorder and there is an order to disorder. The state and the individual use each at will to further their ends. Sooner or later disorder will more actively renew its challenge to the existing system of order, and the shape of society to emerge from that turbulence remains to be seen.
>
> (Paul J. Vanderwood 1992: 181)

Introduction: the War on Drugs is lost

According to a growing body of academic writing the nature of war has been taking a different turn in the last decades.[1] The line of argument that these analysts follow traces the transformation from large-scale inter-state conventional war to new forms of organized violence in which not only states but also "private," non-state actors use violent means to further their goals. The hopeful expectations prevalent at the end of the Cold War that armed conflict would diminish with the end of big-power rivalry have indeed to a large extent been eroded. The continuing proliferation of violent conflicts in a large number of countries in what was known as the Second and Third Worlds, but also in some parts of the most developed world, indicate the difficulties that many states face in maintaining their monopoly on the legitimate use of physical force. In the field of security and peace studies these violent conflicts are often referred to as intra-state wars (Jung and Schlichte 1999). And indeed, organized violence is more confined within state boundaries than ever before in this century. These intra-state conflicts, however, take place in a context of globalization, which links local actors in war zones, their economies, social networks, and military–political power resources to global actors of both a public and a private signature.

With changing actors and opportunity structures, also the means of waging war, the ways wars are fought and financed, and the goals which incite actors to resort to force have been subject to transformations. The conventional conception of war as a large-scale violent showdown between states for the attainment of mutually exclusive political aims thus loses its utility and gives way to a more complex analysis of violent conflict as a mixture of war, organized crime and massive violations of human rights (Kaldor 1999).

Informal criminalized economies are increasingly seen as constitutive to these conflicts. However, the causal link between criminal(ized) economies and (politically) organized violence is poorly understood. The "War on Drugs" is a case in point. As I will argue in this chapter, the War on Drugs is not a mere metaphor but a reality of wide-scale organized violence. This violence does, however, not only take the form of bloodshed. More subtle forms of violence have become necessary and available to wage war. These include human rights abuses, committed by state and non-state actors, massive imprisonment, intimidation, and the infliction of what Johan Galtung called structural violence (Galtung 1969). In general, security becomes a scarce commodity the more states seem to be perpetuating problems that they pretend to be devoted to solving (Rochlin 1995: 338). As an important example of how order and disorder are created in a globalizing world, this chapter will discuss some aspects of the dynamics that underlie conflicts over the drug trade. To put it bluntly: the War on Drugs is lost, but the struggle continues. Within these parameters, however, levels of violence widely diverge between societies. Central to my concerns is thus not only to analyze what the forces are that drive the perverse logic of violent market regulation and excessive state coercion, but also to identify those social institutions that would be able to restrain unbridled drug markets, as well as rein in coercive state practices; and so civilize and pacify society.

In spite of ever-increasing resources dedicated to the reduction of supply and demand of illicit drugs, consumption levels are still rising all over the world. The drug industry is probably the largest and most profitable sector of international crime. The perceived threats of drug consumption and organized crime provide the main justifications for important impulses given in recent years to the development of legislation and the organization of law enforcement. Drug repression thereby increasingly acquires an inter-national character. Unilateral, bilateral and multilateral forms of pressure, intervention and collaboration are proliferating between states in the name of suffocating the ever-swelling drug economy. The prohibition regime is thereby, in a rapid pace, extended with the coercive powers of states to intervene in national and international drug markets, but therewith also in the sovereignty of individuals, peoples and countries. Just as individuals might get addicted to the use of drugs, so the societies in which they live are increasingly addicted to the money that the drug business is generating (OGD 1995: xiii). This seems to be equally true for the agencies that are assigned the task to control it.

As long as demand for illicit drugs exists, the drug war cannot be won, at least not by the coercive institutions of the state. Instead of keeping drug trafficking and organized crime in check, supply repression is likely to increase the profits of illegal entrepreneurs and to give incentives to the professionalization of their organizations. Repression-induced scarcity inflates the price of the merchandise; consequently more people will be attracted to taking the risk and entering the business. When governments enhance their efforts to repress the drug industry, remaining drug entrepreneurs will reorganize their activities so as to limit the risk of detection and prosecution. The end-result seems to be a spiral of growing repression and demand.

Supply reduction therefore seems a dead-end strategy, as it is likely to produce little but counterproductive effects on the supply of illicit drugs and on the organizational strength of the trafficker networks that it attacks. There are, nevertheless, many other regulative functions for the police and other state agencies that might merit their intervention in controlling the problems related to the production, trafficking, distribution and use of drugs. Such problems are basically related to issues of public health and public order. Ultimately, policies aimed at supply reduction must – at least in accordance with official policy goals – be judged by how they affect consumer demand: through the decreased availability of drugs, through an increase in price, or through the deterrent effect of the criminal law (UNDCP 1997: 237). This picture is rather bleak. Over the last decade world-wide production of illicit drugs has expanded dramatically. Opium and marihuana production have roughly doubled, and coca production tripled (Perl 1994: ix). New synthetic drugs find a burgeoning demand in countries all over the world. Nonetheless, what is discussed in the relevant international fora is not so much whether drug policies are on the right track, but how more powers and resources can be assigned to law-enforcement agencies to suppress the drug trade. Thereby the prohibition regime is extending its scope towards the financial sector (money laundering), new drugs, the chemical precursor industry and the disruption of organized crime. Moreover, it is increasingly extending its scope across borders.

In public policy debates, human rights and anti-war on drugs perspectives stand opposed to the belief that only by the strengthening of domestic and international legal instruments can the necessary conditions for the democratization of society be brought about (Dorn *et al.* 1996: 4). As proponents of legalization and those of intensified law enforcement vie with each other in the media and political arenas, the two worlds of crime and law enforcement are increasing their grip on society. Both are extending the scope of their activities, professionalizing and internationalizing their operations. Moreover, they seem to mutually support each other. To understand the perverse dynamics of the booming drug industry and the proliferation of state power to control it, it is my contention that more attention should be paid to the political and economic interests related to both the drug economy and its attempted control. Equally, the intertwined symbiotic and systemic interactions of the upper- and the underworld, which take shape in the international political economy, need to be more closely scrutinized. Most of all, however, we should search for what is missing in this equation: the laws and regulations that assure the protection of citizens and the procedures and institutions that could civilize state–society relations and the relations between states.

It is to this spiraling escalation between two power contenders on different sides of the law to which this chapter intends to draw attention. My quest is to understand how this failure is produced, why this policy is continued and what its consequences could be. Thereby I mainly try to explain the escalation of the drug war and understand its underlying dynamics as deriving from structural changes in the global political economy. I thus look at the drug war as a response to the problems states face in dealing with the decline of their political authority in a globalizing world. I focus on the political and economic stakes of drug trafficking and drug control, and I analyze the flourishing of both the drug industry and the crime-control industry as forms of projecting power and imposing social discipline, as well as mechanisms of wealth accumulation. My core point is that misguided assumptions and the instrumentalization of the War on Drugs – both in the domestic and the international domain – subvert the goals of the prohibition regime and produce not only unintended but also intended consequences that explain its escalation. Such aims and consequences, I claim, have often more to do with subverting the legal rights and protective institutions of citizens and states, than with their defense.

The causes of social conflict in the drug industry and the nature of states' roles in its control may have some very specific features that distinguish it from the regulation of other economic sectors, most notably the global prohibition regime under which relations of production and trade, and forms of state regulation, take shape. However, the patterns of state and non-state violence exhibited in the drug war reflect a governmentality problem that is reproduced in many other spheres of social life and in disparate societies in which the drug industry does not directly play an important social or economic role. As Timothy Luke (1996: 494) observes: "Everyday politics in many places appears to become what power games always were without a pretext of legitimate governmentalizing authority: the conduct of war, crime, and exploitation by other means." The globalized war economy that sustains the war on drugs in all its diverse local emanations follows a pattern that increasingly also affects the political economy of other sectors. In the final section of this chapter I therefore reflect on the insights that can be obtained from my analysis of the drug war in a multitude of other social conflicts that this book addresses under categories of "war economies" and "intra-state war." In a broader sense this chapter thus addresses the multiple tautologies that stem from the "criminalization" of states and economies through both processes of conflict and mutual exclusion between competing state-makers and the imposition of international boycotts on trade with specific countries.

Crime and law enforcement in the "new world order"

Focusing on the international dimension of the interaction between the drug industry and law enforcement practices, this section tries to identify the dominant changes in the international political economy that form the background for an understanding of the dynamics behind the War on Drugs. The internationalization of both crime and law enforcement and therefore their mutual dynamics are an inseparable part of recent changes in the international order generally related to the end of the Cold War: globalization, regional integration and neo-liberal reforms. These transformations have produced new patterns of hierarchy and dominance and have altered the role of the state in the international system. New forms of sovereignty (e.g. economic, multilateral, multinational) and changes in the relationship between economic and political systems (e.g. deregulation, informalization, corruption) have diminished the once established separation between domestic and international frameworks of policy making, as well as of the management of economic affairs (Cerny 1995; Rosenau 1992). Thus the very basis of the accumulation, protection and redistribution of power and wealth has taken unprecedented shapes. In this way globalization entails an increasingly fragmented competition for political and economic resources, engaging more and more non-state actors. It is in this context that the internationalization of and interaction between crime and law enforcement take place and that they influence the parameters of international and domestic political orders, i.e. the very mechanisms through which power is wielded, wealth is accumulated and security is distributed.

Globalization, roughly defined as the intensification of economic, political, social and cultural relations across borders, has to a large extent been facilitated and sustained by technological developments and political decisions to give international exchanges free rein. Together with the partial liberalization of markets, globalization has offered increasing opportunities for the unfettered flow of capital, goods, people and information over the globe. The concomitant increase in the power of market forces and the impact of neo-liberal reforms has debilitated states' capabilities or their willingness to regulate and control these flows. Since the fall of the Berlin Wall in 1989, these developments, uneven as they may be, have been gaining truly global dimensions.

Yet this is only one side of the story. Paradoxically, disintegrative forces relying on the very same technological capabilities and offering unprecedented opportunities for the expansion of criminal enterprises are broadly assumed to have accompanied enhanced global integration. Thereby political turmoil and economic dislocation caused by globalizing processes are said to offer a fertile breeding ground for the drug industry, providing both a way to alleviate economic distress and funds for ethno-nationalist struggles (as is claimed, for example, by both sides in recent conflicts over Kurdistan, Chechnya and Kosovo).[2]

In this respect, globalization may have fostered the expansion of criminal networks and illegal transactions over the globe. Migratory diasporas, for instance, link relatively poor drug-producing countries to consumer markets with very high purchase power. In globalized financial markets the proceeds of crime are easier to hide and increasing trade in general is likely to enhance the opportunities for smuggling and fraud. Both transnational enterprises and organized crime extend their operations and encroach on governments' political authority (Strange 1996: 110). "Mafias," like the Italian *Ndrangheta* and *Camorra*, the American *Cosa Nostra*, Colombian drug "cartels," Chinese and Hong Kong Triads, the Japanese *Yakuza* and, more recently, many more or less nationally or ethnically based organizations from the former Eastern bloc are only the most commonly known examples of criminal networks extending their activities over the globe. Amongst each other, they either compete for markets or establish ways of cooperation. As they are engaged in a multiplicity of legal and illegal activities, drugs may or may not be their most lucrative product. What is important is that these activities not only offer them fast profits, but possibly also the means to exert political power.

In organizing their resources, some drug entrepreneurs establish power structures that challenge the authority of states in specific areas. Moreover, criminal organizations can sometimes supplant and penetrate state institutions and state elites. Ultimately, this affects other sectors of society and endangers the social body in general, where progressively the rule of law and formally regulated relations between states, markets and societies give way to informal arrangements, corruption, violence and intimidation.

The societal consequences of illegal trade and organization are enhanced by their increasing untouchability, which the internationalization of their activities brings about and which makes them such a threat to states' authority. Furthermore, the outlawed or ambivalent legal status of production and transactions in the drug industry severely hinder the regulation of the sector through formal interest associations, civic institutions and administrative laws that – as in most legal industries – could secure the embeddedness of social actors in society through the protection of property rights, the regulation of labor relations, the control of product quality, and the provision of arbitration over conflicts emanating in all market operations. It is my assertion that where drug entrepreneurial networks cannot be incorporated in local or national political and economic arrangements, their impact on society becomes much more detrimental; a situation that is only worsened as the state increasingly resorts to criminalization and repressive means to control their activities. In this context we can observe a seemingly contradictory increase in both the importance of specific criminal or criminalized activities and the coercive powers of states (police, military, customs agencies, fiscal and intelligence apparatuses).

Since the end of the Cold War, the "peace dividend" has to a large extent been absorbed by assigning new tasks to coercive state agencies. In many countries, this was given shape by a rise in expenditure for internal coercion, whereas the cost of defense is increasingly legitimized by the proclaimed need to counter new external threats. In this process, police forces in particular have increased their size, their resources and their legal powers. In many countries also the military has been given tasks in drug repression. The United States in the 1980s and 1990s sufficiently amended the Posse Comitatus Act, which since 1878 had prevented military involvement in civil law enforcement, to enable military engagement in drug law enforcement at home and abroad (Bagley 1992: 130; Drug war facts n.d.). The Dutch, British and French navies are also patrolling the Caribbean to intercept drug shipments. In many countries where the military has always been more important to suppressing internal dissent than to warding off foreign enemies, military involvement in drug control dates back much earlier.

Globalization and liberalization, thus, go hand in hand with new efforts directed at the control and regulation of markets, institutions and societies, notably those related to illegal drugs and migration, and to a lesser extent those controlling capital flows (Andreas 1995). Some of these control mechanisms lie in the remit of state agencies. There is, however, also a tendency to hive off parts of control responsibilities to other levels of political authority, as well as to the private sector (Johnston 1992). Most striking may be a shift from the use of administrative law to criminal law for the maintenance of order in society and for the preservation of national security in general. In this way internal and external security concerns become increasingly blurred, and therewith the tasks assigned to coercive state agencies to protect the sovereignty of the state. The challenges to national sovereignty posed by consequences of globalization have led many governments to believe that the traditional system for the organization of criminal justice policy – the system of individual states – no longer suffices to deal with new problems of international crime (Anderson *et al.* 1995: 40).

Extension and internationalization of state powers, political pressures and foreign interventions in a state's sovereignty, together with a growing share of populations jailed on drug-related charges, however, lead many people to perceive law enforcement itself as a threat to liberal society. Out of the roughly one million people serving jail terms in the United States' state prisons, about 59.9 percent are casual and non-violent drug offenders (Akiba 1997: 607).[3] Many more are in federal, county and other prisons. Their total reached two million in April 2000. In the United States, of every 100,000 inhabitants, 641 are in jail; in the Netherlands, to date, this is "only" 65 (Belenko 1998). The "Americanization" of the War on Drugs is, however, also taking shape in Europe and other countries, particularly in Latin America. International conventions, mutual assistance treaties and – in the European case – institutional mechanisms set up under the three pillars of the European integration process,[4] combine with vastly expanding informal networks among police agencies intended to intensify the suppression of the drug scourge (Sheptycki 1996).

In most European countries, the judiciary has been responsive to the demand and practice of drug law officials to codify in law the investigative techniques and penal power that constitute the tool-kit of their American colleagues. Undercover operations, "controlled delivery" of illicit drug consignments, "buy and bust" tactics, non-telephonic electronic surveillance, and reduced charges or immunity for informants are now standard operating procedures in many countries' drug and crime investigations. Definitions of crime are also broadened, so as to include forms of "criminal conspiracy," membership of an organized crime network, etc. In addition, new and more severe forms of punishment have become part of the accouterment of law enforcement to tackle crime. The promotion and enforcement of drug prohibition laws have played a central role in this development (Nadelman 1997). Not only the individual liberty, but also the property of drug offenders is increasingly targeted. Asset forfeiture took a great leap in the US during the 1980s, and is now experimented with in Europe. Furthermore, a multitude of police agencies are expanding their extraterritorial presence and activities. While military forces and intelligence agencies also assume increasingly international criminal law enforcement tasks.

The drug war – as a core element in the expansion and institutionalization of new coercive state powers – expands the scope of the policing power of states from the domestic to the international domain. To some extent, this tendency reflects a burgeoning of domestic and transnational criminal and criminalized activity. But the relation between crime and repression is, as argued here, a much more dramatic one, where one often breeds the other, and where the activities of criminals become increasingly difficult to distinguish from those of their counterparts on the other side of the law.

Important changes in the international political and economic system that have accelerated in the past decade or two have offered unprecedented opportunities for legal and illegal trade, and for the redistribution of power, wealth and security. These developments incite states, or the elites controlling a state, to look for new ways to accumulate such resources, to control their societies, and to manage the interface with the outside world. Liberalizing some activities thereby seems to go hand in hand with the criminalization of others. The War on Drugs is becoming one of the main legitimization venues for some states to enhance their capacity to intervene, both in the national and in the international domain.[5] How political and economic interests, and interactions between the illegal drug industry and state drug control practices, shape the dynamics and outcomes of the War on Drugs is the concern of the following section.

The political economy of drug law enforcement

The growth of the drug industry and concomitant real or perceived threats to states' authority gave an important impulse to the development of law and the organization of crime control. Beginning with the Shanghai Conference in 1909, step by step a global prohibition regime was created, sanctioning the production, dealing, and trafficking of psychotropic substances. By ratifying international treaties, almost every country in the world obliged itself to adjust national laws in accordance with these treaties, and thereby to suppress the now illegal drug business. The responsibility for control and furthering the design of the regime came to the United Nations in 1946. Still under construction, this regime is targeting new drugs and expanding its organizational devices. It encompasses multinational organizations, state bureaucracies, banks, medical institutions and morality. Thereby a regulatory framework has been established, comparable to the non-proliferation regime for nuclear weaponry. In the evolution of this international regime, individual states attained a high degree of worldwide uniformity and mutual tuning in the regulation of one category of intoxicating, mind-bending substances.

Yet while there does exist a formal global prohibition regime, there is no global criminal justice system to meet the challenge of drug trafficking and globalized crime. Although formal regime control and design are with the United Nations, execution and dedication of control efforts are in the hands of governments and state agencies of individual nation-states. In spite of formal compliance to the predisposition of the prohibition regime, in practice the strategies and tactics for its enforcement are broadly disputed. Historically the conception of the "drug problem" has been subject to dramatic transformations. Fiscal, balance of payment, civic security, public health, social welfare and moral considerations can be found as determining the main diagnosis of the problem. Within and between societies the conception of the problem and the discourses guiding government intervention in the drug industry vary widely, over time and in geographic space. The multidimensionality of the drug problem makes it a very complex policy field. With prohibition in place, repression still is no panacea.

It was only after their dependencies gained autonomy that the major European powers dissolved their colonial monopolies on the opium trade. Prohibition also met with fierce resistance from the pharmaceutical industries in Germany, Japan and Switzerland. State interests in the preparation for war, in which the secured supply of anesthetics plays an important role, often shielded these companies. Coaxing governments into compliance with prohibition has been, and still is, an arduous process. From the beginning it has been the United States that has taken the lead in building the prohibition regime. Especially since the 1980s, unilateral, bilateral and multilateral forms of pressure, intervention and collaboration are proliferating to force governments to comply with prohibition and to stifle the growth of the drug economy. Conditional development aid, extradition treaties (so-called International Mutual Legal Assistance Treaties), new types of financial policing to "chase the money" around the international banking system, financing and advising foreign military and police, political pressure and even outright military intervention count among the plethora of instruments applied in the relations between states in this War on Drugs. In the process, institutional structures (e.g. Interpol, Europol and UNDCP) have been strengthened to intensify international cooperation. Besides that, many informal structures have developed between police, military and intelligence agencies (see Anderson *et al.* 1995; Anderson and den Boer 1994; Benyon *et al.* 1994; Fijnout 1993; Marshall 1991). Many of these are not new. Before the end of the Cold War, countries like France and the United States had extensive programs for the assistance of foreign military and police forces (Fijnout 1993; Marshall 1991). Nowadays, however, such programs are legitimized by the supposed need to strengthen other state's capabilities to fight the drug industry. Since the mid-1980s, through the process of European integration, the European Union has also been asserting itself as a major player in the field.

The internationalizing powers to enforce the prohibition regime are largely legitimized and rationalized by interdependencies that derive from the global division of labor in the illegal drug industry and the concomitant problems this presents to individual states in controlling the drug industry. But forthcoming interdependency does not necessarily mean greater integration (collaboration and harmonization). Interdependency can possibly also mean "dependency," "exploitation," "free riding," and "conflict" (Bühl 1995: 123). International law-enforcement instruments are unevenly distributed and include the exchange of information between law enforcers, international pressures on countries to shape their legislative body (for example, the closure of coffee shops and the lifting of bank secrecy), the provision of military aid and advisors (an important element of the American efforts in Latin America), or the extension of intelligence-gathering by foreign-stationed liaison officers. The control over these instruments ultimately touches on the control that countries have over their economies and political system, and on the control people have over their privacy and security.

The strategies and tactics applied by governments in their drug policies do not only touch upon very different conceptions of "the drug problem," they also affect the distribution of income and the relative power of actors within and between societies. Interventions in drug markets influence the direction, composition and volume of drug streams over the world, and of the flows of money that are generated in this international business. Drug trafficking is, to a large extent, a transnational business. The drug industry consists of various stages: cultivation, refining, transport, distribution, money laundering and investment of proceeds. In every stage of this drug trajectory, from production to distribution, profits are made that are consumed or invested, but often demand some form of laundering to conceal their illegal origins. The transnational dimension of the drug industry is not only a function of the territorial distance between major production and consumption regions. It also consists of the links that are made through networks and organizations with diverse homebases that sometimes develop transnational operations. Thereby differences in countries' legal codes and law-enforcement capabilities shape the opportunities for drug entrepreneurs to evade the risks of prosecution and support the flourishing of their business. Strangely enough, it seems to be exactly the countries with the most stringent legal codes on drugs and with the most eager drug police forces that have the most problems with reducing the harm of consumption, corruption, trade and production; not to mention with state violence itself.

The drug industry constitutes the backbone of many national and local economies, directly and indirectly offering income and employment opportunities for millions of people around the globe. They serve the demand of many more.[6] Countries like Bolivia, Morocco, Mexico and Afghanistan derive incomes from this industry that match their formal export income. Morocco earns an estimated 5.75 billion US dollars, 20 percent of its GNP, from the production and export of cannabis and hashish (Ouazzani 1996: 122), supplying the lion's share of Europe's demand for these products. The Mexican drug economy, based chiefly on the export of homegrown marihuana and poppy derivatives, as well as the transit of Colombian cocaine to the United States, is valued at more than 20 billion US dollars. Such aggregate data for developing countries, estimative and fluctuating as they are, give an indication of the wealth and power that might be derived from criminal sources, and yet they pale in contrast to the late 1980s consumer expenditure on illicit drugs in the United States. This very likely exceeded the total GDP of eighty-eight different countries alone.[7] This tells us that probably the greater part of drug turnovers never leaves the main consumption countries, as they are likely to offer the most lucrative investment opportunities.

Since drug law enforcement – and under-enforcement – influences the international division of labor in the drug industry, it is clear that law enforcement can play a role in disrupting the drug trajectory and, in doing so, can bring about important shifts in the distribution of drug profits. This not only by taking people out, and so creating market space for new entrants (which can be individual entrepreneurs, institutions or whole regions), but also by increasing the cost of maintaining links in the drug trajectory.[8] Drug repression drives up the prices and thus gives an enormous impulse to the profitability of the product and the services rendered to the drug industry. Drug entrepreneurs, be they poppy growing farmers in Pakistan, transport companies in Turkey, or laundering exchange offices in the Netherlands, have to protect themselves against prosecution by police forces, and against competitors. The costs – to decentralize production, bribe state officials, hire protection, create well-camouflaged transport facilities, or convince bankers to take a certain risk – increase with the intensity of repression. Repression of the drug trade thus not only contributes to the growth of the drug economy, but also incites a redistribution of the income from the trade.

Important as contributions of this illicit enterprise may be to overall income and employment levels, the real impact should be measured from its effect on the economy at large, the distribution of its proceeds, and the social costs in terms of health, safety, political transparency, etc.[9] Drug interests are strong enough to create powers that can play a major role in political life and in economic activities. Where many people depend on the drug industry for their income, and where the overall economy is dependent on the influx of foreign currencies from the drug trade, such drug interests, and concrete efforts of drug entrepreneurs to protect their trade, severely limit the margins for governments to deal with the drug industry. Moreover, enhanced drug repression also strengthens coercive powers within state apparatuses relative to each other and the society at large. Drug policies therefore also have an impact on the distribution of power and security in and between countries. On the one hand, they can limit the destabilizing effect of the drug industry on society. On the other hand, they can enhance the resources and legal powers of a state's security forces. In this way policies of drug repression possibly also limit the level of freedom, democracy and human rights that citizens can enjoy.

Drug repression therewith also attains an important political dimension. From the perspective of the ruling elites, it is of concern to prevent power contentions of ethnic, political or clan associations to use the drug proceeds for building their own power structure. In such a situation, they may have little choice but to gain control over the business for themselves, or at least find a way of incorporating such new dynamic sectors into the existing power structure. Drug repression would, in many cases, only strengthen the opposition, as it would leave a good share of the population without means of support. Domestic and foreign drug policies thus touch upon the distribution of power, wealth and security, both within a country and between societies. These interests are informing if not imposing a specific logic on many a state's policies and practices, and lead to symbiotic interactions between the upper- and the underworld that play a (decisive) role in deepening their perverse impact on the relations among states and between states and their societies. The phenomenon of "protected trafficking" here enters the picture (Scott and Marshall 1991: vii), where selective suppression and protection of the drug industry becomes a more likely outcome of drug policies.

Criminal groups and criminally obtained resources are often a deviant element in the national and international dynamics of politics. Illegal violence and authorized force used illegitimately to serve the purpose of one class, clan, ethnic group, region or country against the other is no new phenomenon. It is, however, strongly related to the dynamics and consequences of the growth of drugs markets and state policies to control them. In many countries it is exactly the association of criminal groups with power elites that produces and prolongs such perverse consequences (Hess 1986: 128). In the recent history of both industrialized (e.g. France, the United States and Italy) and developing countries (e.g. Turkey, South Africa, Colombia, Mexico), many examples can be found of cooperation between secret services, political parties and other power groups with – drug trafficking – criminal groups in the repression of domestic opposition, the destabilization of foreign governments, and the support against (geo)-political foes (see Block 1986; Hess 1986; McCoy 1972; Scott and Marshall 1991). Equally, many opposition groups have discovered how important drug income can be to withstanding (foreign) control over their territories (e.g. the PKK in Turkey and the Afghan *Mudjaheddin*).

Forms of "corruption" of a more or less institutional nature often amend such symbiotic relations between drug entrepreneurs and local, national or foreign power elites. The price increase caused by prohibition works effectively as a tax that, however, does not flow straight into the coffers of the state treasury, but is collected by the producers, traffickers and other service providers that sustain the trade. In many countries a prohibition tax is, however, equally levied by "corrupt" enforcement officers and other protectors of the trade within the politico-administrative system. Such state-induced extortion of the trade is not only an activity for private gain (supplementing salaries). In fact, various systems exist that provide for the distribution of such rents within the hierarchical networks through which such money flows. In return, they may facilitate exchange in prohibited markets. Bribery can be a primary method of public finance, alongside taxation, borrowing and inflation (Thornton 1991: 137). From that perspective, it should be less of a surprise to find police officials actively involved in the management and maintenance of black-market monopolies. Through their relations with drug entrepreneurs, police officers (and other state protectors) become responsive to the monopolist. This may lead them to act against new entrants or third parties in the pursuit of maintaining the monopoly and its profits.

Such symbiotic relations are often an outcome of law-enforcement tactics, where drug-enforcement agencies infiltrate trafficking rings, and set up front stores to provide services to the drug industry. The War on Drugs in many countries is literally running out of control. A severe crisis upset the Dutch police and juridical system, for instance, as it turned out that the methods used by police agencies in their criminal investigations on drug traffickers had to a large extent moved beyond the juridical boundaries and parliamentary control. The Dutch parliamentary commission that investigated these methods in 1996 found, for example, that the Dutch police had imported 285 tons of drugs, of which 100 tons had disappeared on the market (Zwaap 1996).[10] The opportunities for bribery and outright extortion, facilitated by the outlawed position of drug entrepreneurs, constitute an important incentive for the escalation of the drug war. In a more formalized way, asset forfeiture laws – directed against the property of traffickers and users involved in a criminal act – have had the same result (Benson *et al.* 1995; Benson and Rasmussen 1996). In fact, the self-financing of police forces in the drug war is now also actively propagated by the United Nations Office for Drug Control and Crime Prevention (Agence France Press [AFP] 31 March 1999).

The narcotics industry has, to a greater or lesser extent, become economically and socially entrenched in almost every country in the world. Drug-related interests have permeated many sectors of society, sectors that often function in the formal economy but derive part of their income from activities connected to the drug trade. Few sectors remain untouched by the drug industry, as drug proceeds are consumed and invested in other enterprises, or as, for example, banks and transport companies provide services to the drug industry and so become part of the drug industry themselves. The drug industry is to varying degrees also socially embedded in many countries. Drug consumption is culturally rooted in certainly not only the most marginalized sectors of the population. Furthermore, drug entrepreneurs increasingly establish themselves as a social force that seeks integration in the formal institutions of the societies in which they live and operate. They thereby often gain if not respectability then at least some leverage to protect their interests. The income and employment the industry generates for a multiplicity of actors and societies at large also provides political clout to drug-related interests, especially when threatened by foreign or domestic repression efforts. Prohibition, however, severely hampers the formal incorporation of the drug industry by means of taxation, interest mediation and forms of market, labor and product regulation. From consequential partial, informal, or denied integration, it is my contention, are derived many of the most harmful consequences of the industries' operations, much more so since police and military institutions are ill-equipped to perform these regulatory roles.[11]

As both the drug industry and drug law enforcement are internationalizing, they put severe strains on the possibilities of the state to incorporate the drug industry in local and domestic arrangements that could limit their destabilizing effects on society. Such a strategy, if applied – and many countries cannot escape such a choice, either by informal arrangements or through "corruption" – is, however, becoming less feasible where the power of organized crime and pressures for intensified law enforcement upset such symbiotic relations. Drug industry and drug repression can therefore have very disruptive effects on domestic political–economic institutions and arrangements. This can come about merely as an unintended consequence of conscientious cross-border supply-reduction efforts. However, in many instances, drug policies are merely part of other foreign policy goals, and are to a large extent shaped by the institutional logic of agencies called in to implement them.

Recent history has shown that, rightly, much more calculation tends to play a role in supply-side policies than zealous supply reduction. Such policies also take into account the interests involved in drug trafficking, and the capabilities of governments to offset the pressure put on these interests by efforts to stifle the drug economy. In this respect the crop-substitution projects carried out by the United Nations, which aim to provide drug farmers with an alternative source of income, are a good example. As soon as drug policies become part of broader policy goals towards other countries they are, however, likely to be subordinated to other priorities that states pursue to protect their national interests. Just as war is the continuation of politics by other means, so the War on Drugs has become an extension of foreign policy by other means (Marshall 1991: ii). International drug policies almost inescapably become enmeshed with geopolitical and economic considerations (LaBrousse and Koutouzis 1996). Also, enhancing the powers of specific law enforcers, such as, in an extreme case, the military in Peru or Colombia, is likely to serve interests quite different from convincing coca growers to limit their output. In its more extreme form, international drug law enforcement can legitimize outright military intervention, as the case of Panama showed in the late 1980s.[12]

Conclusion and corollary: global (dis)order

Since the end of the Cold War, the "new world order," established under conditions of increased globalization and underwritten by neo-liberal reforms, has to a certain extent been shaped by two forces: the visible hand of criminal forms of market control and the extension of the strong arm of the law in the national and international domain. As both increasingly attain transnational dimensions, they become more disposed to prevent themselves from being incorporated into society and, thereby, from being subordinated to democratic control. At the same time, they increase their powers to subvert the sovereignty of societies and the rights of citizens over the globe.

These forces take shape in a competitive world, with unevenly distributed resources, and outcomes of their interactions are also likely to impinge unevenly on different societies and groups within them. The criminal system permeates the political and economic system, thereby undermining the functioning of legal industries and the role and functioning of the state. The extension of states' coercive powers to "control" the drug industry also impinges heavily on the distribution of power, wealth and security within and between societies. The destructive force of the intertwined dynamics of the drug industry and state repression is thereby likely to subvert the existing relations between states, markets and societies. Therewith, the underlying dynamics and outcomes of the drug war are not only shaped by, but are also reshaping the fundamental structures of the world's political economy.

The internationalization of policing and the concomitant proliferation of tools to intervene in the sovereignty of individuals, peoples and foreign countries is highly liable to decrease the prospect of a world order in which peace, justice and freedom could develop. This is mainly due to the uneven distribution of the powers unleashed by the "International Drugs Complex."[13] On the one hand, the globalizing forces of, for instance, smuggling, monetary volatility, and migration decrease the possibilities of protecting the state and the social arrangements that support it. On the other hand, the increasing overlap the criminalization of these flows brings about between internal and external security concerns is likely to lead the formal goals of crime wars to be overruled by geo-political and economic concerns. The coercive powers of states that are called in to maintain internal order and external security tend, to a large extent, to escape democratic control, as their "operational information" needs to be shielded from the outside world. Diminishing accountability goes hand in hand with the increased powers assigned to coercive state agencies. More than this threat of free-floating state powers, however, it is the subversive impact of international criminal organizations that can undermine the very basis of the state and the societies they preside over. If indeed law enforcement directed against the drug industry is counterproductive, and public health and public order considerations are made subservient to quite different political goals, this leaves us with a rather gloomy perspective for the democratization of our societies.

The contribution of the production, trafficking and control of drugs to the intractability and escalation of inter- and intra-state warfare may be a very important one. Particularly when it comes to drug-related incomes for the sustenance of arms procreation by warring parties. In war-torn countries such as Turkey, Federal Republic of Yugoslavia, Myanmar, Colombia, Afghanistan, Tajikistan, or Peru, to name a few of the more lethal "intra-state" hotspots of global conflicts in the 1990s, the drug economy forms a substantial, if not the dominant, part of the war economy. To these essentially rural wars and insurgencies in which the drug economy is important should be added predominantly urban conflicts, which logically tap another flow in the international drug-trafficking chain. Implicating the enemy in the drug trade is, however, also an important tool in war and politics to delegitimize the opponent, securitize the issues at stake and dehumanize the adversary, so as to open the way for his elimination. The importance of the drug economy in war is, thus, most clear-cut where the very survival of the peoples that live under the control of warring fractions is at stake. The relationship between drug economies and war and protracted conflicts is, however, much weaker than these examples might allude to:

1   It is the prohibitive regulations that have added to the geographic conflation of war zones and drug economies. Over the past three decades supply-side policies have contributed substantially to pushing the drug trade around the world (see, for example, Stares 1996: Chapter 2). It should also be no surprise that in those states which already fail to tax and protect substantial parts of their citizenry, violent conflict over the drug trade is more pervasive.

2   Violence not only or even primarily derives from the drug industry as such, but often from the efforts to control or eliminate it. Extensive legal production of opiates on poppy fields and in pharmaceutical industries in France, Australia, India, Spain and Turkey indicate that tight regulations can be maintained without excessive force.

3   The drug industry is an economic enterprise that provides an income to innumerable families that engage in it for reasons of self-sustenance and not necessarily for political aims. Politicization of the drug trade principally comes from threats to people's livelihoods and conflates with already existing social cleavages (class, ethnicity, tribal, religion, age, etc.). Politicization of drug "law enforcement" is therefore best understood in the light of conflicting social entities that use the economic revenues of illicit drugs and the legal war and firepower of their coercive apparatuses to weaken power contenders and competitors.

4   Drug production and trafficking, as well as violent conflicts over its control, are not relegated to remote areas of the world where clear-cut inter- or intra-state wars are fought. Actually, one of the most violent drug wars is fought within the United States, where few people would think of their country's internal conflicts in terms of civil or intra-state wars.

5   There is no inescapable correlation between the establishment of a drug industry and the proliferation of armed conflict. Nor is there a faint possibility of eliminating violence altogether from the drug business. As always, multiple institutions – procedures and rules for interest mediation, political negotiation, law making, taxation, and protection, as well as for policing and warfare – constitute the parameters within which social conflict and exchange take place. Prohibition, far from eliminating the drug trade, rather contributes to such regulatory institutions being replaced by coercive and informal modes of taxation and selective protection. In short, the illicit drug trade is an economic sector that is socially organized, in one way or another.

As with all production and trade, be it legal or illegal, conditions of production and distribution of commodities are wrought with exploitation, fraud, corruption and protective and discretionary regulation, exerted by violent and non-violent means. Resource and trade conflict are part and parcel of the global political economy, in which diverse actors on both the national and international level compete for discretionary market access, extraction opportunities, and comparative advantages. The inflated price of drugs, brought about by prohibition and informal and violent forms of market regulation, may add to the levels of violence pertinent to the drug trade. However, careful scrutiny of historical and even modern examples of drug economies shows that such violence can be minimized, even within the framework of global prohibition (see, for example, Morocco, Bolivia, the Netherlands and the UK).

What I want to establish with these cautionary remarks is that the relationships between drugs and war are established within highly varying contexts that should be studied within the diversity and complexity of the various social, economic and political conflicts in which such relationships take shape. There is no relationship to be taken for granted between current warfare and drugs. An understanding of the dynamics inherent in the various "drug wars" that are fought in the world cannot be attained by separating them from more broadly based patterns of social, economic and political conflict, or cleavage and cooperation within and between societies.

The globalized war economy that sustains the War on Drugs in all its diverse local emanations follows, however, a pattern that increasingly also affects the political economy of other economic sectors. The war logic built into the functioning of the drug economy is reproduced in more and more stages of the production–consumption cycle of other trades like those in diamonds, arms, oil, gold, hardwood, prostitutes, migrants, tobacco and minerals. In these sectors as well, the institutions that regulate production, trade and taxation have been eroded. Relations of production are increasingly determined by coercive labor control, as the capacity of labor unions to protect workers has largely been destroyed by state repression and global competition. Exchange relations in the subsequent stages of production and trade are largely determined by non-market forces that through force or money have acquired the power to set prices. And extortion, bribery and crime increasingly also undermine government control, both in the form of its monopoly on taxation and in its regulative capacity to determine what and how goods and services are produced. Sometimes this takes the form of armed groups that through violence and intimidation enhance the transaction costs of production and trade and so – through extortion – manage to appropriate part of the wealth created. Sometimes it is legal businesses that manage to bribe government officials to obtain a license for exploitation. In other instances, resources are simply stolen or smuggled with the same effect. In all transnational enterprises, entrepreneurs manage increasingly well to shift their resources in such a way as to minimize their tax payments and to demand increasingly better conditions for their investments.

State officials and whole state apparatuses shift to similar strategies – both on the local and the global level – and often in collusion with big investors, to create order and disorder at their behest. What happens in the cocaine industry at the local level between government officials and drug traffickers – which exchange protection for money, to the detriment of local populations – is merely reproduced on the global level when states use their coercive forces to create the conditions under which certain entrepreneurs in, for example, the oil industry can enhance their market power to the detriment of others. From this perspective, destabilizing local communities in the drug war follows much the same logic as the "Great Game" that is evolving over the control of oil and gas resources around the Caspian Sea. Through the use of force, state and non-state actors try to create opportunities for the accumulation of power and wealth, to the detriment of others, although they are often swept away by the very forces they unleashed.

Notes

1 Amongst these, important contributions come from Mark Duffield (1998) and Martin van Creveld (1991).

2 I would argue that the problems mentioned here have much more to do with the structural failure of states to protect parts of their population, not seldom associated with a very substantial restructuring of the institutions that allocate property rights, determine terms of trade, and mediate state–society relations. Such structural changes are sometimes presented as transitions to "democracy" and "free"-market reform. Alternatively, such new structures and opportunities can be presented *and* regulated through concepts such as "mafias," organized crime, smuggling, money laundering and human trafficking. The point I want to make here is that "the law" is by no means neutral or a-political. Neither should we all too readily assume that justice is blind.

3 Between 1980 and 1996, the number of inmates in the United States more than tripled from 501,886 to 1,700,661 (Belenko 1998: 53). A ratio of 1:50 American men are in prison; 1:20 are on parole or probation. In 1993 one in three black Americans who did not finish high-school was in prison (Jacobs 1996: 573). The number given by Mauer (1997) for drug offenders in American state and federal prisons is substantially lower than that provided by Akiba. However, he also notes a considerable shift in law-enforcement priorities toward drug law enforcement. According to his data, from 1985 to 1994 drug offenders accounted for more than a third (36 percent) of the increase in the number of offenders in state prisons and more than two thirds (71 percent) of the increase in federal prisoners. One of the largest increases in arrests has been for violation of laws prohibiting drug sales, distribution and possession – up 154 percent during this time period, from 580,900 to 1,476,100 (Belenko 1998: 55).

4 The three pillars are: European Communities, Common Foreign and Security Policy, and Co-operation in Justice and Home Affairs.

5 The criminalization of entire trade flows, at the same time, severely debilitates more refined forms of government. The control of criminalized trade and

outlawed social sectors inevitably deepens patterns of crime, corruption and coercion, as accountable government is replaced by informal governance. The arms-length, informal and coercive regulation of the drug trade may epitomise what happens in a much broader way to state–society relations in countries under international trade embargoes, or in those where state bureaucracies have been scaled down to their coercive core.

6 According to a recent estimate of the UNDCP, total revenue accruing to the illicit drug industry is equivalent to about 8 percent of total international trade. This comparison is highly deceptive. UNDCP also compares the illicit drug trade to other economic sectors: "In 1994 this figure [400 billion US dollars] would have been larger than the international trade in iron and steel and motor vehicles and about the same size as the total international trade in textiles" (UNDCP 1997: 124). What is actually compared here is the imaginary overall global consumer expenditure on illicit drugs with recorded world imports on other commodities.

7 As cited in Tullis (1995: 2); Akiba (1997) indicates only eighty countries.

8 For example, the US Drug Enforcement Agency estimates that in 1993 the Colombian drug cartels spent 23 percent of their profits on laundering their hard-earned drug money, up from 6 percent in the late 1980s (Foust and DeGeorge 1993).

9 The literature embarking on such assessments is extensive, especially for producing countries. See, for example, the Studies on the Impact of the Illegal Drug Trade, six volumes, undertaken by the United Nations Research Institute for Social Development (UNRISD) and the United Nations University.

10 In June 1999, a new Dutch Parliamentary Commission (Kalsbeek-commission) concluded that double-informants, with the help of drug officers, had managed to import and market an additional 15,000 kilos of cocaine (NRC Handelsblad, June 10, 1999).

11 Like in many other black-market sectors such as illegal gambling and prostitution, exchanges in the drug industry are of a consensual nature. The criminalization of personal vice, as opposed to some of the consequential social harm it inflicts on society, thus leads to what some authors call "victimless crime." Both this consensual nature and the fact that prohibition pushes all exchanges underground has far-reaching implications for the tactics of law-enforcement agencies in the process of evidence gathering, as participants are unlikely to issue complaints or invoke arbitrage from formal institutions, even when disputes arise. Moreover, many of the negative consequences associated with illegal drugs derive from the prohibition rather than the consumption of the prohibited product (Miron and Zwiebel 1995).

12 It may merit here to note that many comparisons with previous efforts at (alcohol) prohibition fall short. Some parallels are obvious with respect to the development of organized crime groups, product quality deterioration and the widespread "corruption" of the criminal justice system (see Woodiwiss 1988 for the US experience). Alcohol prohibition in the US, however, never targeted consumers, or foreign countries and was never associated with the type of mass incarceration and the widespread use of state and non-state violence that characterizes present-day emanations of drug prohibition.

13 A further elaboration on my – as yet incipient – theory of the International Drug Complex can be found in Hans van der Veen (2000).

References

Anderson, M. and den Boer, M. (eds) (1994) *Policing Across National Boundaries*, London: Pinter.

Anderson, M., den Boer, M., Cullen, P., Gilmore, W.C., Raab, C.D. and Walker, N (1995) *Policing the European Union: Theory, Law and Practice*, Clarendon Studies in Criminology, Oxford: Clarendon Press.

Andreas, P. (1995) "Free Market Reform and Drug Market Prohibition: US Policies at Cross-Purposes in Latin America," *Third World Quarterly*, 16 (1): 75–87.

Akiba, O. (1997) "International Trade in Narcotic Drugs: Implications for Global Security," *Futures*, 29 (7): 605–616.

Bagley, B.M. (1992) "Myths of Militarization: Enlisting Armed Forces in the War on Drugs," in P.H. Smith (ed.) *Drug Policy in the Americas*, Boulder: Westview Press.

Belenko, S. (1998) *Behind Bars: Substance Abuse and America's Prison Population*, The National Center on Addiction and Substance Abuse, Columbia University.

Benson, B.L. and Rasmussen, D.W. (1996) "Predatory Public Finance and the Origins of the War on Drugs, 1984–1989," *The Independent Review*, 1(2): 163–89.

Benson, B.L., Rasmussen, D.W. and Sollars, D.L. (1995) "Police Buraucracies. Their Incentives and the War on Drugs," *Public Choice*, 83: 21–45.

Benyon, J., Turnball, L., Willis, A. and Woodward, R. (1994) "Understanding Police Cooperation in Europe: Setting a Framework for Analysis," in M. Anderson and M. den Boer (eds) *Policing Across National Boundaries*, London: Pinter.

Block, A.A. (1986) "A Modern Marriage of Convenience: A Collaboration Between Organized Crime and U.S. Intelligence," in R.J. Kelly (ed.) *Organized Crime: A Global Perspective*, Totowa and New Jersey: Rowman and Littlefield.

Bühl, W. (1995) "Internationale Regime und europäische Integration," *Zeitschrift für Politik*, 42 (2): 122–148.

Cerny, P.G. (1995) "Globalization and the Changing Logic of Collective Action," *International Organization*, 49 (4): 595–625.

Chatterjee S.K. (1981) *Legal Aspects of International Drug Control*. The Hague, Boston and London: Martinus Nijhof.

Creveld, M. van (1991) *The Transformation of War*, New York: The Free Press.

Dorn, N., Jepsen, J. and Savona, E. (eds) (1996) *European Drug Policies and Enforcement*, Houndmills: Macmillan Press.

Drug war facts (n.d.) www.csdp.org/factbook/military.htm

Duffield, M. (1998) "Post-Modern Conflict: Warlords, Post-adjustment States and Private Protection," *Civil Wars*, 1 (1): 65–102.

Fijnout, C. (ed.) (1993) *The Internationalization of Police Cooperation in Western Europe*, Deventer: Kluwer.

Foust, D. and DeGeorge, G. (1993) "The New, Improved Money Launderers," *Business Week*, 28 June.

Galtung, J. (1969) "Violence, Peace and Peace Research," *Journal of Peace Research*, 6(3): 11–33.

Gereffi, G. and Korzeniewicz, M. (eds) *Commodity Chains and Global Capitalism*, Westport: Greenwood Press.

Hess, H. (1986) "The Traditional Sicilian Mafia: Organized Crime and Repressive Crime," in R.J. Kelly (ed.) *Organized Crime: A Global Perspective*, Totowa and New Jersey: Rowman and Littlefield.

Jacobs, Dany (1996) "De Amerikaanse 'crime machine'," *Economische en Statistische Berichten (ESB)*, 26 June.

Jamieson, Alison (1993) "Drug Trafficking After 1992: A Special Report," *Conflict Studies*, 250: Research Institute for Study of Conflict and Terrorism.

Johnston, L. (1992) *The Rebirth of Private Policing*, London: Routledge.

Jung, D. and Schlichte, K. (1999) "From Inter-State War to Warlordism: Changing Forms of Collective Violence in the International System," in H. Wiberg and C.P. Scherrer (eds) *Ethnicity and Intra-State Conflict*, Aldershot: Ashgate.

Kaldor, M. (1999) *New Wars and Old Wars: Organized Violence in a Global Era*, Cambridge: Polity Press.

Labrousse, A. and Koutouzis, M. (1996) *Géopolitique et géostratégies des drogues*, Paris: Economica.

Luke, T. (1996) "Governmentality and Contragovernmentality: Rethinking Sovereignty and Territoriality after the Cold War," *Political Geography*, 15 (6/7): 491–507.

McCoy, A.W. (1972) *The Politics of Heroin in Southeast Asia*, New York: Harper and Row.

Marshall, J. (1991) *Drug Wars: Corruption, Counterinsurgency and Covert Operations in the Third World*, Berkeley: Cohen and Cohen.

Mauer, M. (1997) *Americans Behind Bars: U.S. and International Use of Incarceration, 1995*, Washington: The Sentencing Project.

Miron J.A. and Zwiebel, J. (1995) "The Economic Case Against Drug Prohibition," *Journal of Economic Perspectives*, 9 (4): 175–192.

Nadelman, E.A. (1997) "The Americanization of Global Law Enforcement: The Diffusion of American Tactics and Personnel," in W.F. MacDonald (ed.) *Crime and Law Enforcement in the Global Village*, Cincinnati, OH: ACJS/Anderson.

OGD (Observatoire Géopolitique des Drogues) (1995) *Géopolitique des drogues 1995*, Paris: Editions la Découvert.

Ouazzani, A. (1996) "Le kif au Maroc: de la survie au narco-trafic, le double versant du Rif," in *Drogues et narco-trafic: le point de vue du Sud*, Centre Tricontinental, Alternatives Sud, Cahiers Trimestriels, 3 (1): 115–125.

Perl, R.F. (ed.) (1994) *Drugs and Foreign Policy: A Critical Review*, Boulder: Westview Press.

Rochlin, J. (1995) "Redefining Mexican 'National Security' During an Era of Postsovereignty," *Alternatives*, 20: 369–402.

Rosenau, J.N. (1992) "The Relocation of Authority in a Shrinking World," *Comparative Politics*, 24 (3): 253–272.

Scheptycki, J.W.E. (1996) "Law Enforcement, Justice and Democracy in the Transnational Arena: Reflections on the War on Drugs," *International Journal of the Sociology of Law*, 24: 61–75.

Scott, P.D. and Marshall, J. (1991) *Cocaine Politics: Drugs, Armies and the CIA in Central America*, Berkeley: University of California Press.

Stares, P.B. (1996) *Global Habit: The Drug Problem in a Borderless World*, Washington DC: Brookings Institute.

Strange, S. (1996) *The Retreat of the State: The Diffusion of Power in the World Economy*, Cambridge: Cambridge University Press.

Thornton, M. (1991) *The Economics of Prohibition*, Salt Lake City: University of Utah Press.

Tullis, L. (1995) *Unintended Consequences: Illegal Drugs and Drug Policies in Nine Countries*, Studies on the Impact of the Illegal Drug Trade, Vol. IV, Boulder: Lynne Rienner.

UNDCP (1997) *World Drug Report*. Oxford: Oxford University Press.

Vanderwood, P.J. (1992) *Disorder and Progress: Bandits, Police, and Mexican Development*, Wilmington: Scholarly Resources Inc.

Veen, H.T. van der (2000) "The International Drug Complex: The Intertwined Dynamics of International Crime, Law Enforcement and the Flourishing Drug Economy," in R. Schönenberg (ed.) *Internationaler Drogenhandel und gesellschaftliche Transformation*, Wiesbaden: DUV.

Woodiwiss, M. (1988) *Crime, Crusades and Corruption: Prohibitions in the United States, 1900–1987*, London: Pinter.

Youngers, C. (1990) *La guerra en los Andes: El rol militar en la política internacional de los Estados Unidos sobre la droga*. Series breves de la oficina sobre Latinoamerica en Washington (WOLA)/ CEDIB, December.

Zwaap, R. (1996) "Hassans gecontroleerde doorvoer," *De Groene Amsterdammer*, 14 February 1996.

Part III

Cases of war economies

6 Profiting from war

Economic rationality and war in Lebanon

Jürgen Endres

Introduction: the Lebanese war and its economic dimension

> Faire la guerre il faut trois choses:
> premièrement de l'argent,
> deuxièmement de l'argent,
> troisièmement de l'argent.
> (Moritz, Duke of Saxony)

It is without doubt that the human and economic consequences of nearly sixteen years of wars and armed conflicts in Lebanon (1975–1990) have been devastating. During "*les evénements*" (the events), as the Lebanese still refer to this period of time, over 150,000 people (about 5 per cent of the resident population!) were killed and more than 300,000 were maimed, injured or disabled (Saidi 1994: 199). Tens of thousands of Lebanese became impoverished, displaced or exiled, the basic infrastructure – roads, communications, electricity, water, etc. – was damaged to a great extent. According to Corm, the destruction of public and private property totaled in a range between 20 and 30 billion US dollars (Corm 1994: 218).

It is simply undeniable that the sixteen years of warfare absorbed enormous economic resources. Troops had to be paid, new combatants had to be recruited, costs for the supply of armament and ammunition had to be covered, and administrations as well as social services had to be established in territories newly under the control of the various militias. The Lebanese war[1] demanded vast amounts of money, and the longer it continued, the more economic resources were needed. As it is not possible to calculate the direct economic costs of nearly sixteen years of warfare in Lebanon,[2] the following compiled estimations might give a very first impression of the economic dimension of this war:

1 Traboulsi estimated the direct expenses for a single ordinary day of fighting in the streets at between 150,000 and 500,000 US dollars (1993b: 571). Taking into account that there have been periods of time

without armed clashes, according to these estimations the direct costs totaled somewhere between 800 million and 2.7 billion US dollars.

2   Couvrat and Pless – quoting French experts – estimated the value of the yearly import of weapons between 1978 and 1986 at about 400 million US dollars, summing up to 3.6 billion US dollars for the nine years inclusive (1993: 95).

3   Picard rated the direct costs for warfare in Lebanon at between 150 million and 1.5 billion US dollars per year (1996: 76), oscillating between relatively peaceful years and years in which major combats occurred.

Evidently, in economic terms, the Lebanese war unfolded enormous destructive and money-absorbing potentials; yet at the same time, the years of warfare showed a second, quite antagonistic economic dimension. The ongoing war also formed the basis for newly evolving economic systems which, developed into a source of wealth, and thus war became a "continuation of economics by other means" (Keen 1998: 11). Parallel to the human and economic costs, highly profitable economic structures evolved in the shadow of the war. In the midst of a general nightmare, the various Lebanese militias in particular developed economic strategies that enabled the fighting factions not only to cover their direct costs of warfare, but also to gain enormous financial profits from waging war. Thus the main thesis of this chapter suggests that the analysis of these financial profits might provide us with a better understanding of the dynamics and developments behind the Lebanese war, as well as with an insight into the mechanisms behind its prolongation.

So far, only few academic studies have dealt with the "beneficial" economic effects of the so-called "civil war" in Lebanon.[3] Taking this lacuna into account, the central questions of this chapter are: Which economic strategies and economic systems enabled the Lebanese militias to cover all expenses for equipment, salaries, administrations, etc., over a period of nearly sixteen years? What consequences did the evolution of war-related economic strategies have for Lebanese society and the armed conflicts themselves? Who profited from war and which social groups were the "losers?"

Focusing on the economic dimensions of war and armed conflicts in Lebanon, the chapter first introduces a general concept of "war economies." Second, it briefly presents the genesis of the various Lebanese militias, as well as a description of some of their most important representatives. Then, the decay and the fragmentation of the Lebanese state and some characteristic features of the Lebanese war system are discussed. In the main section, some economic strategies of the Lebanese militias to finance warfare are analyzed. It will be shown that the militias' economic strategies were (nearly exclusively) based on the situation of war; the militias thus created the respective conditions for their economic activities by waging war. Furthermore, this study points at forms of economic cooperation between the warring militias, as well as at political, economic and social aspects through which the militias could profit from warfare. The conclusion analyzes the impact that the evolving forms of war economies had on the armed conflicts themselves, and discusses the thesis of an "economic rationality" behind the Lebanese war.

War economy as a general concept

The following brief conceptualization of war economies serves as a general explanatory framework for the set of central questions that guide this analysis. Here, the term "war economies" refers to economic strategies applied by irregular military forces such as guerrillas or party militias. These economic strategies are only likely to evolve under the circumstances of war. It is the decay of states and their respective governmental structures, as well as the dissolution of the state monopoly of the legitimate use of physical force, that form essential preconditions for the evolution of such war economies.[4]

To a large extent, the situation of war or armed conflict determines the basic conditions of the forms of economic reproduction. At the same time, the protagonists that are directly involved in the armed clashes adjust their modes of economic reproduction to the new situation. In this way, market-regulative state institutions vanish and a "radical free market economy" evolves (Elwert 1997: 92). War economies are characterized among other things by the domination of short-term economic strategies over long-term strategies, as well as by the appearance of new entrepreneurs and "new economies." Physical force – in peace times ideally regulated by state institutions – becomes a "free-for-use" economic instrument and, in an appropriation of economic resources that is no longer subject to social restrictions, the distinction between "legal" and "illegal" economic methods loses its relevance.

Thus the protagonists of war create the respective conditions for their economic activities by waging war. Evolving under the circumstances of war and out of the necessity to finance military equipment, war economies in the above-defined sense often develop a remarkable structural persistence. The Lebanese experience will show how the gradual breakdown of institutionalized security can be turned into a lucrative source of income for those who are waging war. From this perspective, the dimension of an "economic rationality" is rather likely to be added to the initial political causes of wars and armed conflicts. The situation of war becomes an intrinsic part of the protagonists' economic strategies and therefore the necessary basic condition for the evolution of war-related economic systems. Violence thus assumes the character of "economic violence" in the sense of Keen who defines this term as follows: "Economic violence is violence from which short-time profit is made. Its motivation may not necessarily be purely economic. It may be encouraged or tolerated for political reasons, although ultimately it is provoked to defend economic privileges" (Keen 1998: 11).

Due to this "economic rationality" of violence, the fighting troops are not necessarily pursuing the establishment of a new government or a new state. On the contrary, instead of shaping new political orders, militias as entrepreneurs rather aim at the paralyzation of existing state institutions or the restriction of their functions. In this case, the aim of armed combat is not to win a war, but to perpetuate it (see also Jean and Rufin 1996; Keen 1997, 1998; Rufin 1994, 1995).

"Lebanonization" of Lebanon: the war system, 1975–1990

The continuing situation of war and armed conflicts on Lebanese territory developed into a rather persistent war system. Previously, the country was known as the "Switzerland of the Middle East" and its capital Beirut had been labeled as the "Paris of the Middle East." Yet the course of the Lebanese war changed this image drastically. Now, the term "Lebanonization" entered the vocabulary of political discourse as a synonym for state decay and the complete fragmentation of society.[5] The years of war left visible imprints on the country and transformed the Lebanese society to a high degree. Lebanon broke up along sectarian lines and became extremely "militarized." In developing into persistent institutions, the Lebanese militias implemented their own systems of rule and controlled large parts of the country. Yet, although the institutional setting of the Lebanese state decayed, it nevertheless remained as a political façade. As the evolution of this war system and of specific forms of war economies were closely interrelated processes, a more or less simplified sketch of the Lebanese war system can help to grasp the Lebanese "reality" that emerged in the years between 1975 and 1990.

"Militarization" of Lebanese society: opposing forces

Long before the first clashes between members of the Christian *Kata'ib* militia, also called *Phalange Lebanese*, and armed Palestinian forces spurred the war in 1975, a variety of clan-, party-, and confession-related militias existed in Lebanon. Regarding the conceptual core element of all states, their monopoly of the legitimate use of physical force, the occurrence of these first violent clashes did not therefore indicate – as frequently suggested – the beginning of the decay of the Lebanese state. Rather they were the first violent climax of a long-lasting process in which the core requisites of Lebanese statehood decayed.

In spite of its image as a democratic and pluralist polity, as an island of democracy in the sea of Arab authoritarianism, the Lebanese state had actually been unable to acquire an efficient monopoly of physical force.

Lebanese state formation was characterized by the establishment of quasi-autonomous territories under the control of feudal landlords and sectarian groups (cf. Jung 1992). This situation of "shared control over the means of force" became particularly precarious following the so-called "Black September" in 1970,[6] after which Palestinian guerrilla forces built up their presence on Lebanese territory. Previously, the Palestinian guerrillas that now began to fight their war of liberation against Israel from Lebanese soil had not been perceived as a major threat to the security and stability of the Lebanese state. In 1969, for example, the Lebanese government signed the Cairo Agreement, which entitled the Palestine Liberation Organization (PLO) to the establishment of refugee camps, the creation and maintenance of armed forces, as well as to wage war against Israel from Lebanese territory. But soon the Palestinian troops surmounted the Lebanese Army in strength and number.[7] Within a short time, the Palestinian refugee camps had developed into autonomous military bases and achieved a virtually extraterritorial status. In short, Palestinian organizations formed – together with their military wings – "states within the state" (Rotter 1986: 195). Facing the state's inability to install state sovereignty over the armed Palestinian organizations and their territorial entities, the Lebanese Christians perceived the enforced presence of armed Muslim Palestinians as a fundamental threat to their own Christian communities, as well as to the fragile Muslim–Christian balance in the country. Thus, the Christian communities re-enforced existing and formed new militias, shortly followed by the Lebanese left as well as parts of the Muslim communities (Hanf 1988: 663).

The increasing fragmentation of Lebanese state and society along confessional, social and political lines, together with a persistent threat to physical security, enhanced the "militarization" of Lebanon, leading to the existence of an estimated dozen major and some 40 minor irregular armed forces (Rotter 1986: 192). With regard to the military capabilities of these militias, the estimations vary widely. In their very careful estimation, Marchal and Messiant suggested that these irregular forces did not comprise more than 2,000 to 3,000 "permanent full-time" combatants (Marchal and Messiant 1997: 13). Yet given the fact that most militias were made up of "part-time" fighters, their numbers somehow distort the overall picture. More accurate seem the figures of Kliot, who estimated the number of militia fighters at its peak of about 100,000 (Kliot 1987: 66). Taking into account that the estimated population of Lebanon was, at the beginning of the war, around 3.2 million (Reinkowski 1997: 501), the militarization of the country reached a relatively high degree.

The armed struggle between the two major militia coalitions, the Lebanese Forces and the Lebanese National Movement, was often characterized as a war between Christians and Muslims. Yet, in reality the particular compositions of these coalitions were far more complex. The "pro status quo" Lebanese Forces included primarily the Christian-Maronite militias of the

Jumayyil, Chamoun and Faranjieh clans, with a total number of about 30,000 fighting men and women. The most noticeable militias within the Lebanese Forces were, among others, the Phalangist Party,[8] the Marada Brigade,[9] and the Guardians of the Cedars.[10] The Lebanese National Movement, which was far less cohesive and organized than its opponent, comprised a multitude of different militias, from confessional- and community-based organizations, such as the Popular Socialist Party (PSP)[11] and *Amal*,[12] to a variety of leftist groups,[13] as well as to guerrillas from different Palestinian organizations.[14]

In addition to these two major militia coalitions, a number of "independent" militias appeared during the war, pursuing their particular interests by violent means. Most prominent amongst those were the predominantly Christian South Lebanese Army (SLA) and the Shi'i *Hizbullah* (Party of God). While the first was collaborating with the Israeli occupation forces and controlling the so-called security zone at the Israeli–Lebanese boarder, the *Hizbullah*, founded in 1982, received massive support from Iran and was able to put more than 7,000 men under arms (Chevalérias 1997: 156).

"Cantonization" of the Lebanese state

With the outbreak of the Lebanese war in 1975, the fragmentation of Lebanese society dramatically accelerated. Triggering massive waves of expulsions, the war led to an unprecedented fragmentation along religious and communal lines. Confessionally almost homogenous entities and territorial islands under militia control emerged whose boundaries were only reversed by massive military interventions from outside (by the Syrian army and the Israeli Defence Forces [IDF]). In 1985, ten years after the outbreak of the first armed clashes, the Christian militia Lebanese Forces, the Shi'i militia *Amal* and the Druze militia PSP had firmly established their own cantons (Hanf 1990: 428). The Lebanese Forces controlled East Beirut, the coast between Beirut and Al-Batrun, as well as parts of Mount Lebanon. The Druze PSP ruled over the Shouf mountains, whereas *Amal* competed and cooperated with *Hizbullah* in controlling major parts of South Lebanon and the Shi'i-dominated suburbs of Beirut.

However, at that time the largest part of the country was under the military domination of regular external forces. In changing alliances involved in the armed conflicts since 1976, the Syrian army dominated the coastal strip north of Al-Batrun, the Biqa' valley and the territory along the Syrian–Lebanese border. The IDF, in turn, intervened in Lebanon 1978 and 1982 and occupied large parts of South Lebanon, in particular the area south of the Litani river.

During the war, some of the militia-controlled cantons developed into highly organized "mini-states." Formally, the militia leaders respected the legitimacy of the official Lebanese governments, which as a formal representation of the Lebanese state never ceased to exist. In a speech delivered

in 1987, for instance, the leader of the Druze PSP, Walid Jumblatt, proclaimed:

> In creating the civil administration in 1983, with the help of the martyr
> Halim Takieddine, we had neither intentions of secession, nor did we
> aim at the creation of any canton by an autonomous management,
> because we consider the [Shouf] mountains to be an integral and
> inextricable part of Lebanon.
>
> (*L'Orient – Le Jour*, 24 March 1987)[15]

In practice, however, the militias exercised in their respective cantons governmental authority and functions (partly with the assistance of state
institutions), and they built up their *de facto* rules (Tueni 1991: 19). The
militias formed their own administrative and legal systems, they raised taxes,
tolls and fees, took over police functions, took care of water and electricity
supplies and established public hospitals and health centers.

In this way deprived of essential state functions, the Lebanese government itself performed more or less as a passive spectator. In military terms
unable to re-establish control over the country, it had politically been
paralyzed between the fighting militias and the interests of their communities. Moreover, in only remaining in its rudimentary function, the official
government was condemned to cooperate with the militias in almost all
fields. Thus the Lebanese state offered only little resistance to militia rule
and failed to stop the ongoing fragmentation of the country.

Characteristics of the Lebanese war system

In general, studies on the objectives of military factions in intra-state wars
focus on three different assumptions:

1   Militias aim at the domination over the whole state territory;
2   Their interest is to eliminate the opposing factions;
3   Military struggle is engaged in to establish a new state, to create a new
    state order, or to secede from an existing state.

In the case of Lebanon, however, it is apparent that none of these assumptions sufficiently explains the logic behind the armed conflicts (cf. Corm
1991a: 16). On the contrary, in the course of the Lebanese war, the warring
militias increasingly developed strategies that gave this war a specific logic
that could briefly be described by the following characteristics:

1   *No pact and no alliance were impossible*: the Lebanese war was mostly
    perceived as a war between Muslims and Christians, but in reality the
    picture of this war was far more complex. Christian forces fought
    against Muslim forces, Christian militias against Christian militias,

Sunni Muslims against Shi'i Muslims, Shi'i Muslims against Shi'i Muslims, the Syrian army together with Christian militias against Muslim militias, Christian militias against the Syrian army, communist or Nasserist militias against Christians, etc. Virtually, no military pact and no military coalition was deemed to be impossible. The ally of today could be the enemy of tomorrow and vice versa.

2   *The fighting militias did not aim at the establishment of a new state*: the opposing Lebanese militias did not want to (re-)establish a state or a new state order. None of the Lebanese militias was interested or militarily able to gain control over the whole Lebanese territory. The motivation for continuing warfare was not the vision of shaping new, but the interest in the ongoing paralyzation of existing state structures. The continuing paralyzation of the Lebanese state became the essential precondition for the militias' mere existence and for the rise of a new political elite.

3   *The militias were not seeking the elimination of their adversaries*: the fighting Lebanese militias were not aiming at military victory over opposing forces. Not the elimination of their adversaries, but the maintenance of their existence was in their interest. In this way, they were able to perpetuate the security threat to their own communities, providing them the necessary justification for their own armed presence and the domination over their respective territories. Thus, waging war was a means of providing the militias with political legitimacy and of stabilizing the structures of violence, i.e. the system of insecurity.

Against this background, it is nevertheless important to underline that the war in Lebanon also had clear limitations. The frequently made equation of Lebanon with Thomas Hobbes' state of nature, i.e. the notion of a war of everybody against everybody, does therefore not adequately reflect the Lebanese reality. There were periods of "neither war nor peace," and there were regions that were less or even not at all directly affected by armed clashes. Furthermore, the years between 1975 and 1990 were not characterized by a total chaos of random violence, but rather by a structured system of the application of physical force. Military struggle was not always omnipresent and various forms of regulating and controling the means of physical force emerged. Not only did the militias themselves provide security and social services, but also most Lebanese learned to arrange themselves with the war-system situation and had to adapt everyday life to the persistence of the structures of violence. In addition, despite the fragmentation of the Lebanese territory into militia-controlled cantons and the creation of confessionally almost homogenous territorial entities, personal contacts across the various frontlines persisted. These forms of continuation apply equally to the existence of national markets. Thus goods that were produced in one canton were "exported" into another regardless of the existing hostilities. Moreover, the nation-wide subsidization of some imported goods through the Lebanese government never fully ceased.

Economic strategies of the militias: from covering needs to making profits

The continuing military activities, as well as the maintenance and consolidation of the cantons, demanded immense economic resources. Armament and ammunition had to be permanently provided, troops to be paid and administrations to be established in the territories under militia control. Thus, "the first concern of the militias was to build a material base which would enable them to finance their drive for domination" (Corm 1994: 216). Facing this economic challenge, the militias developed economic strategies and established systems of war economies which built on both the use of physical force and social structures that were in themselves a result of ongoing warfare. At the same time, the Lebanese militias were fighters, thieves, tax collectors and entrepreneurs. In a vicious circle, steady access to economic resources enabled continuing warfare, and the ongoing war, as well as the decay of the state, guaranteed the persistence of the new-born militia economies.

Given the informal character of war economies, it comes as no surprise that the estimations concerning the militias' economic profits vary widely in range. In October 1990, for instance, the Lebanese daily *an-Nahar* estimated the profits from the militia economy at a minimum of 14.5 billion US dollars for the years 1975–1990, that is to say about 900 million US dollars per year (Harris 1997: 294). In qualifying the Lebanese militias as "confession-related criminal syndicates" (Labrousse 1991: 132), Corm calculated that the Lebanese militias obtained with their war-adapted economic strategies about two billion US dollars per year. According to his figures, about one-half of the money was of external origin, comprising both the financial support of foreign states and contributions by the highly organized Lebanese diasporas. The other half (one billion US dollars per year!) he estimated as coming from internal sources and was the remarkable result of a diversified system of war or militia economies in the previously mentioned sense (Corm 1991a: 17).

External financial and military support

Foreign intervention in Lebanese affairs was not a new phenomenon. Long before its independence in 1943, Lebanon's internal and external affairs had been subject to external interests, and external powers always cultivated client relationships with Lebanese partners. Consequently, with the outbreak of the armed clashes in 1975, Lebanon became the "bloody arena" not only for conflicts within Lebanon but also for conflicts that originated outside Lebanon. Facing an increasing demand for economic resources, the militias were able to benefit from traditionally existing or newly established client relationships to foreign forces, and at the same time they played the role of local "spearheads" for external interests, thus becoming agents of foreign interference. In addition to direct military intervention, i.e. of the IDF and the Syrian army, various other states were indirectly involved in the Lebanese war and supplied the various militias with armament and provided financial support for their respective allies.

The two militias profiting most from external donor states were the Christian militia coalition Lebanese Forces and the Shi'i militia *Hizbullah*. The Lebanese Forces benefited from the financial and military support of different countries, including Arab states such as Saudi Arabia, Jordan and Egypt. Considering the Lebanese (Christian) Maronites as their "natural allies" in a region dominated by Muslims, Israel mainly supported the Lebanese Forces and Israeli military assistance peaked in the years between 1976 and 1982 with some 25 million US dollars per year (Picard 1996: 77).[16] Traditionally allied with the Catholic Christian communities in Lebanon, France is another Western country that is said to have provided support for Christian militias.[17] During the last years of the war (1987–1990), the Lebanese Forces even received armament supplies from Saddam Husain's regime in Baghdad, which hoped to counter Syrian influence in Lebanon with its support of Christian militias (Corm 1994: 218). Finally, it was the Shi'i militia *Hizbullah* that depended most on external funding. Financed almost entirely by the Islamic Republic of Iran, *Hizbullah* received about 100 million US dollars per year from Tehran (Corm 1994: 218).

Internal forms of militia economies

As previously mentioned, the Lebanese militias did not only depend on external resources, but established their own economic systems in Lebanon. At an early stage, the economic strategies of the Lebanese militias rested almost exclusively on the forced extraction of economic resources from the Lebanese population. Yet given the limitations of these resources, more efficient and less limited ways of economic extraction had to be developed. Thus the Lebanese militias created a system of war economies linking different strategies of economic extraction to local, national and international markets. The following presentation of three of these various forms of war or militia economies might give an idea of the highly efficient practices employed by the Lebanese war entrepreneurs.

Pillaging, confiscation of private property and theft

Pillaging, the confiscation of private property along with the "cleansing" of confessionally heterogeneous areas and the establishment of militia-controlled cantons, as well as militia-organized theft, provided a substantial part of the economic resources on which the Lebanese militias relied. A spectacular act of predation was, without any doubt, the pillaging of the "British Bank of the Middle East" in Beirut in April 1976. As the world's largest bank robbery to this day (estimated between 20 to 50 million US dollars), it even entered the *Guinness Book of Records* (Traboulsi 1993a: 61). The militia members' possibilities of making at least modest economic fortunes by pillaging their fellow countrymen were widespread, and the desire for booty frequently even led to the interruption of the fighting. Messara, for example, describes a more or less typical combat situation as follows:

> According to concurrent reports, Lebanese who were fighting in the streets of the city center, after having pillaged all the shops behind them, concluded an armistice based on a pure compromise in order to be able to also plunder the shops that were between their lines. They came together, formed a bilateral committee and sent out joint groups that systematically plundered the shops. Once they had finished their venture, they resumed fighting. The distribution of the booty among the partners, associates and rivals became an established rule.
>
> (Messara 1989: 86)

Applying these methods of pillaging and theft, Lebanese militias seized in the period from 1975 to 1990 between 5 and 7 billion US dollars (Corm 1994: 217).

Cultivation, processing and trading of drugs

Parallel to the ongoing war and the progressing decay of state institutions, the cultivation, processing and trade of illegal drugs became an important economic activity in Lebanon. According to Favret, the drug business amounted to at least 50 percent of all economic activities in wartime Lebanon (Favret 1986: 190). Harris, for example, estimated that the militias' annual profit from the drug economy was about 600 million US dollars (Harris 1997: 207). Without any doubt, the drug business was a major source of income for practically all militias and therefore an essential financial resource for the purchase of arms (cf. Labrousse 1991: 132).

During the years of war, Lebanon developed not only into a nodal point for drug trafficking, but it also became a leading drug producer. For years, the country was the world's largest producer of hashish and an important cultivator of poppy, which was almost in its entirety processed to heroin on the spot. The progressing decay of the state, as well as the consolidation of militia-dominated cantons, made this steady increase in drug production possible. According to Picard, the area under cultivation with hashish quadrupled from 1976 to 1988 (1996: 67). Marchal and Messiant estimated that in 1988 the area under cultivation with hashish reached about 25,000 hectares (1997: 14). With an average yield of 36 kilograms of hashish per hectare, the yearly Lebanese production of hashish was about 900 metric tons.[18]

Poppy is said to have been introduced in Lebanon by Kurdish experts in 1984. Initially cultivated on an area of 60 hectares, this picture changed dramatically. According to Couvrat and Pless, the poppy cultivation reached about 4,000 hectares during the war with an average yield of 15 kilograms of opium per hectare, an amount which is sufficient to produce 6 metric tons of heroin (Couvrat and Pless 1993: 66). Parallel to the extension of drug-cultivated areas, the drug business also became more diversified. In addition to the more or less "traditional" production of hashish and opium, heroin, cocaine and amphetamines were produced on and distributed from Lebanese territory.[19] With a production of 900 metric tons of hashish and 6 metric tons of heroin, the profits from the drug business have been estimated as much as 2 billion US dollars per year, a sum that does not include incomes from Lebanon's role as an important transit country for drugs from East Asia (Couvrat and Pless 1993: 94).

Depending on their respective capabilities and facilities, the militias participated in a multiplicity of ways in the Lebanese drug economy. Some militias were directly involved in the cultivation of hashish and poppy and they ran their own drug-processing laboratories. Other militias concentrated more on drug trafficking to all parts of the world, thereby benefiting from their international (political and economic) contacts. Another way to profit from the drug business was the forced collection of protection money in exchange for safeguarding fields under cultivation and drug laboratories. In addition, the militias also raised special taxes on drugs. In this way, the price for hashish doubled or even tripled on its way from the Biqa' valley to the coast owing to the taxes that were raised at the barrages of different militia checkpoints (Favret 1986: 96).

Taxes, duties and other fees

The more the Lebanese state lost its capacity of extraction, the more the militias themselves appeared as tax collectors. With the decline of the state, duties and other fees became one of the main economic sources of the militias, and they gradually deprived the Lebanese state of its original power resources (Perthes 1993: 39). The militias developed an efficient system of taxation within their cantons over the years of war, and most former governmental resources were now collected by the fighting militias. While in 1980 90 percent of the duties and taxes went into the Lebanese treasury, in 1983 this figure was only 60 percent. In 1986, not more than 10 percent of the taxes were left for the official authorities, while the rest fuelled the war budgets of the militias (Picard 1996: 67).

In fact, there was nearly no industrial production, no economic trans-action, no trade and no administrative or other services on which the militias did not impose taxes. The fighting factions taxed exports and imports, public services, restaurant bills, theatre or cinema tickets, tobacco, cigarettes, gasoline and flour. At their barrages, they levied tolls on the passage of goods and individuals from one militia-controlled zone to another. The following examples might give an idea of both the efficiency and the high level of organization with which this militia system of taxation worked.

The Lebanese Forces imposed a tax of 20 Lebanese pounds on each liter of gasoline and 20,000 Lebanese pounds on each metric ton of flour. On tickets for cinemas and theaters they levied 4 percent tax. The largest source of revenue in the "service sector" came from the "Casino of Lebanon," which was situated in the area under control of the Lebanese Forces. It provided them with a monthly cash influx of approximately 30 million Lebanese pounds (about 80,000 US dollars). In the territories under its control, the Shi'i militia *Amal* raised 13.5 Lebanese pounds as tax on each liter of gasoline, apartments were taxed 100 Lebanese pounds, super-markets with 1,000 Lebanese pounds per month.

Due to the significance of import and export taxes for the militia economy, the control over official or unofficial ports[20] became vital for the Lebanese militias.[21] For instance, the ports under the control of the Druze militia PSP (the ports of Jiyeh and of Khalde south of Beirut), provided together approximately 21 million Lebanese pounds (about 60,000 US dollars) per month. The Christian Lebanese Forces controlled various ports, including the fifth basin of the Beirut port the main source of income with about 30 million Lebanese pounds per month.[22] Altogether the income of the Lebanese Forces from taxing and raising duties at the country's borders reached about 60 million US dollars per year (Picard 1996: 93).

Forms of economic cooperation among the warring militias

Though fighting each other fiercely on the battlefield, the Lebanese militias did not hesitate to cooperate on the field of commerce. At the same time, they were enemies and business partners, waging war against each other and sharing mutual economic interests. Thus, the maintenance of the status quo became the main linkage among the fighting Lebanese factions: the continuing paralyzation of the state institutions, the continued existence of their own cantons, the control over the communities they pretended to represent, the persistence of various forms of war economies, and, of course, the continuation of the armed conflicts on Lebanese territory. Due to this specific war logic, the Lebanese militias shared over a long period of time the "opposition to everything that promised to bring back a legal system, such as the reconstruction of the administration, the development of police forces and the reopening of normal economic channels" (Picard 1993: 26).

The Lebanon-specific situation of this war – the territorial and functional fragmentation of the Lebanese state along with the persistence of a Lebanese national market – represented the ideal conditions for the Lebanese militias to pursue their economic ambitions. Therefore, the mere fact of a country divided into different territories that were controlled by seven main militias should not mislead the observer. Behind this apparent political fragmentation was still a vital national market on which the different militias cooperated in order to maximize their economic profits (Picard 1996: 91). Despite the numerous victims of war, despite all existing political differences and hostilities, the forms of economic cooperation between the Lebanese militias were various and the militias "generally respected one another's turf" (Harris 1997: 204). A typical tale, often told in Lebanon, is of a businessman who avoided paying taxes to militia x while on his passage from the canton controlled by militia x into another canton controlled by militia y. In canton y he was later visited by representatives from militia y and ordered to pay the charges to militia x he previously had tried to circumvent (Harris 1997: 204). The direct financial cooperation in the form of debt collection guaranteed each militia that nobody could escape their financial requests, even if the respective person or company resided outside the canton under the militia's control.

In particular the highly profitable drug business became a major field of economic cooperation and bound together the material interests of militias that were normally engaged in heavy military clashes: "Mainly cultivated by Shiites, transported towards the ports of Tripoli, Chekka and Jounieh by Sunnites, Druzes and Christians, shipped abroad by mainly Christian boatmen – the drug is the domain where militias of all sides cooperate and collaborate" (Traboulsi 1993b: 572). Realizing that only direct economic cooperation guaranteed the large scale of the Lebanese drug business and therefore the high profits for the militias, the Shi'i militia *Amal* cooperated with the Druze militia PSP, the Shi'i *Hizbullah* with the Christian Lebanese Forces, the militias controlling Tripoli with *Hizbullah*, etc. (Picard 1996: 91).

Profiting from war

In October 1989, the Ta'if Agreement paved the way towards an end to the Lebanese tragedy. In comparison with the political structures of the pre-war period, the agreement itself entailed no major political changes. It was rather due to massive external pressure and to the growing war-weariness among the Lebanese that most of the militias accepted the regulations of the Ta'if Agreement and ended the hostilities. In October 1990, with the defeat of General Michel Aoun, who with his mainly Christian troops resisted the Ta'if Agreement, the Lebanese war finally came to an end.

For a large part of the Lebanese population, the human, political, social and economic consequences of the various wars and armed conflicts have been devastating. In sharp contrast to this vast majority of the Lebanese, however, many of the militias and their leaders were on the winning side. Although none of the militias could claim that they had won the war, nearly every militia profited in political or economic terms from its military engagement. In this regard, they even proved that the most destructive war can also produce wealth (cf. Picard 1996: 73).

More important, however, within the militia system a "new Lebanese elite" had emerged which was not willing to renounce the privileges they had been able to acquire during wartimes. This new elite – heavily armed as it was – demanded the transformation of their privileges into post-war Lebanese society. In exchange for the militias' willingness to cooperate and to disarm, the Lebanese government accepted their integration into the re-established state institutions. "The new government and the new parliament granted them [the militias] a place in the sun" (Kiwan 1994b: 59). In a package deal some militia leaders were appointed to the cabinet of Umar Karami, while almost 20,000 militia fighters were integrated in the Lebanese army, the police forces and the new state administration. Today, the Lebanese militias – except for the Shi'i militia *Hizbullah* – are disarmed (at least to a great extent) and some of them transformed into legal political parties. Evidently, the spoils of war were successfully transferred into spoils of peace.

An illustrative example of a more or less "typical" Lebanese war and post-war career is without doubt the success story of Walid Jumblatt. Born in 1949 the only son of the charismatic Druze leader Kamal Jumblatt, he was not politically active until his father, whom he succeeded, died in 1977. Whereas his political inheritance was shaky at the start – he lacked the experience, the political stature and the charisma of his late father – it was mainly the victory of the Jumblatt-led PSP militia over the Lebanese Forces in the "war of the mountains" in 1983 that made Walid the undisputed leader of the Druze community and therefore an important player on the Lebanese political scene. Due to his military and political importance, he became Minister of Tourism in 1984 and Minister of Public Works in 1989. In 1990 he was appointed Minister of State and in 1992 Minister of Displaced Persons – an office he held until December 1998.

In addition to these political and social gains, the militias also made large economic profits. Given the fact that the economic surplus of Lebanon's war economy surmounted the direct costs of warfare, the Lebanese militias were able to invest and reinvest their profits in Lebanon and abroad.[23] "The bigger militias, which were able to accumulate fortunes during the war, turn today toward the creation of holdings and the participation among business companies. Some of them are already a part of the negotiations among companies which are interested in the reconstruction of Beirut" (Kiwan 1994b: 71). It is only against this background that the successful implementation of the Ta'if accord – the abrupt, and for many experts surprising, end of the hostilities, the dissolution of the existing militia system, and the more or less successful transformation of the Lebanese war society into a post-war society – can be explained. However, the necessary precondition for this was, above all, the disentanglement of violence from its political and social origins – the "banalization" of violence during the years of the Lebanese war.

Taking into account the numerous individual human tragedies, the enormous economic destruction, and the growing impoverishment of the Lebanese population, the formula *"la ghalib wa la maghloub"* (neither winner nor loser) on which the Lebanese armed factions agreed in Ta'if seems to be a rather cynical interpretation. While in sixteen years of armed confrontations a small group of war entrepreneurs secured high economic profits, the majority of the Lebanese had to foot the bill.

Conclusion

This study has shed some light on the various forms of war or militia economies that Lebanese militias developed and from which they could not only finance their military activities, but also realize large economic profits. The ongoing violent clashes prevented the re-establishment of the Lebanese state and enabled the Lebanese militias to build up quite profitable economic systems. Only on the "heap of ruins" of the Lebanese state, could the militia economy evolve and persist in the way it did between 1975 and 1990. Thus, war and the evolving forms of war economies determined each other and interacted. Yet what were the consequences of these existing forms of war economies for the war itself? What impact had the war economies on the course of the armed quarrels?

First of all, there is no doubt that the existing forms of militia or war economies contributed to the perpetuation of the war. In particular, the war economies provided the necessary financial means to cover the rising costs of arms and ammunition. Second, the revenues of war supported the Lebanese militias in claiming legitimacy for ruling their respective cantons. Being able to provide social and administrative services, as well as to reallocate parts of the revenues to the population living under their domination, the militias could not only justify their mere existence but also claim to represent legitimate political authorities. Without these redistributional mechanisms based on the various forms of war economies the Lebanese war system could not have lasted for such a long time.

This brings us finally to the question of whether there was an "economic rationality" behind the Lebanese war. Did the various Lebanese militias wage war for economic reasons? The enormous profits of some militias, the military logic of some armed clashes, and the fact that despite all arduous hostilities, forms of economic cooperation existed between the militias strengthen the thesis of an intrinsic "economic rationality" to the

Lebanese war. Nevertheless, the violent breakdown of the Lebanese state was primarily a result of historically developed political, social and economic contradictions within Lebanese society. It was only under the conditions of protracted warfare itself that the primary causes turned into secondary and the use of force tended to lose its political aims. The evolving forms of war economies, which initially were the result of the dire economic necessity to cover the costs of warfare, developed their own dynamics and turned into a major purpose to wage war. Therefore it would be an exaggeration to interpret the years of war in Lebanon as strictly economically motivated. It was under the conditions of war (which formed the absolute precondition for a large-scale militia economy) that the militias used physical force as an instrument to pursue their economic ambitions. Realizing that the situation of war guarantees wealth, as well as political authority, the Lebanese militias had only few reasons to end their bloody business until the accord of Ta'if gave them a guarantee of also participating in the political and economic spoils of peace.

In the light of this conclusion, the importance of war economies for a comprehensive understanding of current intra-state wars should not to be underrated. A scholarly approach to explaining the social phenomenon of war therefore demands more than a limited investigation under the sole question "why war?" In order to reach a sound understanding of the violent logic of protracted conflicts such as the war in Lebanon, the dynamics, developments and social changes that evolve during a war have to be taken into account. For this reason, the fundamental question "why war?" has to be completed with the equally essential question: "who profits from it?"

Notes

1 It is only a matter of convenience that this study uses the term "the Lebanese war." As a matter of fact, the term hides a multiplicity of violent conflicts and armed clashes which were characterized by changing fronts and alliances. Therefore the term "Lebanese war" sums up a complex and interwoven set of armed conflicts.

2 Direct economic costs are defined as expenses for armament, ammunition and other military equipment, salaries, etc. They do not include the economic consequences (destruction of public and private property, losses of the Lebanese political economy) that the various armed clashes inflicted.

3 The frequently used classification of the violent clashes between 1975 and 1990 in Lebanon as "the Lebanese civil war" does not correctly represent the Lebanese reality during this period of time. First, not *one* war was waged, but many different wars or armed conflicts which followed each other, merged, interwove or overlapped. Second, the classification as "civil war" entails problems. The violent clashes occurred not only between Lebanese organizations, but also between Lebanese actors and external actors like the different Palestinian armed organizations, the Syrian army and the Israeli Defence Forces (IDF).

4 It is important to emphasize that it is not the forms of the chosen economic systems and strategies that are decisive for the definition of war economies but the preconditions under which they evolve and persist. The same applies of course to the "economic protagonists" themselves. This is important to mention, because in many cases forms of war economies are similar to economic strategies and systems employed in so-called "organized crime." In other cases, the way of economic action is not war specific in itself, i.e. the traded goods do not have any war-specific characteristics. In those cases only the existing circumstances (dominated by the situation of war), the economic protagonists themselves (militias, guerrillas, irregular troops) and the way of appropriation of economic resources make economic actions a "war economy."

5 Meanwhile the French equivalent to "lebanonization" (libanisation) formally entered the French language, defined in *Larousse* as "processus de fragmentation d'un État, résultant de l'affrontement entre diverses communautés" (Harris 1997: 1).

6 In September 1970, the Jordanian government under King Husain of Jordan decided no longer to tolerate the Palestinian forces which waged their war against Israel from Jordanian territory. The armed clashes between the Jordanian army and the armed Palestinian organization led to the expulsion of the Palestinian troops from Jordan and to the influx of thousands of Palestine Liberation Organization (PLO) militants into Lebanon. Thus, Lebanon became the only territory from which Palestinian troops could wage their war against Israel (Harris 1997: 154).

7 At the outbreak of the war in 1975, the Lebanese army was about 15,000 troops strong (Sigaud 1988: 54).

8 The Phalangist Party, known in Arabic as *Kata'ib*, was the mainstay of the Lebanese Forces. Founded by Christian patriarch Pierre Jumayyil in the 1930s and modeled on the German and Italian fascist parties, the militia could muster up to 20,000 troops, of which 3,000 were full-time soldiers. It evolved into a formidable and highly organized fighting force.

9 The Marada-Brigade, also called the Zhagartan Liberation Army, was about 3,500 troops strong and represented mainly the interests of Sulayman Faranjieh, president of Lebanon at the outbreak of the armed conflicts in 1975. It operated mainly out of Tripoli and other areas of northern Lebanon around Zhagarta.

10 The militia Guardians of the Cedars was led by Etienne Saqr, a former police officer. It consisted of about 500 fighters.

11 The PSP militia was mainly Druze. It consisted of about 2,500 men and was led by Kamal Jumblatt and, after his assassination in 1977, by his son Walid Jumblatt.

12 The Shi'i militia *Amal* (Arabic for "hope" as well as an acronym for *Afwaj al Muqawamah al Lubnaniyah*) was founded in 1975 and comprised approximately 1,500 men. Its original leader, Musa as-Sadr, disappeared under mysterious circumstances in 1978.

13 I.e. the Popular Guard, the Communist Action Organization, and the Nasserite militia *Murabitun*.

14 During the years 1975 to 1990 dozens of Palestinian military entities operated in Lebanon, totalling about 25,000 men under arms.

15 All quotations from French texts have been translated by the author.

16 Israeli objectives in Lebanon centered among others on the maintenance of a Christian-dominated Lebanese government and on the security of its northern border.

17 According to *Le Commerce*, the municipality of Paris supported the *Kata'ib* militia with about 90,000 US dollars (16 June 1989).

18 At that time, Pakistan, Afghanistan and Morocco together produced about the same amount of hashish (Couvrat and Pless 1993: 90).

19 *Table 6.1* Area under cultivation with hashish and poppy, in hectares

Year	1984	1985	1986	1987	1988
Hashish	16,000	15,000	15,000	22,000	25,000
Poppy	60	120	1,500	600	3,000

Source: *Le Commerce*, 20 May 1993.

20 Traboulsi lists fifteen illegal ports (1993b: 565–567).

21 The control over the ports was not only important for the militias due to the economic revenues they guaranteed, it was also vital as "an open door" for the import of armament and ammunition as well as for the trafficking of illegal goods.

22 Figures out of: *Les Cahiers de l'Orient*, revue d'étude et de réflexion sur le Liban et le monde arabe, deuxième trimestre 1988, 10 : 271–287.

23 The treasurer of the Lebanese Forces stated in 1989 that the Lebanese Forces had invested approximately 100 million US dollars, 60 percent of that amount in real estate (*Le Commerce*, 26 February 1989).

References

Abou-Rjaili, K. (1989) "L'émigration forcée des populations à l'interieur du Liban. 1975–1986," *Monde Arabe: Maghreb Machrek*, 125: 53–68.

Azar, E.E. (ed.) (1984) *The Emergence of a New Lebanon: Fantasy or Reality*, New York: Praeger.

Boustany, A. (1991) "Guerre et drogue au Liban [entretien]," *Cultures et Conflits*, 3: 99–104.

Bulloch, J. (1977) *Death of a Country. The Civil War in Lebanon*, London: Weidenfeld and Nicholson.

Chevalerias, A. (1997) "Le Hezbollah libanais, une force politique," *Stratégique*, 2 (3): 145–159.

Collings, D. (ed.) (1994) *Peace for Lebanon? From war to reconstruction*, Boulder: Lynne Rienner.

Corm, G. (1991a) "Hégémonie milicienne et problème du rétablissement de l'État," *Monde Arabe: Maghreb Machrek*, 131: 13–25.

—— (1991b) "Le centre ville de Beyrouth. Ou est l'état?," *Les Cahiers de l'Orient*, 24: 97–110.

—— (1992) *Liban: les guerres de l'Europe et de l'Orient*, Paris: Gallimard Folio.

—— (1994) "The War System: Militia Hegemony and Reestablishment of the State," in D. Collings (ed.) *Peace for Lebanon?*, Boulder: Lynne Rienner.

Couvrat, J.F. and Pless, N. (1993) *Das verborgene Gesicht der Weltwirtschaft*, Münster: Westfälisches Dampfboot.

Deeb, M.K. (1980) *The Lebanese Civil War*, New York: Praeger.

Dupuis, S. (1994) "Palestiniens au Liban. Une précarité source d'instabilité," *Les Cahiers de l'Orient*, 35: 121–131.

Elwert, G. (1995) "Gewalt und Märkte," in W. Dombrowsky and U. Pasero (eds) *Wissenschaft, Literatur, Katastrophe*, Münster: Westdeutscher Verlag.

—— (1997) "Gewaltmärkte. Beobachtungen zur Zweckrationalität der Gewalt," in T. von Trotha (ed.) *Soziologie der Gewalt*, Kölner Zeitschrift für Soziologie und Sozialpsychologie, Sonderheft 37/1997, Opladen.

Endres, J. (1997) "'Wirtschaftswunder' im Krieg. Formen der Kriegsökonomie im libanesischen Bürgerkrieg," *Beiruter Blätter*, 5: 35–41.

—— (2000) "Vom 'Monopoly' privatisierter Gewalt zum Gewaltmonopol? Formen der Gewaltordnung im Libanon nach 1975," *Leviathan*, 28 (2): 221–234.

Favret, R. (1986) "Liban: j'ai assisté aux vendages de l'opium," *Actuel*, 85: 94–194.

Fawaz, A.I. (1987) "Sectarianism and Lebanon's National Dilemma," *Orient*, 28 (1): 22–37.

Hamdan, K. (1991) "About the Confessional State in Lebanon," in L. Fawaz (ed.) *State and Society in Lebanon*, Oxford: Centre for Lebanese Studies.

Hanf, T. (1988) "Libanon-Konflikt," in U. Steinbach and R. Robert (eds) *Der Nahe und Mittlere Osten. Politik, Gesellschaft, Wirtschaft, Geschichte, Kultur*, Bd. 1, Opladen: Leske und Budrich.

—— (1990) *Koexistenz im Krieg. Staatszerfall und Entstehen einer Nation im Libanon*, Baden-Baden: Nomos.

Harris, W. (1985) "The view from Zahle: Security and Economic Conditions in the Central Bekaa 1980–1985," *Middle East Journal*, 39 (3): 270–286.

—— (1997) *Faces of Lebanon. Sects, Wars, and Global Extensions*, Princeton: Markus Wiener Publishers.

Jean, F. and Rufin, J-C. (ed.) (1996) *Économie des guerres civiles*, Paris: Hachette.

Jung, D. (1992) "Der Krieg im Libanon. Exemplarischer Versuch einer gesellschafts-theoretisch fundierten Kriegsursachenanalyse," *Arbeitspapier* Nr. 61 der Forsch-ungsstelle Kriege, Rüstung und Entwicklung, Universität Hamburg.

Kassir, S. (1994) *La guerre du Liban: de la dissension nationale au conflit regional (1975–1982)*, Paris: Karthala.

Keen, D. (1997) "A Rational Kind of Madness," *Oxford Development Studies*, 25 (1): 67–75.

—— (1998) "The Economic Functions of Violence in Civil Wars," *Adelphi Papers*, 320, London: International Institute for Strategic Studies.

Khazen, F. el (1991) "The Communal Pact of National Identities: The Making and Politics of the 1943 National Pact," *Papers on Lebanon*, 12, Oxford: Centre for Lebanese Studies.

—— (1997) "Permanent Settlement of Palestinians in Lebanon: A Recipe for Conflict," *Journal of Refugee Studies*, 10 (3): 275–293.

Kiwan, F. (ed.) (1994a) *Le Liban aujourd'hui*, Paris: Éditions CNRS.

—— (1994b) "Forces politiques nouvelles, système politique ancien," in F. Kiwan (ed.) *Le Liban aujourd'hui*, Paris: Éditions CNRS: 57–72.

Kliot, N. (1987) "The collapse of the Lebanese State," *Middle Eastern Studies*, 23 (1): 54–74.

Labrousse, A. (1991) *La drogue, l'argent et les armes*, Paris: Fayard.

Maila, J. (1986) "Liban: onze ans après," *Les Cahiers de l'Orient*, 2: 111–127.

Makhlouf, H. (1994) *Culture et trafic de drogue au Liban*, Paris: L'Harmattan.

Marchal, R. and Messiant, C. (1997) *Les chemins de la guerre et de la paix. Fins de conflit en Afrique orientale et australe*, Paris: Karthala.

Messara, A. N. (1986) "État et communautés au Liban," *Les Cahiers de l'Orient*, 1: 85–100.

—— (1989) "Le citoyen libanais et l'état. Une tradition tenace de constitutionnalisme menacée," *Monde Arabe: Maghreb Machrek*, 125: 82–99.

Norton, A.R. (1987) *Amal and the Shi'a. Struggle for the Soul of Lebanon*, Austin: University of Texas Press.

Perthes, V. (1993) "Der Libanon nach dem Bürgerkrieg. Von Ta'if zum gesellschaftlichen Konsens?," *SWP* – S 385 (Mai 1993), Ebenhausen.

Picard, E. (1988) *Liban. État de discorde. Des fondations aux guerres fratricides*, Paris: Karthala.

—— (1993) "Le Lebanese Shi'a and Political Violence," *Discussion Paper*, 42, United Nations Research Institute for Social Development (UNRISD).

—— (1996) "Liban: la matrice historique," in F. Jean and J-C. Rufin (eds) *Économie des guerres civiles*, Paris: Hachette.

Rabinovich, I. (1985) *The War for Lebanon, 1970–1985*, rev. ed., Ithaca and London: Cornell Paperbacks.

Reinkowski, M. (1997) "National Identity in Lebanon since 1990," *Orient*, 38 (3): 493–515.

Rieck, A. (1989) *Die Schiiten und der Kampf um den Libanon. Politische Chronik 1958–1988*, Hamburg: Deutsches Orient-Institut.

Rotter, G. (1986) "Die Milizionarisierung des Libanon," *Saeculum*,. 37: 192–198.

Rufin, J-C. (1994) "Les économies de guerre dans les conflits de faible intensité (1re partie)," *défense nationale*, décembre, 50e année: 45–61.

—— (1995) "Les économies de guerre dans les conflits de faible intensité (2e partie)," *défense nationale*, janvier, 51e année: 15–25.

Saidi, N.H. (1994) "The Economic Reconstruction of Lebanon: War, Peace, and Modernization," in D. Collings (ed.) *Peace for Lebanon?*, Boulder: Lynne Rienner.

Sigaud, D. (1988) "L'armée libanaise. Éclatement ou destin national?," *Les Cahiers de l'Orient*, 11: 47–68.

Traboulsi, F.N. (1993a) "De la violence. Fonctions et rituels," *Stratégie II*, Peuples Méditerranéens, 64/65: 57–86.

—— (1993b) *Identités et solidarités croisées dans les conflits du Liban contemporain, thèse de doctorat d'histoire*, université de Paris VIII, (unpublished), Paris.

Tueni, G. (1991) "Looking ahead," in L. Fawaz (ed.) *State and Society in Lebanon*, Oxford: Centre for Lebanese Studies.

7 Between ethnic collision and mafia collusion

The "Balkan route" to state-making

Francesco Strazzari

Introduction: the "fog of war" in the limelight

Throughout the 1990s the soldering of politico-military interests and mafia investment represented the fortune of the entrepreneurs of violence in all former Yugoslav territories. Although dismissing these complex and somewhat obscure processes as "the inevitable side effects of all wars" may be. tempting, this would seriously prejudice our understanding of the cycle of Balkan wars that concluded the twentieth century. Moving from this insight, the following analysis is an attempt to delve into these processes, bringing them back into the main picture out of which they have often been relegated.

Most of the academic and journalistic accounts have treated the Bosnian war, for example, as a relatively uniform conflict among two or three ethnically distinct warring parties that were involved in diplomatic and military confrontation along a 1,000-km long front line. However, once one moves down from bird's eye representations and analyzes particular trouble spots, the intertwining of newly emerged ethnically-defined institutions, mafia-style war economies and elite connivance patterns becomes more tangible and easier to identify. Upon closer inspection, this war can also be seen as a collection of local wars along which state-dismantling and state-building projects have been articulated.[1] The presence of international mass media made part of the devastation visible to the public. However, the pouring of a large number of journalists into crowded press conferences that were held in the region's capitals proved to be no guarantee of complete information. This was the case, for example, concerning the war in Mostar, whose moon-like scenario of devastation and segregation had been deliberately eclipsed by the parties. Once the fog of war cleared and the disaster of Mostar's Croat–Muslim war emerged, relatively few attempted an explanation. Indeed, many observers limited themselves to list this case under the rubric "inhuman degenerations." In doing so, they were in fact archiving this case as one whose analysis could tell us little about the logic of the whole Bosnian war. This stands in stark contrast to the fact that it was precisely with the brokering of a fragile agreement in Mostar that in early 1994 the US strategy of involvement in the Balkans began to unfold. Possibly, examining warfare in Mostar was a risky exercise for most observers' cognitive consistency. Around the project of creating the state of Herceg-Bosna, warfare patterns did not follow the logic of most "top-down" diplomatic representations, and the elites were making deals while conducting campaigns of terror. Thus, it is perhaps precisely from the analysis of escalations like the one that took place in Mostar that one should start to gain an understanding of the nature of war-making and state-making in Bosnia and, inasmuch as Bosnian events illuminate regional dynamics, of the other Balkan wars (Bjelakovic and Strazzari 1998: 74–75).

Likewise, it has to be noted that while a lot of ink has been used to dissect the suffering of the victims and the sadism of the perpetrators, relatively little has been written about the choices of political economy that accompanied and accelerated the dismantling of Yugoslavia in the years 1990 and 1991.[2] These choices had a visible impact on the traumatic modalities of the Yugoslav agony, if not on the fate of the Federation as a whole, which a decade later was still continuing. Given the difficulty in collecting and verifying data, this exploration has to be considered as a preliminary attempt at identifying and interpreting some empirical patterns. Accordingly, its focus is limited in scope, the following pages being essentially concerned with investigating the nexus between Balkan conflict patterns and the underlying illicit geoeconomic flows. In overall terms, this chapter aims to shed some light on the conflict in the south-eastern Balkans during the second half of the 1990s; this is done in the reflected light of the wars that were fought in the north-west Balkans in the first half of the same decade. Accordingly, it rests upon interpretive categories that were developed by (part of) the scholarly and investigative literature on the Bosnian war,[3] and it seeks to widen the picture to broader regional dynamics that unfold around the Kosovo knot and the broader Albanian question.

Given the peculiar character of this "radiography," a proviso is in order. This reading into the dynamic of underground and criminal economy is not carried out with the intention of claiming for itself the merit of uncovering the "true causes" of a war that was being prepared in secret, as one sometimes reads elsewhere. The root and proximate causes of the patterns of peace and war in the Balkans are extremely complex and could in no way be reduced to this by such an operation. Nonetheless, one can maintain that it is difficult to interpret and explain the historical trajectory of the Balkan region during the 1990s without accounting for these dynamics, if nothing else because they proved able to move an amount of money that in many cases is comparable to the gross domestic product (GDP) of one of the ethnophobic micro-states that emerged from the political seismic waves that shook this region, not to speak of their state budgets. It is perhaps worth remembering that a note from the US Drug Enforcement Agency dated 1997 assessed the amount of money controlled by the Kosovo Albanian mafia as triple the GDP of the state of Albania (Provvisionato 2000: 96).

Evidence from the Balkan region and from other areas struck by ethnonational conflicts shows that it would be a mistake to postulate the existence of a direct, unidirectional link between market opportunities, political decision-making and war-waging. Dismantling Yugoslavia was not an economic bargain for former Yugoslav peoples. The dissolution of the country was also the dissolution of an integrated market: the breakup of its economic continuities had a severe impact on the economy of each secessionist republic and predetermined the course of subsequent reforms. Like elsewhere in eastern Europe, the prospect of a gradual integration in the West proved to exert an irresistible attraction for small-sized new states that were rallying around identity politics. More than once, political decisions proved effective in cutting quite abruptly well-consolidated productive, financial and commercial links. In the meantime, the new regimes were faced with the task of sustaining the costs of war. This often entailed the annihilation of family savings through a number of financial maneuvers (e.g. the case of the *Ljubljanska Banka* at the time of the Slovenian secession), thus increasing uncertainty and further nurturing a sense of emergency. In a systematic way, rump and self-styled state entities systematically operated first through predatory practices to ensure control over productive resources, and then through covert and illegal channels to consolidate themselves.

An aspect that has to be taken into account in understanding the link between war and economic activities in former Yugoslav territories is the peculiar role played by the pre-existing, self-management type of socialist economy. As the country was sitting on a fulcrum, both political and economic reforms were perceived to be no longer deferrable. While nationalist politics derailed the path of democratization, the introduction of a market economy often meant the unleashing of plundering practices: in this context, the predominance of socialistic forms of "social property" made the conquest of the levers of political power synonymous with the opportunity to control the process of (re)allocation of property rights. The Yugoslav model differed considerably from the centralized Soviet model, also in the fact that it ended up encouraging the formation of local economic elites and of a client system that often followed ethnic demarcations.

Formal and informal economic and administrative practices that took root in the late days of Yugoslavia often happened to play a key role in the priming of war dynamics. The Bosnian elites knew each other rather well at the onset of the war, and most times hostilities did not interrupt contacts and bargaining amongst them. In this regard, analyses that are premised on factors such as "the collapse of communication" prove to be quite misleading. A case in point is Fikret Abdic, the Muslim leader of the Bihac pocket in north-western Bosnia. He was able to mobilize an army that stood against Sarajevo's uncompromising line toward the international plans and was eventually defeated militarily. Abdic was an influential businessman with good connections to the Kraijna Serbs. A grotesque but telling note on the margins of the vicissitudes of this corner of Bosnia is the fact that Abdic's self-styled "minister of foreign affairs" was in fact an Italian truck driver from Tuscany.

Against this background, the mushrooming of different types of militias (Bougarel 1996a: 103) can be interpreted as a function of the decomposition and recomposition of the state's monopoly on force, and as a bridge toward new armies and new forms of political legitimacy. This process coincides with the rise of the parastate, that is a force acting *against* the state, *within* the state or *in place of* the state, often laying claims of legitimate succession to an expiring order by seeking either to transform itself into a state or align with larger states (Liotta 1999: 26–27). As a result of war activities aiming to draw new social and ethnoterritorial borders, statehood is transformed according to patrimonial conceptions that deny autonomy to state institutions. At the same time, the public sphere is swept away by an all-too-familiar admixture of irrationalist ethnic dictates and hyper-rational predatory calculations that can work only if the population is homogenous and pacified because both assisted and intimidated by an all-encompassing mafia system.

The following two sections are an attempt to reconstruct almost narratively the spatial and temporal coordinates of the intertwining of ethnic collision and mafia collusion by focusing on two crucial cases for the stability of south-eastern Europe: the "Albanian question" and the "Yugoslav question" across the current borders of the southern Balkans. The last section, by contrast, will build on this reconstruction to suggest some interpretive insights on the relationship between transnational organized crime and the violent rise of Balkan states and parastates.

The borders of the Albanian question

Although not self-evident, part of Kosovo's destiny was encoded in a statement on the 1991 report that Interpol issued in Lyon in 1992. This report signaled a slump in heroin seizures, only a year after the Croatian police had been praised for being the most efficient in Europe in carrying out activities of control and repression against drug trafficking (Rastello 2000: 172). To find a partial explanation for this circumstance one has to consider that on the eve of the war, illegal activities appeared to become vital for the maintenance of the new separatist entities. In particular, the Croat Herzegovinan mafia clans – which soon turned out to be the main stakeholders in Tudjman's ruling party even in Zagreb – began to demand a policy of non-interference in their illicit activities. There was more, however. It is no exaggeration to argue that up to 1990, Belgrade's establishment had been able to present itself as an efficient actor *vis-à-vis* the international drug trade networks; in doing so, it had been able to extract a significant profit from trafficking activities that were accompanied by corruption and big money-laundering investments.

Behind the surface of events, Zagreb was now making a clear choice. So far the strategy adopted by the new Croatian elite had consisted of hampering the huge movements of heroin that traditionally constituted the "Balkan route" connecting Turkey to Europe via the Belgrade–Zagreb backbone. It should be borne in mind that according to Interpol, during the 1980s, approximately 70 percent of the heroin consumed in western Europe was channeled though the "Balkan route" (Provvisionato 2000: 92). The breakup of the federative structures of Yugoslavia, and the attack on Belgrade's attempts to introduce reforms that would re-centralize the country had an impact at all levels of economic life. In this phase, the seizures of drugs on Croatian territory marked the emergence of an increasingly self-confident political power that contested the interests managed by the center in Belgrade. Coincident with the secessionist birth of the Croatian state, now the tremendous influx of money that was granted by the river of Turkish narcotraffic aroused the appetites of the new Croatian political elite.[4] Quite tellingly, this is also the period in which emissaries of the Sicilian *cosa nostra* appeared more and more frequently on the Croatian coast. One of them, Giambattista Licata – an important referent for the *mafia del Brenta* in northern Italy – was even in possession of a Croatian passport. Given this context, it did not go unnoticed in Italy that the Semtex that was employed to explode the car of the famous judge Giovanni Falcone during the heaviest offensive conducted by *cosa nostra* was of Croatian provenance.

In other words, it was not so much the outbreak of war in the region that modified the geoeconomy of illicit activities in the Balkans, but rather the diminished convenience of the traditional Balkan route. Along this route, far too many predatory interests were now demanding royalties because of the emergence of more fragmented and complex regional geopolitics.

In Albania, the parallel rise to power of Sali Berisha, the US-backed leader of the Democratic Party and expression of the interest of the northern *Fares*,[5] can be viewed as an important transformation in the local criminal landscape. After fifty years of unchallenged prevalence of southern *Fares* under Enver Hoxha's tough dictatorship, the previously marginalized northern factions were now in control of the capital and of its political relations. Territorial proximity and a number of common interests with the Albanian population of the formerly autonomous Serbian province of Kosovo opened wide the border on the Serbo-Montenegrin federation, which was struck by an international embargo to sanction its role in the wars that were burning outside its borders. The Yugoslav–Albanian border had been a hot spot throughout the Cold War, and both the tense situation in Kosovo and the existence of an international embargo would induce one to think that it was kept hermetically closed in the early 1990s. Things went in a different way. For example, it is estimated that in the years 1993–1994, when approximately 200 boats were crossing the waters of the lake of Skhoder every day, oil-smuggling activities would account for a daily influx of approximately one million US dollars. In addition to oil and fuel, these borders saw the crossing of arms and Turkish heroin. In particular the drug traffic began to beat the old routes of tobacco, reaching the Adriatic ports of Bar (Montenegro) and Durres (Albania) along a way on which Kosovo was a crucial junction.

At the same time, Kosovar businessmen were increasingly seen in Tirana, where an explosive admixture of politics, private interests, and illicit transactions was being prepared. As revealed by a number of intelligence and police sources, *Vefa*, the most important Albanian holding until the implosion of 1997, was heavily involved in both funding the national political system and trafficking drugs and weapons. Thanks to contacts with Puglia's mafia, the *sacra corona unita*, its managers even developed an investment strategy in southern Italy.

In and around Slobodan Milosevic's mini-Yugoslavia, international sanctions had been the main propellant for illicit activities. Along the same Balkan directrix of colossal traffics, a pervasive melting of vital interests took place between the new Albania, the new Yugoslavia, and the criminal organizations that were able to provide all the necessary services to insure a relatively easy access to all sorts of commodities. As it emerged later during international investigations, Albanian organizations usually enjoyed high-level protection in Belgrade. This situation of mutual gain and connivance is important for a sound understanding of the relatively pacific situation in Kosovo until 1997. On the one hand, there was the repression by the Yugoslav authorities, and the firing of ethnic Albanians from public offices. On the other hand, however, while the visible side of Kosovo's economy followed rigid patterns of ethnic exclusion and self-ghettoization, the province also grew into a crossroad for all sorts of trades that were able to engender large profits. Contrary to widespread perceptions, poverty was not a major problem in Kosovo, thanks to a dense network of private activities: in late 1998, the average income among Albanian Kosovars was two or three times the average salary of the Serbian citizens of Pristina.

One pillar of this paradoxical Serbian–Albanian *pax mafiosa* was undoubtedly the axis that came into being between Zeljko Raznatovic, better known as Arkan, and Enver Hajin. While the former was a well-known Serbian criminal boss and a paramilitary chief who had won the seat to the Yugoslav Parliament in Pristina, Hajin was an ex-officer of Enver Hoxha's secret police who had become a prominent figure among the Albanian criminal bosses operating around the Skhoder lake.

The salience of the criminal profile assumed by Kosovo's organizations is illustrated by a number of police operations that were conducted throughout Europe between 1992 and 1997. A case in point was "Operation Macedonia," a joint Italian, German and Swiss effort directed at deciphering the rising prominence that Kosovo Albanians were assuming in the European criminal scene, thanks to the capillary rooting in their communities of expatriates and migrants.[6] The close link between heroin trafficking and the financing of the Kosovo insurrection, especially since 1997, has been documented in different countries and at different levels by a number of intelligence reports and journalistic investigations.[7] "Operation Macedonia," however, is also important because it shed light on mafia financial activities in Zurich, pointing to the collaboration that emerged between 1995 and 1998 between Kosovar mafias and the Italian *'ndrangheta*. The arrest of Albanian politicians tied to Berisha's milieu, of important Kosovo bosses (e.g. Agim Gashi in Milan), and of leading figures of the *'ndrangheta* (e.g. Giuseppe Morabito and Domenico Branca) revealed the organizational capabilities and the modalities of territorial control of a criminal network that was extended throughout Europe and that united even wider interests in illicit activities. The Kosovar Albanian organizations were winning the underground war over the drug market against the Albanians from Albania, and they emancipated themselves from the role of being a mere connection ring between the Turkish mafia and the allocation on the Western market. Moreover, the strategic alliance with the Italians and even with Russian and Ukrainian groups rendered these organizations, which soon became famous for the ferocity of their methods, an autonomous actor.

This is also the period during which an increasing role was assumed by so-called "oriental" and "northern Balkan" routes, which offered alternative and safe bases running through Bulgaria and well north of the Danube. "Operation Africa," carried out by the Italian police in June 1998, unmasked a number of tracks that were converging in Bratislava. By the second half of the 1990s, heroin was no longer running on big Turkish TIR (Transport Internationaux Routiers) trucks across Yugoslavia. A more sophisticated net of small couriers had come into being under the control of the Kosovo groups in alliance with the *'ndrangheta* along the axis Turkey–Budapest–Bratislava. Capital would arrive in Vienna already clean, accompanied by bosses that had changed their clothes and were now wearing elegant Italian fashion (*Diario*, 3 February 1999).

A relatively famous ramification of this "northern Balkan route" goes through Bulgaria, and then into Serbia. In December 1996, at the border post of Dimitrovgrad-Gradina, the Yugoslav police intercepted 365 kilograms of heroin on board a truck carrying green peppers from Plovdiv. To fully appreciate this figure, one can compare it with the 20 kilograms that the Yugoslav police declared they had seized during the year 1998, or with the 14 kilograms intercepted by the Macedonian police in 1999. Remarkably, the Plovdiv-based society turned out to be owned by Nazim Delegu, an Albanian from Kosovo who was known as a godfather of a wide mafia net extended to the former Yugoslav territories, to Albania and Italy (Miletitch 1998: 124).

Another early signal of the subsequent tragic bent of Kosovo's destiny was the murder of the aforementioned Enver Hajin at the hand of Darko Asanin in 1996, a criminal element sharing with Arkan the reputation of a leading *mafioso* and war hero. New equilibria were being formed and the wind was turning on Albania. There, Berisha turned his attention toward Europe, most notably Germany, thus irritating some of his early open American sponsors. Perhaps this step was an excess of self-confidence, resting on the "financial miracle" that was fueled by speculative capitals and family savings invested in blatantly unsustainable financial "pyramids." These were pioneered by figures such as Hajdin Sejdia, a Swiss-based Kosovar businessman who put together a capital of some 40 million US dollars that had been stolen from peasants and workers. At any rate, now Daimler Benz opened new plants in Albania, while American advisors were replaced with German officers. As Washington jettisoned the increasingly cumbersome Berisha, an inspection of the main financial pyramids by the International Monetary Fund (IMF) announced the storm that prompted the sudden shutting down of such societies. This meant the disappearence of the savings of the majority of Albanians that had trusted in the "capitalist miracle" whereby "money breeds money." Needless to say that this event propagated panic. What followed, with a climax in March 1997, is remembered as a quasi-civil war. In its course, Berisha's Democratic Party, whose fingerprints were quite evident on the pyramids, lost power to the Socialists led by Fatos Nano, a man from the south with solid connections to the southern *Fares*, who was quite close to Tirana's criminal boss Nehat Kulla. With the collapse of the pyramids, power had moved to a political family far less involved in the Yugoslav plight, and inclined not to consider deals with the Kosovar "cousins."

Beside the Macedonian town of Gostivar, the lake of Ohrid, on the border between Albania and Macedonia, now became the neural node of traffics that would modify the course of regional politics. As a matter of fact, this lake offered a way out for the Turkish heroin that was now being deviated away from Kosovo. As had happened with the traditional Balkan route, maintaining the whole system of Kosovo connivance and collusion had become too costly. During Dayton, international diplomacy had carefully avoided addressing in a plausible way the Kosovo issue. Therefore the Kosovar Albanian elite's grand and yet gradualist project of constructing a parallel state, a parallel economy, and a parallel society was now in a dead hand. The income tax of 3 percent that each Kosovo *emigré* was contributing to the "Republic of Kosova" via its government in exile, led by Bujar Bukoshi, ceased to arrive in the coffers of the Pristina-based, nonviolent presidency of Ibrahim Rugova. In this situation, the light weapons that had disappeared during the implosion of the Albanian state structures were cheap and easy to obtain through the porous borders of Macedonia. Parallel to these developments, the trafficking route through Kosovo became obsolete. The southern Albanian ports of Saranda and

Vlora were now offering a more convenient outlet to the sea and to hard currency markets. The new route that took shape under the auspices of the Kosovo warring factions connected Bulgaria with Macedonia and Albania.

Perhaps it was partly by coincidence that in this crucial phase Albanian armed formations began to act in Kosovo. The Albanian leader Fatos Nano, who a few months earlier had been vociferously attacked by Macedonian and Kosovar Albanian political circles for not being supportive to their cause, now turned into a fervent sponsor of the Kosovo Liberation Army (UÇK). Furthermore, Berisha made an attempt to create a professional army (FARK) in alliance with Bukoshi, and a brief underground battle was fought between Kosovo Albanian factions also in Albania. After some murderous episodes, Hashim Thaçi's UÇK remained almost unrivaled and ready to take over through an extended net of self-appointed mayors throughout the province as soon as open hostilities would cease.

If the strategic position conquered by the Kosovo criminal organizations may reveal itself as not very solid in the fluid geopolitics of the international drug market, one can nevertheless rule out a period of decadence for Kosovo organizations in the near future. On the one hand, there is a tendency towards the unification, at least in ideal and commercial terms, of Albanian societies in the southern Balkans. This tendency could fuse a dangerous conflict in the Republic of Macedonia, a country whose pharmaceutical products in the past few years have been used to produce heroin, and in whose western districts Albanian activities are well rooted and permeated by nationalist slogans. In this area illegal activities and incidents along the border with Albania have always been a major problem. A more recent development that is somehow correlated with the growth of the economic and Western military presence in this area is proliferation of criminal organizations that thrive on the trade of women from Ukraine, Moldavia, Romania, Bulgaria and Serbia. It is in anonymous rural areas around border villages (e.g. Veleshta) that these women, who have already been deprived of their documents and sold from gang to gang, are temporarily "stocked," *de facto* forced to prostitution, and eventually channeled into the streets of the European Union.[8]

Even the counterposition between southern and northern clans in Albania seems to be less and less a decisive factor. This can be explained by the magnitude of the business in transit in Albanian territory. Unlike the situation in Serbia, in Albania the availability of a plurality of national, transnational and international interlocutors provides an abundance of resources for all actors taking part in those illegal transactions that are part of the process of "globalization of criminal economy." As a result of this, even the southern Mediterranean route – i.e. Greece, Cyprus – is open to Kosovo Albanian investors. According to the Italian *Direzione Investigativa Antimafia*, the structuring of cartels between groups that control different portions of the Albanian territory is a development that is well in sight. Thus it is not too hazardous to hypothesize that among other possible directions of state-making the gradual emergence of a new pan-Albanian elite, solidly anchored in uncontrolled economic flows, is looming behind these geoeconomic processes. This elite could develop into a political referent for Albanian nationalism and, consequently, into a main actor in defining regional relations. By way of mere example, one can mention Behgjet Pacolli, a successful Swiss-based businessman from Kosovo, who turned out to be involved as a key figure in the big corruption scandal that struck the Kremlin and Yeltsin family in 1991 (*La Repubblica*, 19 January 2001). Pacolli is extremely popular among his co-nationals also because of his marriage to Anna Oxa, a famous Italian pop singer of Albanian background. Furthermore, one has to underline that Albanian criminal organizations seem to have attained a global reach, as witnessed by the dismantling, in early 2001, of a Colombian–Albanian axis that was geared to ship some 40 tons of cocaine a year, thanks to the protection offered by some high-level police officers in Tirana (*La Repubblica*, 10 February 2001).

On the other hand, one year after the end of hostilities in Kosovo, it was evident that the making and unmaking of states in the region was far from concluded. The volatile situation in Montenegro, to quote only one example, may lend new oxygen to criminal activities in and around Kosovo. Another interesting case is the Presevo area, a mainly Albanian-inhabited valley that runs through Serbian territory next to the border with Macedonia. Here, a number of roads connect the quasi-protectorate of Kosovo with Albanian border cities, western Macedonia, central Serbia and Bulgaria. Demilitarized by the technical agreement signed between NATO and the Yugoslav army, the illicit flows of which this region became a center some decades ago (e.g. the small town of Veliki Trnovac) soon began to suffer from Kosovo's pacification. This induced local clans to blow on the fire of Albanian irredentism, so as to fuel rewarding forms of conflict and control over population and economic activities. Among those, Shaban Shala, a businessman with solid connections with the UÇK, is a prominent figure (*La Repubblica*, 24 March 2000). For months, the Presevo demilitarized strip has been a dangerous area of instability, in which Albanian snipers have targeted Yugoslav soldiers claiming the liberation of "Eastern Kosovo." In spite of the American presence in the territorially adjacent sector of Kosovo, hundreds of armed troops of the "Liberation Army of Presevo, Medvedja and Bujanovac" were even able to launch a new guerrilla offensive in December 2000, stipulating an alliance with Macedonian clandestine factions such as the "Albanian National Army" (AKSH).

In the spring of 2001, following the mutual recognition of borders between Skopje and Belgrade and a series of armed incidents in the mountain village of Tanusevci, right on the Kosovo–Macedonian border, an armed offensive was launched in west Macedonia against the central government by a newly born UÇK. Quite tellingly, Tanusevci is home to

Xhavit Hasani, an Albanian–Macedonian boss who had become a war hero during the Kosovo war, transforming this area into a logistic base for the Kosovar combatants. After four months of violence, the strategy pursued by the Albanian–Macedonian UÇK was eventually rewarded with a number of concessions made by the central government at the prodding of international mediators. As a result, one year after the offensive the districts of western Macedonia had become in many regards an Albanian-dominated autonomous region: as its leaders in Tetovo were intent on an intestine power struggle that involved some episodes of violence often perceived by observers as "criminality," the separateness of ethnic Albanian and Macedonian societies and economies had become more distinct, and the fact that no formal demands of independence were advanced appeared to be a matter of political and economic convenience (Strazzari 2001: 15–35).

The survival of the last federation

The distinction between legal and illegal market activities became quite irrelevant, at least from Belgrade's point of view. After years of sanctions and regional turmoil, the borders between legal, gray and criminal economies looked increasingly fuzzy. The war mood and the survival priorities that had become preponderant in 1999 in coincidence with NATO's bombing campaign marked the overcoming of formal institutional dialectics and the sliding into pure power politics and open authoritarian repression of dissent. Among other things, the shrinking of political and economic spaces meant a dramatic rise in the killings of prominent politicians and businessmen.

Descending to Belgrade's mafia underground, one can note that the structures of Serbian organized crime throughout the Yugoslav wars rest in a significant way upon pre-existing networks. These were connected to the counter-espionage apparatus, the police and the army, and in the past they were employed in the war against a host of enemies abroad. The latter were to be found among those nationalist circles that as a matter of fact managed to place their men in leading positions during the secessionist wars. A good example is Gojko Susak, the first Croatian Minister of Defense. He used to be a businessman in Ottawa, Canada, a position from which he had been particularly active in organizing anti-Yugoslav provocations and the funding of nationalist factions, also by strategically manipulating the remarkable flows of pilgrims visiting the Catholic sanctuary of Medjugorie (Rastello 1998: 63–77).

With the spiraling of wars and sanctions, the Yugoslav state began to collaborate with those local mafia organizations that had nothing to do with the security apparatus, aiming at using them as liaisons for international business. Meanwhile, Milosevic's government was quite efficiently raking up family savings and foreign currency, resources that were needed to sustain wars and withstand international isolation. This was made possible through speculation schemes that were quite similar to the Albanian pyramids, and through a strict control of the net of street moneychangers. In addition to these maneuvers, banking societies such as *Jugoskandik* and *Dafiment* revealed themselves as Trojan horses for a firmer grip on the productive apparatus. Predictably, once this objective was achieved, they eventually sank in a climate of total impunity. A paradoxical destiny, in this context, was that of the Bank of Kosova. Its bankruptcy was disguised and hidden by Belgrade, but loudly brought up by the Kosovo Albanians as a debt that they would be quite eager to pay back. It goes without saying that this act would have implied responsibility toward what was portrayed as a national bank, and therefore the request of an invitation to the tables where problems related to the international succession to Yugoslavia were being negotiated.

With the economic indicators plummeting and Yugoslav forces increasingly endangered by UÇK snipers and ambushes, the costs of maintaining the massive security apparatus in Kosovo had become increasingly high. What made such costs for the budget of a sanction-struck country more unbearable was the fact that its leadership was aware of the end of the implicit pact with Rugova, who ran parallel Albanian institutions to those of the Yugoslav state, as well as of the impossibility of keeping control over two million Albanians who had embarked upon an intransigent political project. In this light, the fears of the "international community" that Milosevic would try to seize as hostages the Organiz-ation for Security and Co-operation in Europe (OSCE) monitors upon their departure, in order to keep a grip on the whole region, proved to be quite misleading. Everybody was ready, so the war could begin. As the first bombs fell and the Yugoslav army proved able to suffer only minimal losses, Belgrade gave priority to a plan of violent and brutal forced expulsions and "minority reduction" that was improperly called "ethnic cleansing" or even "genocide." Moreover, it attempted to retain a hold on those strategically important resources, such as the huge Trepca mining metallurgical complex in the vicinity of Mitrovica, that could have been used tactically in future – i.e. once it was clear that the borders of Yugoslavia, formally speaking, were still there.

Looking at Belgrade's financial situation, the close relationship with Cyprus banks, which had played a crucial role in the survival of the country, was progressively interrupted as a result of closer international inspections conducted at US prodding. Nicosia, which had already offered a shelter to capitals escaping the Lebanese war, was now paving its accession track to the European Union. Consequently, it felt little need to get further embroiled in Yugoslav affairs. Some oxygen for the agonizing Yugoslav treasury came thanks to the privatization deal that was concluded, not quite transparently, with the Italian and Greek companies *Telecom* and *Ote* (*La Repubblica*, 17 February 2001). As the Kosovo storm approached and the coordinates of almost all Cypriot accounts were disclosed, Belgrade turned its attention toward China, in particular to Hong Kong and Shanghai, where Yugoslav consulates were opened. In spite of the alarmism of certain Atlantic circles, the announced transfer of some 300 million US dollars to Belgrade, which was announced in December 1999 after a visit to China by the Yugoslav Minister of Foreign Affairs (*Jane's Intelligence Review*, February 2000), could in large part be regarded as Yugoslav capitals on their way back. Be that as it may, coincident with NATO's attack on Yugoslavia, the Chinese presence in Belgrade became increasingly visible. While the influx of Chinese emigrants of rural background was no novelty,[9] Yugoslavia became, in 1999, a destination for Chinese businessmen engaged in key sectors of post-war reconstruction. Some payment problems with *Sinochem* – a provider of Libyan, Iranian and Russian oil – were overcome (Institute for War and Peace Reporting [IWPR], 1 February 2000), and despite the devastating attacks on oil refineries and chemical plants, fuel tanks and bottles for sale disappeared relatively soon from Belgrade's streets. Eventually, Milosevic's government was able to announce that the country was endowed with abundant reserves.[10]

Godmother of the "Chinese way" was Mira Markovic, Milosevic's wife, who came back fascinated by Beijing's model in 1996, while a wave of protests was sweeping Belgrade's streets. China saw a clear interest in keeping a European ally that did not bend to reiterated Western dictates and that could later prove to be a springboard for investments and commercial penetration in Europe. It is not only for Albania's Sinophile past, or for NATO's would-be accidental bombing of the Chinese Embassy to Yugoslavia that Chinese policy-makers kept an interest in this region. Also telling were the maneuvers through which the little Republic of Macedonia – a faithful American client with lingering recognition problems – broke the international consensus by recognizing Taiwan, in exchange for a promise of Taiwanese direct foreign investment. While NATO was warming up its airplanes, Macedonia struck an escalatory note in both regional war politics and in strategic competition. It is worth noting the amount of money that Taipei, according to some speculation circulated in Skopje, had promised to help Macedonia's refugees' plight: precisely 300 million US dollars. In order to grasp the nature of state-making in the Balkans, it is quite instructive to take note of how the blatantly opportunist survival strategy of a neophite state interacts with great powers' intervention and competition patterns. In the end, quite predictably, Taipei's money did not flood Macedonia, but the UN preventive contingent had to leave the country following a Chinese veto in the UN Security Council, thus leaving the Macedonian scene entirely to NATO. Seen from a perspective of *longue durée*, this episode confirms expectations of external backing and intervention that tend to be associated (both as a remedy and as a cause) with violent conflict and destabilization dynamics as the most powerful factors shaping state-making in the Balkans.

It is undeniable that the history of the Balkans is also one of imperial ambitions and decadence, hegemonic manipulation, benevolent intervention, and aggressive nationalism. If one reads these war episodes in the light of the redefinition of the order of international relations, it is possible to say that encouraging Belgrade's war economy appeared to be a cheap way for China to engender obvious advantages. At the same time, the influx of Chinese commodities (shoes, clothing, low-tech, food) can be situated in the wide gray area that stands between market and underground economy. United in the production and import of counterfeit goods, the expansion of this sector performed a double function. First, it allowed relatively high profits by virtue of low costs. Second, and most important, it insured a modicum of social stability, granting a level of market offer that surrogates the need for consumer goods.

In respect to the question of international sanctions, the case of the warlord Arkan remains emblematic of how the embargo against Belgrade was turned into an asset for criminal gangs. At the moment of his assassination in Belgrade, the criminal profile of Arkan – whose Tigers are accused of the worst crimes in Croatia, Bosnia and Kosovo – stood in striking contrast to the one of a blood-thirsty fanatic, and was more in line with the one of a skilled service provider. He was on the side of the Belgrade regime and could manage a good share of the pie of oil and derivatives. Increasingly active in the importation to Serbia of German and Swedish-made fertilizers through Hungary, his Montenegrin acquaintances finally allowed him some involvement in the cigarette-smuggling business (IWPR, 28 February 2000). Given the extent to which criminal gangs were in a symbiotic relationship with the regime, it shows the way the central regime took care of its own perpetuation. The binomial sanctions borders in a context of shrinking state budget became a crucial factor for the Milosevic family, including not only the presidential couple, but also their son Marko, who was heavily into transborder activities. In short, by manipulating the embargo, the Milosevic family got control of all the financial and commercial arteries that connected the country with the outside world. While the relationship between sanctions and the crumbling of Belgrade's regime in October 2000 remains open to debate, the fact that the strategy (or lack of it) that has been pursued *vis-à-vis* the "Serbian question" has contributed heavily to reinforcing the dynamics of criminalization of the public sphere can be hardly denied.

In spite of this empirical record, until Milosevic's defeat, the Bureau for International Narcotics and Law Enforcement Affairs of the US State Department claimed that any measure going in the direction of lifting the embargo on Serbia–Montenegro would boost illegal flows in the region. It is perhaps worth remembering that in order to intervene on the side of the UÇK, the US administration first had to remove it from its own list of terrorist organizations, thus laying a veil over the heavy involvement of the UÇK in drug trades.

Generally speaking, the management of illegal traffics entails a number of activities that can engender frictions if local counter-powers stand up and claim border-control prerogatives. In this respect, the dispute between Belgrade's federal authorities and the Montenegrin government over the patrolling of the borders, including the Podgorica airport and the economic blockade on Montenegro,[11] can be read in terms of friction over "who is in control of what" in a state-making perspective. Summing up, the reality seems to be, once again, that territorial militarization and criminal activities fostered by embargoes and sporadic but frequent escalatory dynamics go hand in hand. A good example is the *de facto* exemption from sanctions that the secessionist Montenegrin government had been able to extract after the end of the bombing campaign. Up to this moment, the independentist elite gravitating around the premier Milo Djukanovic had been trying to distance itself from any form of dependency on Belgrade. Yet given the strictures on Montenegro's small market, he ended up, on the one hand, in the hands of the criminal organizations of the Adriatic coast.[12] On the other hand, acting upon the recommendation of US economic advisors in October 1999, Djukanovic announced the adoption of the Deutsche Mark (DM) as the official currency of the Republic of Montenegro. Meanwhile, Washington was financially supporting the government's payments deficit.

Thanks to the entrepreneurial profile of societies such as *Zetatrans* or *Monti*,[13] the Montenegrin Republic became the most important stocking area for loads heading for Western markets that elude taxation through a number of passages from American, Swiss, Dutch and above all Belgian depots via Ukraine, Poland, Romania, Macedonia (*il Manifesto*, 31 August 1999) and later on via Greece, Cyprus and Croatia (*La Stampa*, 9 November 2000). According to a report issued by the Italian parliamentary Antimafia Commission, the tobacco companies Philip Morris and R.J. Reynolds operated from Basel, Switzerland, through two organizations. One of them, Export Two, was tasked with sending cigarettes to Montenegro along channels that proved to be rather permeable to drug and weapons smuggling as well (*Panorama*, 16 November 2000). While the treasury of Montenegro was being put safely away in Switzerland along with private capital, a state tax euphemistically defined on export–import was being levied on cigarette smuggling activities (10 US dollars per case).

Historically, the process making Montenegro a safe haven, if not a veritable pirate colony, for Italian *mafiosi* of various affiliations, began in 1993. Between 1994 and 1995 some 450 protagonists of Italian organized crime found a shelter around Podgorica which had then no contacts with Interpol. The tobacco business toward Italy was estimated to engender profits of some 2,000 billion Italian lira (approximately one billion US dollars, not to mention the damage to the fiscal revenue system) and work for some 26,000 people. An alarm bell was rung when the head of

Podgorica's police, Vaso Bausic, was caught in Bari during his initiation rite to the local *sacra corona unita*. In 1999, the Tribunal of Napoli documented the close relationship between the Montenegrin government and the clan headed by Ciro Mazzarella, a *camorrista* that settled in Lugano, Switzerland. Interestingly, at the end of 1999 the investigation brought the indictment of the then Minister of Foreign Affairs of Montenegro, Branko Perovic, who was accused of collusion with the Napolitan *camorra*. One year later, upon a mandate of the Italian police, the almost legendary Swiss referent for the huge cigarette smuggling and money laundering business of a number of mafias, Gerardo Cuomo, was eventually arrested in Zurich (*Mafianews*, 9–16 May 2000). Active through a host of financial societies based in Aruba (Dutch Antilles) and Cyprus, Cuomo was able to deal directly with tobacco multinationals and was the titular of an import–export license of the Republic of Montenegro. Subsequently, the police carrying out an investigation on illegal international trades and money laundering brought to prison among others a Swiss judge who was officially supposed to watch over international smuggling and money laundering. Eventually, in November 2000 the EU Commission announced legal moves against Philip Morris and Reynolds for their involvement in tobacco smuggling and tax evasion.[14]

While helping polish up the reputation of Montenegro as a Mediterranean Tortuga by eliminating the most grotesque and out-of-control aspects of the independentist circles, Western economic, political and security support to Podgorica introduced a new ambivalent dividing line. It is across this new division that criminal activities associated with regional war making are likely to thrive. Being crossed by the various Balkan routes, at the end of the 1990s, Montenegro had became a land of competition between different sovereignties, mafias and security apparatuses.

Conclusion: peripheries, paramilitaries and parastates

The current mainstream security discourse tends to represent transnational crime as a recent (if not unprecedented) challenge. Alarms about the growing tentacles of organized crime are often heard, usually in association with the indication of ethnic and religious fanaticism as a potent source of destabilization in the otherwise orderly and peaceful post-Cold War world.[15] Needless to say, the hotbeds of international crime and ethnopolitical fanaticism are often to be found along the borders of what was once described as the "evil empire." Yet, inside the folds along which the security discourse is articulated, it is not difficult to find representations of mafia activities as something archaic, a lingering feature, a phenomenon painted in gangster caricatures and treated as a piece of tradition that has to be overcome by complete modernization.

In reality, as far as war-mongering is concerned, the history of criminal enterprises accompanies the complex (and certainly not recent) process of the emergence and consolidation of modern states. In this sense, then, the intertwining of "black economy" and war-related activities that has been investigated here is extremely modern. At the same time, however, when faced with patterns of warfare displayed by the last round of Balkan wars – such as cities besieged, "ethnic cleansing," the plundering of productive resources, and the predation on commerce – one is tempted to prefer the pre-modern idea of "sack" to that of "war" (Bjelakovic and Strazzari 1998). Used *lato sensu* – that is, to designate the strategic use of civilians and the communicative infrastructure – categories such as post-modern warfare do seem to capture part of the reality of the Balkan wars.

The Balkan route to state-making has displayed the emergence of a number of recognized and unrecognized state entities cut in the opaque mold of economic depredation, elite collusion and external intervention. The history of wars, and Balkan wars in particular, is also the history of small and big deals that are cut with the irreconcilable enemy. It comes as no surprise that across the sieges implicit and explicit economic and military deals were quite frequent. It is well known, for instance, that the defense of Sarajevo was first organized by street gangs that were physically eliminated as the state monopoly of force was being reconstructed through the Bosnian *Armija*. If one focuses on the processes in which the institution of state sovereignty has been molded – and looks into the role that was played by international piracy, by chartered companies with license to wage war, and by privateering practices – then the Balkan wars assume a somehow familiar coloration. Used by state powers in the interstices of the international order to reinforce their monopolies and sovereign preroga-tives, such agents were eventually liquidated or neutralized as the state's monopoly became complete and the international order changed (cf. Thompson 1994).

Staying within the realm of private companies that interact directly with the state's claimed monopoly of force, it is worth noting that the crafting of a client state system in the Balkans has also been accompanied by the extensive incorporation of security firms (e.g. MPRI) in strategic thinking.[16] These private security providers serve as intermediaries in relations between strong and weak states, thus overcoming the reluctance that the former often show in providing direct military assistance to areas of no strategic interest (Reno 2000: 59). These phenomena have revived the debate on "failed states" (Thuerer 1999: 731), i.e. on states that in a period of deep crisis entrust certain functions to non-state actors. However, once the crisis has gone, they are incapable of recuperating those sovereign state functions that they had delegated away, thus losing their institutional integrity.

Today's challenge is to understand how the nexus between war-making and state-making changes (and the role played therein by illegal and criminal enterprises) as a response to the transformation of sovereignty and intervention practices, as well as the globalization of economic and political order. Looked at from this perspective, Montenegro's trajectory, going from the hands of traffickers straight into those of Western economic and military advisors in a situation of continued tension with the mini-Yugoslav federation (even after the fall of Milosevic in Belgrade), can possibly be taken as paradigmatic of wider trends. A considerable number of the states that have emerged from the explosion of federative links along the central-eastern and south-eastern European peripheries are weak states in a region where minority problems have been a detonator for wider international crises. Moreover, they are small entities, numbering some two to three million inhabitants on average, and led by elites that are legitimized by more or less ambivalent nationalist claims, and endowed with few resources and disrupted economic links. Having in mind models of state and national epics that are often extrapolated from the history of the nineteenth century, these local elites perceive the opportunity to extract more for themselves and their constituencies by sitting for would-be negotiation with the emissaries of the "international community" than by being the opaque administrative class of an obscure province. In this situation, protracted conflict and the prospect of war can often be an asset for raising negotiation prices. In addition, influencing the conduct of a little state that is part of a fragmented periphery is relatively easier and not particularly expensive for external powers. Although involving high stability costs, these seemingly prove to be functional in creating a "demonstration effect," and in shaping the consensus for giving a thrust to the otherwise heavy machine of military Keynesianism.

Contrary to a widespread perception, not unlike other mafias, Balkan mafias do not come into being where the market and the state are absent, but they accompany the unfolding of market and state structures. The emergence of small, almost stifled states, devoid of institutional autonomy and of margins of maneuver in the international arena, seems to be the condition in which mafia structures and practices thrive. In this way, mafias can often go as far as to take hostage the development of state structures. Organized crime has always been a provider of war services, and in protracted ethnopolitical conflict it develops a strong interest in fostering the festering of violence. The mix between the current prohibitionist and sanctionatory structure of international relations and the constraints to nationalist elites because of a lack of resources offers to mafia structures the opportunity to put their hands on types of business that are extremely lucrative and enabling. Drugs, fuel, migrants, tobacco, arms and other smuggling activities across several borders become typical tools by which mafias emancipate themselves from the role of mere provider and become able to intervene directly in the management of political violence (Armao 2000: Chapter 5).

The shrinking of the Serbian economic space accelerated the criminalization of Serbian politics and the terms of the competition (which became a chain of domestic violence) between power groups that were used to widen margins of action and higher profit. In 1999, one of the more lucrative activities in Serbia consisted of the smuggling of agricultural products, most notably berries. Measured on this scale, and read against the background of the resources mobilized during both escalatory dynamics and post-war reconstruction, it was quite apparent that if the Serbian mafias lost, Kosovo and Montenegrin clans would win.

A working hypothesis that is corroborated by the parabola of Balkan military reversals over the 1990s is that mafias prove to be an extremely efficient link between the local and the global. Mafia organizations in the Balkans have emerged principally from the clientelistic degeneration of the state. As the Yugoslav crisis was deepening, political obligation was replaced by personal bonds and *ad personam* credits. Nestled in territorial, economic and social interstices at local, state and international level, mafia structures have gradually been able to handle the growing demand of speculative capitals. These developments correspond to the present financial phase of capitalism, and have accompanied and influenced the molding of new state structures. At the same time, a mafia-dominated *modus vivendi* also emerges from eroded state welfare systems, closely related to both war and post-war reconstruction policies. The "black economy" is not only made up of intimidation and blackmail, but it also represents a safety net for many people, and one can easily measure in person the local degree of popularity of many of its protagonists. These processes have been accentuated by the peripheral character of the Balkan region, making the Balkans especially exposed to illicit trades and economic transactions, while external intervention practices seemed to be unable to graduate from a "more-borders-more-police formula" which, especially when it comes to questions such as the nexus between criminal and political agendas, regularly fails to keep its promises. In this landscape, it does not take much to draw a conclusion about the victims of new mafia states: any universalistic practice of citizenship and any idea of socio-economic sustainability.

Notes

1 A problematization of the nature of the Balkan state and state-making in the Balkans is beyond the scope of the present reconstruction, which is limited to the analysis of the role of some actors and *clientèles*: nevertheless, it is perhaps worth underlining that I do not see the "Balkan route to state formation" (and the agents that operate inside this complex) as following a cyclical, or even Hegelian, progression toward the state as a final point of culmination.

2 An exception is Woodward (1995), see also Chossudovsky (1996).

3 In this direction goes the work of authors such as Xavier Bougarel (1996b), Nicolas Miletitch (1998) and Luca Rastello (1998).

4 *Turkish Daily News* (Ankara, 5 May 1997) reports that the American DEA estimated that every month, 4 to 6 tons of heroin left Turkey to be introduced in Europe.

5 Family-based enlarged clans along which the Albanian mafia organizations are structured. Unlike Serbian nationalism, which during the "Ottoman yoke" took inspiration from the French and above all the Piedmont administrative model and which can be defined without hesitation as state-centric, Albanian nationalism entertains an ambivalent relationship with the Ottoman legacy and is certainly more society-centered, where Albanian societies are quite differentiated across the Balkans.

6 Unlike Hoxha's Albania, Tito's Yugoslavia never put obstacles to the emigration of its citizens, thus providing a safety valve for unemployment and political discontent.

7 Balkania.Net provides an archive of 35 articles published since 1985 in different international newspapers and academic journals, see: http://members.tripod.com/Balkania/resources/terrorism/kla-drugs.html.

8 During the month of April 2000, a number of journalistic investigations drew attention to the business of forced prostitution in and around Kosovo: *AfP*, 5 January 2000; *The Times*, 5 April 2000; *La Repubblica*, 3–4 April 2000, *Mail on Sunday*, 15 April 2000; *il Manifesto*, 19 April 2000, *Washington Post*, 24 April 2000; *Corriere della Sera*, 25 April 2000.

9 Some of those immigrants could be found even in the so-called "neglected areas" of the Bosnian *Republika Srpska,* many others were in the hands of mafia organizations that provided for a clandestine entry in EU countries.

10 For an analysis of the oil situation in Serbia, see: http://www.eia.doe.gov/emeu/cabs/serbmont.html

11 After some measures that were taken during the fall of 1999 as Podgorica announced a separate financial and economic course supported by the West, in February 2000 Belgrade decided on a blockade of food "exports" to Montenegro.

12 In a number of interviews dated January 2001, the Italian Minister of Treasury, Ottaviano del Turco, denounced the connivance between Montenegro's leaders and the trans-Adriatic smuggling organizations.

13 The latter was controlled by the powerful mafia boss Francesco Prudentino, who was arrested in Thessaloniki, Greece, in December 2000 after years of investigations.

14 In 1999 5,690 tons of illegally traded cigarettes were seized inside the EU borders. EU experts are convinced that this figure represents approximately 10 percent of the cigarettes actually smuggled (*La Stampa*, 13 January 2001).

15 For example, Canada's Minister of Foreign Affairs, Lloyd Axworthy, in *Nato review* (Winter 1999: 9).

16 Military Professional Resources Inc. is a Pentagon-licensed private firm based in Virginia, mostly made up of retired US military personnel, who act under the tacit consent of Washington. It has been active with a number of military training programs in Croatia, Bosnia and Macedonia. Following revelations on

offers of weapons and mercenaries to the UÇK, Scotland Yard opened an investigation on the British security firm Aims Ltd., which is also accused of involvement in activities in support of anti-Kurd military repression by Ankara (*Sunday Times*, 31 October 1999).

References

Books and articles

Armao, F. (2000) *Il sistema mafia. Dall'economia-mondo al dominio locale*, Torino: Bollati Boringhieri.

Bjelakovic, N. and Strazzari, F. (1998) "The Sack of Mostar, 1992–1994. The politico-military connection," *European Security*, 8 (3): 73–102.

Bougarel, X. (1996a) "L'économie du conflit bosniaque: prédation et production," in F. Jean and J-C. Rufin (eds) *Economie des guerres civiles*, Paris: Hachette.

—— (1996b) *Bosnie, Anatomie d'un conflit*, Paris: La Decouverte.

Bove, A. and Durante, G. (2000) "E la camorra sbarcò in Montenegro," *Limes*, Quaderno Speciale: 41–48.

Carimeo, N. (1998) "Montenegro o Montecarlo?," *Limes*, 3: 171–180.

Chossudovsky, M. (1996) "Dismantling Yugoslavia; Colonizing Bosnia," *Covert Action*, Spring 1996.

Corti, A. (1999) "Serbia o Tortuga? Palingenesi politica di uno stato criminale," *Limes*, Quaderno Speciale: 43–48.

Del Re, E. (2000) "Crimine e stato in Albania," *Limes*, Quaderno Speciale: 49–64.

Gambino, M. and Grimaldi, L. (1995) *Traffico d'armi. Il crocevia Jugoslavo*, Roma: Editori Riuniti.

Gustincic, F. (2000) "Segnali di fumo fra Serbi e Albanesi," *Limes*, 5: 191–198.

Kaldor, M. (1999) *New and Old Wars. Organized Violence in a Global Era*, Cambridge: Polity Press.

Karup, D. and Pecanin, S. (1998) "Cosa Nostra bosniaca," *Limes*, 3: 225–242.

Liotta, P.H. (1999) *The Wreckage Reconsidered. Five Oxymorons from Balkan Deconstruction*, Lanham: Lexington Books.

Miletitch, N. (1998) *Trafics et crimes dans les Balkans*, Paris: PUF.

Morozzo della Rocca, R. (1997) *Albania. Le radici della crisi*, Milano: Guerini e Associati.

—— (1999) *Kosovo. La guerra in Europa*, Milano: Guerini e Associati.

Observatoire Géopolitique des Drogues (1999) *Annual Report 1997–98*, Paris (www.ogd.org).

—— (2000) *Annual Report 1997–98*, Paris (www.ogd.org).

Ostojic, S. (1998) "Vaticano 1991, la vera storia della lobby croata," *Limes*, 3: 295–300.

Peleman, J. (1999) "Gli stati-mafia: dietro le quinte dei regimi balcanici," *Limes*, Quaderno Speciale: 59–72.

Provvisionato, S. (2000) *Uck: l'Armata dell'ombra*, Rome: Gamberetti Edtrice.

Rastello, L. (1998) *La guerra in casa*, Torino: Einaudi.

—— (2000) "Il crocevia dei traffici," in F. Strazzari, G. Arcadu, B. Carrai and L. Rodriguez-Pinero (eds) *Kosovo 1999–2000, la pace intrattabile. Una radiografia del dopo-bombe*, Trieste: Asterios.

Raufer, X. (2000) "Come funziona la mafia albanese," *Limes*, Quaderno Speciale: 65–73.

Reno, W. (2000) "Internal Wars, Private Enterprise, and the Shift in Strong State–Weak State Relations," *International Politics*, 37 (1): 57–74.

Silber, L. (1999) "Milosevic Family Values," *New Republic*, 30 August 1999.

Strazzari, F. (1999a) "Macedonia, requiem per uno stato-caserma," *Limes*, Quaderno Speciale: 79–86.

—— (1999b) "Una, due, molte Macedonie," *Limes*, 2: 225–236.

—— (2001) "Il triangolo macedone," *Limes*, 2: 15–35.

Strazzari, F. and Dognini, G. (2000) "Geopolitica delle mafie jugoslave," *Limes*, Quaderno Speciale: 21–40.

Thompson, J.E. (1994) *Mercenaries, States and Sovereigns. State-Building and Extraterritorial Violence in Early Modern Europe*, Princeton: Princeton University Press.

Thuerer, D. (1999) "The 'Failed State' and International Law," *Revue Internationale de la Croix Rouge*, 81, December.

Tilly, C. (1985) "War Making and State Making as Organized Crime," in P. Evans, D. Rueschemeyer and T. Skocpol (eds) *Bringing the State Back In*, Cambridge: Cambridge University Press.

Woodward, S. (1995) *Balkan Tragedy: Chaos and Dissolution after the Cold War*, Washington: Brookings Institution.

Newspaper and newsletter sources

Abate, C. and Crimi, B., "I segreti della tabacco connection," *Panorama*, 16 November 2000.

Barbacetto, G., "Milano? Chiedete all'Fbi," *Diario*, 3 February 1999.

Bonini, C. and D'Avanzo, G., "E la Cia avvertì Roma: Sappiamo di Telecom," *La Repubblica*, 17 February 2001.

Caprile, R., "Una nuova Uçk ai confini della Macedonia," *La Repubblica*, 24 March 2000.

D'Avanzo, G., "Dal Cremlino all'Isola di Man, tutte le ricchezze di Pasha," *La Repubblica*, 19 January 2001.

Didanovic, V., "Polémique autour du niveau de vie en Serbie," *Reporter/Le Courrier des Balkans*, 5 April 2000.

Filipovic, M., "Sumadija Takes on Belgrade," *IWPR's Balkan Crisis Report*, 28 March 2000.

Harris, P., "China Re-establishes Balkans Influence," *Jane's Intelligence Review*, February 2000.

Indolfi, R., "Ha uno yacht di 11 miliardi il manager della tabacco-connection," *il Mattino*, 3 March 2000.

Kusovac, Z., "Crime and Culpability in Milosevic's Serbia," *Jane's Intelligence Review*, February 2000.

Mastrogiacomo, D., "Le navi della cocaina," *La Repubblica*, 10 February 2001.

Rozen, L., "Belgrade's China Rescue," *IWPR's Balkan Crisis Report*, 1 February 2000.

Ruotolo, G., "Emissari USA incoraggiano la secessione," *il Manifesto* 27 August 1999.

—— "Sulle coste del Montenegro, regno dei contrabbandieri," *il Manifesto*, 31 August 1999.

—— "Contrabbando, accuse alle banche," *La Stampa*, 9 November 2000.

Sensini, M., "Sul tabacco un affare da 11 mila miliardi," *La Stampa*, 13 January 2001.

Silvestri, F., "Il papavero e la guerra," *Narcomafie*, March 2000.

Staletovic, S., "Arkan's Smuggling Empire," *IWPR Balkan Crisis Report*, 28 February 2000.

Vasovic, M., "Serbia's Self-imposed Sanctions," *IWPR Balkan Crisis Report*, 15 March 2000.

8 Assisting structures of violence?

Humanitarian assistance in the Somali conflict

Joakim Gundel

Introduction: being sucked into the dynamics of violence

Humanitarian assistance represents a substantial resource, which in the context of intra-state war and extreme scarcity can be subject to attack and predation. This was the case in Somalia, where the resources brought in by the humanitarian agencies made a difference in other ways than saving lives: they also contributed to sustaining the structures of violence in Somali society rather than helping to get rid of them. This happened because the agencies felt compelled to deal with the warlords, whereby they risked becoming sucked into the political economy of violence. The aggregate result was that since 1991 the humanitarian assistance interventions have contributed to the propping up of "warlords" in southern and central Somalia. Hence the proposed hypothesis of this chapter is that by being involved with the political structures of violence in Somalia the agents providing humanitarian assistance played a significant role in impeding a long-term solution to the conflict.

The argumentation follows three steps: first, a theoretical section will define the concept "structure of violence" and the two notions that are required for understanding the dynamics of the Somali conflict, namely "clannism" and "spoils politics." The linkage between the political structure of violence and humanitarian assistance is provided by using an approach which argues that relief agencies are subordinated to politico-military actors in conflict, whereby the resources of the former serve important economic and political functions for the latter. Second, the background to the conflict in Somalia is described historically by showing the significance of clannism and spoils politics in the main phases of the conflict. Third, the main part of the chapter follows and examines the linkages between the humanitarian agencies and the political dynamics in Somalia. This comprises the following issues: food aid distribution, security arrangements, diversion and externalities of aid resources, and, finally, partnership. The concluding section deals with the long- and short-term consequences that the influx of humanitarian aid had on the structures of violence in Somalia.

Political structures of violence

When humanitarian assistance is provided in the context of intra-state wars, it inevitably becomes integrated into the dynamics of warfare, acquiring political and economic functions that potentially benefit the very structures in which the direct application of physical force serves as a political instrument. I argue that "clannism" and "spoils politics" were the dynamic elements in the structures of violence which (re-)produced the intra-state war of Somalia. Therefore, first I will provide a brief definition of the concept of "political structure of violence."

This concept is different from yet nevertheless inspired by Peter Uvin's application of the much broader concept of structural violence. He defines structural violence as the institutionalized inequalities of statuses, rights and power which are not the result of freedom of choice by individuals and groups. Rather, it is a consequence of the more powerful group's use of coercion, and it becomes institutionalized in the legal system, and justified through mythology, religion, ideology and history (Uvin 1998: 103–104). While structural violence focuses on unequal life chances caused by injustice, discrimination and marginalization, the term political structure of violence refers to political configurations, workings and dynamics which reproduce structural violence. Thus, a structure of violence is composed of the configuration of power relations, political, military and economic actors and their specific internal dynamics of violence.

Chris Allen, for example, recognizes that political violence in Africa, on the one hand, can be attributed to the adaptation of local actors to global economic and political processes. On the other hand, he emphasizes that at the roots of political and social violence are the internal dynamics of "spoils politics." In his analysis, spoils politics constitutes structural violence, becoming in its later stages "the dominant feature of political interaction and change" (Allen 1999: 381). Thus, spoils politics plays a dynamic role in a political structure where violence is endemic, and it performs as the prime means of action (Allen 1999: 381). In the clan-based segmentation of Somali society, however, this term has little meaning if associated with the Chinese warlord system of the 1920s from which it has been derived (Compagnon 1998: 74). Rather, the leaders of the clan-based factions are "political entrepreneurs" working clannism as an instrument for their political aims.

Clannism

I.M. Lewis wrote in 1961 that "the segmented clan system remains the bedrock foundation of pastoral Somali society and 'clannishness' – the primacy of clan interests – is its natural divisive reflection on the political level" (Lewis: 1961). In this sense clannism is often seen as the most important constituent social factor in Somali politics, and it is generally believed to be the core element for any explanation of Somali political dynamics. Clannism is primordial, but only in terms of its basis in real kinship relations, language and common cultural traditions. These traditions are based on the communal mode of production, which again is governed by traditional cultural and political norms and institutions such as the *reer* and *xeer*, which both regulate intra- and inter-clan relations and conflicts. *Reer* refers to the smallest clan family unit, whilst *xeer* stands for a social contract between all the *reer*, which also outlines the size of *"diya"* payment. *Diya* means blood payment, which is the compensation that one clan pays to another for an offense committed by one of its members. In addition, all clans have respected elders who may come under different names such as *"Ugaas"* or *"Suldaan."*

While "clannishness" pervades the political system in Somalia, its segmented nature has the potential of creating instability. According to Ken Menkhaus, clannism, which is the political manipulation of the clan system, is inherently centrifugal (Prendergast 1997: 93). This means that a clan conflict can easily fragment further on the basis of sub-clans. However, clannism can only become centrifugal if it is subject to political entrepreneurship, as Daniel Compagnon pointed out (1998: 83). Clannism is not static, but it is a dynamic and workable phenomenon. In its modern forms, clannism matured, so to speak, with the imposition and evolution of the modern state-form by its political agents. However, clans can only be manipulated when asymmetric inter-clan balances upset their traditional egalitarian nomadic values. If that happens, then a struggle to re-establish a new balance is almost inevitable. In other words, it is the interplay between political entrepreneurship and clannism that is the dynamic behind factionalism in Somalia. Yet it is the competition for spoils that is the motive for conflict between the factions (Compagnon 1998: 85).

Spoils politics

Chris Allen's (1995) notion of spoils politics can describe the dynamics that emerge out of the conflicting relations between different groups of Somali elite and their clan-based networks aiming at positioning themselves most favorably within Somalia as a political entity. Spoils politics is the competition between political actors for the goods (Allen 1995), or booty, which can be derived from access or domination of public office or directly through warlord activity (Reno 2000: 47). Spoils politics originates in clientelism, which is the personal networks of political dependents built up by politicians. Such networks became one of the basic forms of relationship between the post-colonial Somali state and its society (Thomson 2000: 111). They became ever more profound during the socio-economic crisis of the 1980s, because it produced a sense of social insecurity, leaving people with no other option than to rely on their clan-based networks for both survival and enrichment. The combination of clientelism and clannism in Somalia produced a regime characterized by being personalized and opportunistically corrupt (Marchal 1996: 26). Elite networks abused the state and eventually Somalia found itself in the midst of a clientelist crisis that turned into spoils politics with the following characteristics (selected from Allen 1995):

1   A winner takes all principle, entailing that the winning and dominant political faction tries to deny all other factions access to resources;
2   Corruption and the use of public office for private or factional (clan) gain;
3   Growing competition within the political elite for the spoils leading to further economic crisis and declining real incomes;
4   Communalism (clannism) extensively and increasingly used as a basis of political mobilization for factional activities.

Ultimately, spoils politics can engender new dynamics in which violence becomes endemic and may reproduce itself and thereby also the structures of violence (Allen 1999: 375). It is into this process that humanitarian assistance enters when it is provided to the victims of violent conflict. According to Francois Jean (1996: 573–589), the possible impact of humanitarian assistance is based on the premise that it constitutes a key resource for the legitimacy of the armed politico-military actors (political resource function) and their military activities (economical resource function). Thus humanitarian aid often benefits the most influential actors in conflicts. The main premise that enforces this is that humanitarian agencies are subordinated to the political and military actors, and international agencies rely on these local actors for access, security, authority and distribution of aid (Jean 1996: 566).

Background to the Somali political emergency

After Somalia's independence in 1961, the first decade of Somali politics resulted in a clientelist crisis that was caused by a profound clan-based proliferation of political parties. Thus, when Siad Barre became president through a *coup d'état* in 1969, he claimed that the new socialist system was to put away political clannism. The result was an intermittent solution to the crisis. Yet Siad Barre did not do away with clientelism. Instead he began to entrench his power, basing it on his own *Darood/Marehan* clan. He centralized power in the Office of the President, which also was used to regulate clientelist competition. Clientelism, however, is only viable as long as there are sufficient (external) resources to feed it. These necessary resources dwindled rapidly with the war against Ethiopia in 1978 and the oil and debt crises of the 1980s. In the resulting downward spiral, people turned to their kin for support and internal trust. While searching for new external alliances, they were at the same time deepening the institutional role of clans in defending their members (Adam 1992). With the end of the

Cold War and the decrease in aid in 1989, it became clear that the cliente-list crisis had remained unresolved (Rawson 1994). Siad Barre could no longer feed his client networks and turned towards spoils politics, which resulted in the clan-based war for which he had sown the seeds (Marchal 1996: 24–32; Prendergast 1997: 93).

Somalia became a prime example of how unresolved clientelist crisis can lead to political breakdown, crude military repression, and counter-insur-gencies (Allen 1999: 377). Thus, open intra-state war broke out already in 1988 when the Somali National Movement (SNM) dominated by the *Isaaq* clan carried out an insurgency towards "their" capital Hargeysa in northwestern Somalia, today known as "Somaliland."[1] Siad Barre retaliated by bombing Hargeysa to rubble. The Somali Salvation Democratic Front (SSDF) of the *Darood/Majerteen* clan operated in arid northeastern Somalia. The *Hawiye* clan groups, who also inhabited some of the most arid parts of Somalia, did not organize themselves militarily before General Aideed entered the scene and turned the United Somali Congress (USC) into an armed faction of the *Hawiye*. USC was the major armed faction that pushed towards Mogadishu in 1990 and finally ousted Siad Barre on 27 January 1991. However, USC soon split into two alliances: the Somali National Alliance (SNA) of General Aideed (the sub-clan *Habr Gedir*) and Ali Mahdi's (*Abgal* sub-clan) Somali Salvation Alliance (SSA). Conse-quently, the regime collapsed, and all governmental institutions literally ceased to exist. Somalia was thrown into an indefinite process of political, social and economic disintegration, ensuing clan-based fragmentation and the growth of new endemic structures of violence. Somali politics has since then been described as shifting and highly fluid (UNDP 1998: 36). A simple breakdown of the following Somali complex political emergency into three distinct phases may be useful for an understanding of the historical dimension (UNDP 1998: 29).

The first phase, from January 1991 to December 1992, was character-ized by high-intensity fighting, resulting in mass displacements and famine, mainly in the interriverine area. After Siad Barre fled Mogadishu, the USC militias pursued him to the Kenyan border, but without being able to defeat his forces. The result was that the forces allied to Barre, now called the Somali National Front (SNF) of the *Darood/Marehan* clan and the *Darood/Ogaden* Somali Patriotic Movement (SPM) could strike back. The resulting fighting moved across the interriverine regions several times, and each time the *Rahanwein* agropastoralists and the *Bantu* agricultural minority suffered immensely by being assaulted, raped and displaced. Their harvests and storage rooms were plundered, and new crops could not be planted. This, and not drought, was the prime cause for the disastrous famine. In their pursuit of both existing and prospective spoils (of a resurrected state), the militarily strong factions deliberately targeted those clans who inhabited the most fertile lands in the interriverine regions in an outright conquest on their lands. Consequently, it was the interriverine agropastoralists and the already displaced people who suffered most during the famine of 1991–1992, and not the pastoralist nomads (de Waal 1997: 159–160).

The famine caused an urgent need for humanitarian aid, but the international community had evacuated Somalia when Mogadishu became too insecure. Only a few agencies returned to provide insufficient but needed assistance to the victims. State collapse was a new situation to the agencies, and the collapsed economy created an urgent need for a substitute economy. Humanitarian assistance was an obvious resource that simply had to be preyed upon, causing more insecurity. The state collapse raised a new issue: with whom could the agencies negotiate access and security, and who could possibly be implementing partners. Nevertheless, the famine was bound to attract international humanitarian assistance, and the first international intervention, dubbed the United Nations Operation in Somalia (UNOSOM I), was launched in April 1992, one and a half years after Siad Barre was ousted. The international assistance in this period was not appropriate. Funds did not correspond with the appealed amounts. Even more important, the cause of the famine was incorrectly attributed to drought rather than to the armed conflict (NDC 1994: 72 and 93).

The second phase, from December 1992 to March 1995, began with the replacement of UNOSOM I with the United Nations Task Force (UNITAF), which was a military intervention under the leadership of the United States. The purpose of UNITAF was to protect the distribution of relief aid. UNITAF was replaced by UNOSOM II in May 1993, and was given the responsibility of establishing a transitional government, and facilitating a better groundwork for humanitarian assistance. The new "warlord" leaders did not pay any serious attention to the humanitarian emergency, and due to their preoccupation with capturing the state instead of transforming it, the Somali conflict was prolonged indefinitely. Bryden and Steiner found reason to state that "for Somalia's emergent warlords, government meant little more than access to state resources, in principal those associated with international recognition and foreign aid" (1998: 15). The intervention became sucked into the conflict turning the Somali crisis into a true "complex political emergency." UNOSOM II was withdrawn in March 1995 because of its political failures.

The third phase, which may be called the post-intervention period, has now lasted since March 1995. The failure and frustrations of the 1992–1995 international intervention led to a reduction in aid (UNDP 1998: 13–14). After UNOSOM, all the international operations were run from new headquarters in Nairobi. While the self-declared Republic of Somaliland and the Puntland administration emerged in northern Somalia, southern and central Somalia remained in a quagmire of fragmented political structures of violence.

Humanitarian action and political dynamics

Food aid

Food aid was considered the most important relief item in the first phase of the complex political emergency in Somalia, because of the perceived famine. Food aid did not commence until early 1991 because of insecurity, and the International Committee of the Red Cross (ICRC) was the main food provider. A few other International Non-Governmental Organizations (INGOs) contributed as well, but the effort was insufficient. ICRC found that 40 percent of the population in southern Somalia risked starvation by November 1991 (Milas 1997: 31). The food aid operations became subject to attack, diversion and manipulation. Shipments of food aid were prevented from discharging at ports by armed belligerents. Warehouses were looted, and truck convoys with food were hijacked by militia forces and bandits. While distributing food, relief workers were killed, making most agencies reluctant to handle food aid on the ground in Somalia (Milas 1997: 31).

The international community did not respond to the Somali crisis before the UN Security Council adopted its first resolution (UNSC Resolution 733) on 23 January 1992. This resolution urged the parties to a cease fire and to facilitate humanitarian assistance. The United Nations' plan to deploy 550 military peacekeepers and to distribute 23 million US dollars of humanitarian aid was a message of great interest to all those factions who could gain legitimacy from large flows of food aid into the areas under their control (Milas 1997: 35). After an agreement between General Aideed and Ali Mahdi was signed in March 1992, a cease-fire did take effect, and UNOSOM I was launched in April. Relief aid was instrumental in achieving the cease-fire because all sides needed the supplies badly. Food aid could relieve the daily pressure from civilians for whose basic needs the political factions increasingly were unable to provide. Thus, food aid was seen as a strategic resource that could both legitimize the faction leaders and strengthen their military capacities for the next stages of the conflict.

In April 1992, the UN launched a 90-day action plan. The first World Food Program (WFP) food aid ship arrived on 3 May 1992, and the Lutheran World Federation (LWF) began to operate the airlift in the same month. The airlift ended in November 1993. ICRC, WFP and UNICEF delivered more than 80,000 tons of food during the first half of 1992 (Milas 1997: 37). The performance by the UN was very poor in this phase, and except for UNICEF they did not maintain offices in Somalia. The ICRC and the INGOs were far more efficient, and their effort contributed significantly to the humanitarian improvements in the famine-stricken areas (African Rights 1992: 9). The WFP had by mid-July only delivered less than one-third of the amount of food they themselves had pledged to do. ICRC had delivered three times as much.[2] When UNITAF was deployed, food could again be transported safely through the security corridors which the American marines had established. However, UNITAF and UNOSOM II failed because they came too late to address the famine. They also failed in building peace, but that is described elsewhere (see Clarke and Herbst 1997). Thus, immediately after UNOSOM II arrived, ICRC pulled out because they found that the famine was over and that they had accomplished their mission (NDC 1994: 111–128).

When the first food aid arrived in May 1992, it came in large quantities, and triggered large-scale looting because it was the first food in six months and the value was very high. There was a clear relationship between availability of relief items and the interest in looting them. For instance, when sorghum later became abundant, looting of that item ended while high-value food stuffs such as rice, pasta and oil could led to looting frenzies (Milas 1997: 38). By flooding the market with low-value food, Andrew Natsios argues, both security and famine is addressed simultaneously because food will be so abundant that it loses its trading value (Natsios 1997: 87). Nevertheless, the predation of humanitarian assistance continued, leading to competition between factions and clans. This resulted in an exacerbation of conflict and security and an increased need for protection of relief operations.

Creative food distribution

Outside UNITAF- and later UNOSOM-controlled areas, the predation of humanitarian assistance continued. Furthermore, food could often not be delivered directly to the beneficiaries. As a consequence, food was often distributed indirectly through the militias who had looted it, or it had to be delivered directly from the gates of the relief agencies. The result was that the poorest, the ones really starving, seldom had any benefit from the food aid. They were often too exhausted to collect food at the gates of the agencies. They were also at the bottom of the social hierarchies, making it doubtful how much food actually reached them, especially when distribution was controlled by the factions.[3] Because of the unresolved security situation, humanitarian access remained a primacy for the agencies, and they simply had to find alternative ways of delivering aid. The effort at finding alternatives included cross-border channels, small ports and beach landings. In an effort to prevent food aid from ending up with the warlords, ICRC began to set up soup kitchens. Looting was thus immediately reduced, since stealing prepared food was not of interest. Unfortunately, this tactic had, according to Andrew Natsios (1997: 88), another disastrous effect on local agriculture, and displaced people to the immediate locations of the kitchens. More important for the future course of events, most of the kitchens were located in the areas of General Aideed, whereby he could gain an advantage by controlling these populations, including denying recruits to the other warlords.

Competition for food aid spoils

According to Daniel Compagnon, the rationality of predation, or in his words "culture of loot," stems from the spoils politics of the Siad Barre regime, but in the context of a collapsed society, it is a rational way of life (Compagnon 1998: 85). Predation had an important function in the patrimonialized regime of Siad Barre in feeding the clientelistic networks. In this way, the army diverted humanitarian assistance that was destined for the large refugee camps near the borders to Ethiopia throughout the 1980s (Maren 1997). This did not end in civil war, but set a precedent and was later practiced by the non-state actors of the contending clan-based factions instead of governmental officials. This culture of loot had another effect, which was to have pronounced significance for relief aid in Somalia. The personalized networks of clientelist spoils politics erased in the minds of people the distinction between public and private goods. Increased competition to loot before others was the direct implication. As I will show in the example below, this also had an interesting effect in reviving traditional jurisprudence.

Predation and jurisprudence

Throughout 1990 and 1991, food aid entered Somaliland through the port of Berbera, or at a small ancient port near the town Erigavo. Most of that food either never left the region or was looted completely by local clan militias claiming that what they found was their fair share.[4] In 1991, a shipment of emergency food came through the port of Berbera for distribution by the German Emergency Doctors. But Hargeysa-based militias looted all the food destined for Hargeysa. After that incident, most of the local humanitarian agencies decided to abandon food aid.[5] After the SNM victory, and when people came back to their homes in Somaliland, nothing was left: no businesses, destroyed houses, no income possibilities, etc. Still, the new Somaliland government, which declared its independence in May 1991, decided that international aid agencies should stop food aid and begin rehabilitation instead.[6] Yet despite the governments' request, food aid continued to enter Somaliland, and it became the immediate cause for re-igniting the war there.[7] Most of the renewed fighting in 1992–1993 around Berbera was strategically about food aid and contributed to the re-ignition of war in Somaliland. International food aid had a very destabilizing influence because it was perceived to be external to the local traditional jurisprudence.[8] Since it did not belong to any clan, it was perceived as "public" and everyone wanted a share. At the same time, local merchants in Somaliland imported and distributed food privately, and were never targeted by the militias. This safety of local merchants was due to the fact that they were a part of the local clan structure and their actions embedded in the norms regulating clan behavior according to the traditional social institutions of the *reer* and *xeer*. The clan-based militias knew that any attempt to loot them would trigger an inter-clan war.

Sub-contracting local distributors

Later the lesson of northern Somalia did reach the international agencies. In 1997, WFP decided to sub-contract its food deliveries to private Somali merchants.[9] This method involved a private Somali contractor who deposited an amount of money equivalent to the value of the food he was in charge of delivering. After the food had been delivered, the deposit was returned together with payment for transportation. The contractor was fully responsible for security and delivery.[10] In this way, WFP and other food distributing agencies could avoid the responsibility and negative associations that occurred when a security incident hit a food convoy. In the beginning, the system seemed to work quite well. However, the context in the south is different than in the north. There, traditional authority and practice are not as strong as in the northern regions, and the competition and fragmentation between business groups, sub-clans and warlords is more intense. Contractors used the traditional Somali nomadic means of communicating and securing a convoy into the countryside (Marchal 1996: 40). In spite of such new methods of food distribution, incidents such as killings and fighting about the food transportation continued.[11] The reason is that food transports have become the focal element in the ongoing feuds between clan-based factions. For instance, a contractor may be good, cheap and reliable, but he may also be a *Warsangeli* of the *Hawiye* clan group. The *Warsangeli*, however, are feuding with the *Abgal*, and the transport has to pass through *Abgal* land. Another example is that most of the contracts may go to *Hawiye* business people in Mogadishu or Merca. But the *Rahanwein* recipients in Baidoa may find it difficult to accept that the food meant for them has to be contracted to members of their enemies.

Food aid and structures of violence

Although food aid does not in itself cause war, in Somalia it did, and still does cause armed skirmishes. When food aid arrives in a conflict, it easily becomes one of the central objects of fighting. Thus, during the big famine and during UNOSOM, the massive influx of food aid caused even more than only local skirmishes. It was also easier for the authorities to reject inappropriate food aid in Somaliland than in the south. Today the opinion in Somaliland is that free food is no good when it is not really needed.[12] The best thing is when the clans can support their own members fleeing war on the basis of their traditional coping mechanisms. In the south the situation is different from Somaliland. There the need for food aid is much greater because of the interriverine agropastoralists' vulnerability to conflict. The competition for spoils in the south, especially among the dominating warlords in Mogadishu, was far more intense than in the northern parts of Somalia. Food aid came massively to the south and represented a major business opportunity, which the emergent warlords (political entrepreneurs) were swift to exploit (Prendergast 1997: 123–124). Their dominant position achieved at gunpoint was ultimately legitimized by UNOSOM and UNITAF. Thus, the humanitarian agencies continued to find themselves in an insecure environment and in a position subordinated to the factions, local authorities and NGOs, which the political entrepreneurs controlled.

Security arrangements

As Francois Jean asserts, insecurity and the humanitarian imperative of access to victims makes the agencies subordinate to the factions with whom they have to negotiate access and protection (1996: 566). Due to the very complex, volatile and insecure conditions in Somalia, all expatriate UN and INGO staff, as well as that of diplomatic missions, were evacuated in January 1991 (Refugee Policy Group 1994: 14–15). Only Médicins sans Frontières (MSF) and ICRC returned. UNICEF was not authorized to reopen its office in Mogadishu until December 1991. However, a few relief agencies continued to work in Somalia. These agencies contributed considerable assistance under very difficult conditions throughout 1991 and 1992.

The general insecurity that followed the civil war was supplemented by localized clan-conflicts and banditry, and all this contributed to the difficulties faced by the humanitarian agencies. They were deliberately targeted by both faction militias as well as gangs who, in the absence of public security forces, could loot them with impunity. Obviously, the agencies made themselves prey of high value because of the resources they brought in the form of money, cars, expensive equipment and scarce goods such as medicine and food. Furthermore, they contributed to the difficulties themselves via negotiations with warlords. These negotiations were required to get relief supplies through military checkpoints, or to hire so-called "technicals" (heavily armed pick-up trucks) to accompany the relief convoys. The lack of security compelled the agencies to hire armed guards to protect themselves, their cars, and their relief items. In Somalia, ICRC hired armed protection for the first time in its history.

These local security arrangements, or "protection rackets" as Jean calls them (1996: 574), became systematic and extortive. Thus, a substantial part of the agencies' budgets went to secure relief provision and to provide the payments for safe access to the people in need. All this was negotiated with the factions, or with their proxies (Yannis 1999).

UNITAF did create a secure space for humanitarian assistance during its three months of operation, but only in certain narrow transport corridors. It was also criticized for not disarming the Somalis right away as most Somalis actually expected them to do (Refugee Policy Group 1994). Security gradually worsened after UNOSOM II took over from UNITAF, which was partly due to unclear mandates and unclear command structures. UNITAF was under the sole leadership of the USA, while UNOSOM II was a multinational force without a clear leadership. The Americans insisted on having a say in UNOSOM II, which in turn antagonized the European contingents. Furthermore, the approaches of the military wings of UNOSOM II collided with the objectives of the humanitarian agencies. For instance, the military intervention in Kismayo was counterproductive in solving the security problems MSF had in running the local hospital. Instead it further deteriorated the relations between the local population and the humanitarian agencies (Clarke and Herbst 1997: 239–250).

When UNOSOM II left in 1995, the security that they had provided for the aid agencies' operations was no longer there, thus leaving the international agencies with a major security problem. The most common solution seemed to be to fall back to the pre-UNOSOM kind of security arrangements with local Somali militias, or to find a local NGO (LNGO) co-partner that was on good terms with the local *de facto* authorities.

Project managers under the impression of severe insecurity felt compelled to give in to the pressure from clan-factions to hire their people, contractors, security arrangements, compounds, cars or whatever one could think of. Yet, in the Somali context of a very egalitarian tribal society, no group or clan would leave any goods solely for the others without themselves making a bid for it, thus the security arrangements developed into another object of conflict. The spoils politics element contributed to extreme competition in this field as well. Either way, the combined dynamics of clannism and factional spoils politics meant that the INGOs had to respect these authorities and often were perceived as being "owned" by the clans and the factions in that given place.

Especially food, fuel and vehicles created more insecurity in the context of extreme conflict. Although the INGOs learned to reduce or stop bringing in food, cars and fuel, they still entered local security arrangements. In Somalia there was a trade-off for security, and this situation remains in the south, where security is still a major problem.[13] Here the local security arrangements became an integral part of the vicious circle of socio-political instability that regenerates community dependence on the militias, not only for security, but also for income when an international agency is the contractor. In accepting these conditions, and the pressure of local communities to hire security packages (usually you hire a package of four guards who come with the car that is needed), international humanitarian agencies have been contributing to the structures of violence.[14]

Diversion and externality

The intra-state war in Somalia continued to be funded, in part, by rich local traders and by Somalis living abroad, although at later stages of the conflict the traders were no longer in a position to support the various militias as much as at the beginning of the conflict. New resources were needed, and they were provided by the international relief agencies. Thus, the militias extracted resources from international agencies in the form of bribes or direct payments, all this in exchange for granting the relief organizations operational freedom in their respective areas of control (Augelli and Murphy 1995: 346–347).

To be sure, aid diversion techniques existed already before the civil war. They were even utilized by the Somali government. Later, however, the political entrepreneurs (warlords) developed an interest in perpetuating conflict by diverting aid resources into buying land or building military capacities (Compagnon 1998: 86). The economic resources associated with humanitarian aid were able to set free resources for military use (Keen 1998), a phenomenon that is also described by the substitution thesis. Other observers point at humanitarian assistance as contributing to an "artificial economy" or at various ways in which it can become integrated into war economies (Jean 1996; Prendergast 1997).

In general, the literature describes the following four techniques of aid diversion, which were also able to be found in Somalia:

1   There is the rather primitive form of predation, i.e. theft and looting often perpetrated from road blocks (Anderson 1999: 39).
2   A more sophisticated form is levying taxes and fees at road blocks, or on airfields, usually collected by armed militias. Although being almost as direct as predation, this form is more "regulated" by factions or local authorities.
3   The third form are the previously described protection rackets, or extortive security arrangements.
4   Finally, there are even more sophisticated ways to extract revenue from the aid operations, mostly derived from house rents, car hire, jobs, etc. (Prendergast 1997). I call these forms the "externalities" of humanitarian aid.[15]

The problem of "negative" externalities exploded in Somalia with the international military intervention, generating highly inflated prices for labor, rents, vehicle hires and other local services. Augelli and Murphy found that the warring factions appropriated "some hundreds of thousands of dollars a month in Mogadishu alone" (1995: 347). Armed escorts were rented for protection and relief transports had to pay militias to insure protection from their own men. In this security business, 2,000 US dollars were paid for each security guard per month, an armed "technical" cost around 300 US dollars per day. In addition, offices and houses were rented at high prices. During the UNOSOM period, the monthly rent for houses was between 10,000 and 12,000 US dollars. Considering that UN agencies and INGOs rented at least 100 houses and that around 380 "technicals" were used in Mogadishu per day, the externalities business was thriving. Moreover, personnel was hired in greater numbers than needed and they were, as a rule, overpaid. In 1994, UNOSOM spend more than 40 million US dollars in salaries, employing roughly 17,000 Somalis (Prendergast 1997: 113). Food was transported in stolen trucks rented back from those who had stolen them. Levies were put on everything from landing fees, cargo, ships entering the port, etc. For instance, at one point the *Xawaadle* clan was able to conquer and control Mogadishu's international airport, which was actually far out of bounds of their traditional territory.[16] Finally, the international actors concluded numerous service contracts with local Somalis. For instance, one notorious Somali became a millionaire by disposing of garbage from the UNOSOM compounds.[17]

As it is not possible to find any reliable statistics indicating the actual magnitude of these externalities of relief aid, one must rely on estimations such as Augelli and Murphy did. It is also difficult to collect any reliable data on the total amount of aid provided to Somalia.[18] Yet the figures from the Refugee Policy Group provide at least a general impression of the substantial rise in the amount of assistance from 1991 to 1992. According to them, in 1991, the USA granted 29.6 million US dollars in humanitarian assistance, a sum that increased to 95.1 million US dollars in 1992.

In 1992, the international assistance to Somalia was at its peak.[19] Nevertheless, even today the externalities of aid represent the most direct type of spoils that can be achieved from international agencies. To illustrate this, Action Contre la Faim (ACF), which is operating in Mogadishu, estimated that they alone support up to 10,000 people through the staff they have hired and the security arrangements, including cars and guards, they have made.[20] These unfortunate externalities of the humanitarian practices, both before and during UNOSOM, paved the way for many future security incidents. Moreover, they consolidated the dependency on international aid agencies, which again caused serious problems of disengagement for the international aid community (Yannis 1999).

The dilemmas of delivering food aid, especially concerning security and respect for public assets, applies for other types of assistance as well. Food and seeds in the agricultural sector, valuable drugs in the health sector, motorized pumps in the water and sanitation sector, in southern Somalia all have been either looted or they formed the basis for cultures of bribe and extortion, and this was silently accepted by the INGOs at large.[21] For instance, the Sheikh Hospital in Somaliland was looted completely,[22] and the militias were selling looted food at low prices. Against this background, it is evident that a fair distribution of all resources is necessary to prevent escalations of conflict. Given the extremely egalitarian norms of the Somali context concerning the perception of "public goods," most communities expect a careful and fair distribution of assets.

Partnership

Undoubtedly, the political entrepreneurs (warlords) had a specific interest in entering partnerships with international agencies. By positioning themselves as guarantors of relief, they could simultaneously elevate their popularity (legitimacy), maintain their clientelistic network and channel resources to their war capacities. The warlords did not only value relief aid in terms of money, but also with regard to the human resources it represents. For instance, drugs and health service equipment require expertise and knowledge to use. If a warlord or a "politician" can attract health assistance of vital importance for survival, this may give him an important leverage for his political legitimacy and ambitions.[23] Yet as direct partnerships might have been too obvious, the strategy of the warlords was to access the aid resources indirectly via LNGOs under their control. The insecure conditions on the ground in the context of state collapse were not conducive for finding appropriate partners (Yannis 1999).[24] Nonetheless, the Somalis were quick in exploiting a situation in which the international agencies were left in bewilderment as to who they could interact with legally. The factions who filled the vacuum used their newly acquired positions to negotiate access to relief aid with the INGOs and UN agencies (Compagnon 1998: 89).

In this process, the ICRC and most of the INGOs perceived their role as being impartial and neutral, which also meant that they defined their role as having a right and an obligation to collaborate with all local power structures, including direct negotiations with warlords. This in fact jeopardized their impartiality. It also caused friction with the UN, because it questioned who had the right or mandate to negotiate deals with the warlords, and where, how, why and on what basis such negotiations should take place. To a certain extent, the UN agencies were also confronted with a different problem because they were used to dealing primarily with governmental institutions. Thus INGOs were more used to working with local partnerships. In the light of civil society and local participatory approaches, the role of LNGOs as implementing partners increased within the international aid community in the beginning of the 1990s; with them the INGOs seemed to have an alternative to government institutions. The UN embraced this idea by sub-contracting INGOs and LNGOs to carry out the relief tasks. This had another consequence. The vast amounts of money spent during UNOSOM II together with the sub-contracting policy led to a wild proliferation of LNGOs in Somalia (Abdillahi 1998). Forming LNGOs became a business and these non-governmental organizations mushroomed throughout Somalia.

After UNOSOM II left and the aid flow shrank to below a quarter of what it was before, the international agencies developed a more critical stand in choosing their partners. Many LNGOs turned "stand-by," and became nominal. The idea of strengthening civil society was not always an appropriate approach. For instance, an INGO which is the major social service provider in the water and sanitation sector may enter a partnership with a "nominal" LNGO.[25] The implication can be that the INGO via the LNGO supports a political structure, which formally is vested in the regional council, but which in reality is little more than the puppet of the local politicians, warlords and supreme elders who maintain the real political and military power. The consequence is that the local power structure is maintained and legitimized by external agencies, functioning as the local authorities' social welfare provider.

Unfortunately, many humanitarian agencies did not use traditional authorities as partners, and they are still not used unequivocally. It can be very wise to address the local elders on all matters of doubt concerning rentals, hiring and any aspect of operations. The elders can advise so as to prevent conflict, misunderstandings and other trouble in advance. It is especially important that the security arrangements are clarified with them. However, the trouble is that security arrangements usually play into the hands of militias. Thus, if the elders do not have full control over them because they have lost their authority, then such arrangements may contribute to keeping the local communities under the domination of the factions. Furthermore, some elders are also political entrepreneurs who have used their personal attributes such as education, money or trade to enhance their elder status.

The resulting configuration of power in the various "partnerships" seems to be vested in the odd constellation of warlord political entrepreneurs, certain elders, and the employees in local and international NGOs. This may be good if we are dealing with people who possess a high level of personal integrity and morality. The problem is that the dependency on the flow of resources through the international agency reduces the sense of responsibility of the Somali leaders, on the one hand, and keeps the logic of spoils politics alive on the other. Thus, the involvement of INGOs may prevent the Somalis from establishing a local polity on which fair balances of power could rely, and which is sustained by local sources of income and a peaceful stability.

Conclusions: feeding localized structures of violence

Humanitarian assistance was a strategic resource in the first and second phases of the complex emergency in Somalia, and the factions speculated on how to get part of it either directly by predation or by exploiting the spoils of externalities. The Somalis did benefit from the vast resources of UNOSOM II to such a degree that people in southern Somalia still wish the UNOSOM II period back.[26] But the political efforts of UNOSOM II at buying political agreements through direct payments to local Somali leaders contributed to shaping the Somali perception of international assistance as a source of competition. This, ironically, undermined the very same peace process it was originally supposed to promote. During the major international intervention of UNOSOM II, a political and military turn was taken, and all its mistakes in fact created and legitimized the southern and Mogadishu-based warlords (Compagnon 1998: 86–89). After the end of UNOSOM II, the external resource flow shrank, and so did the UNOSOM-dependent Somali economy. Therefore, when new agencies move in today, and with them money and resources, then the chase for spoils begins all over again. In this context the "peace dividend" approach launched after UNOSOM II did not create sufficient leverage for peace in Somalia. Nor did it become a sufficient and forceful mechanism for engendering peace in a situation in which the warlord syndrome had been established.[27] It is significant that in areas with no assistance, and no other external interference, life seems to pass by much more smoothly and peacefully. In the south, in the context of relatively weak and highly fragmented local polities, international assistance had a greater impact regarding the type of formal political structures that it sought to establish, and these local polities function fundamentally as interlocutors to the international community. They therefore become the main arena for political competition about the spoils of social and welfare services.

Short-term fuelling of conflict

The political significance of humanitarian assistance should not only be seen in terms of its magnitude or in terms of saving lives, but also concerning the role it plays in the dynamics of socio-political processes. Of course, the importance of humanitarian assistance varies depending on what type of assistance we are talking about, which sector we are within, and on what is at stake between the belligerents. In Somalia humanitarian assistance turned into business. Therefore, as a function of the extreme localization of politics, it became a significant element in "low politics." If certain events in the low political "sphere" occur in a quantitatively significant number this may even turn into a new qualitative situation in "high politics." For instance, food transports can escalate intra sub-clan conflicts when they pass through. A possible result is the spreading of such conflicts to all the places where the belligerent sub-clans are found. The sub-contracting of food transports to only one sub-clan in a conflict can strengthen it economically in contrast to another. Or it may be perceived to be threatening the fragile power balance, which can be just as serious. Thus, fighting can be triggered only for that reason, or simply because of jealousy, as the very egalitarian sub-clans would rather see that no one gets anything than their neighboring sub-clan receives something while they themselves do not. Andrew Natsios concluded that "saving lives over the short term may increase deaths over the longer term, as well as damage to civil society" (Natsios 1997: 93).

Longer-term structural impediments

The direct impact of short-term instability is that it legitimizes the use of armed force and thus confirms the rationality of the structures of violence. From this perspective, humanitarian assistance does have the capacity of entrenching structures of endemic conflict. Furthermore, by focusing on the faction leaders as the "legitimate" authorities to negotiate with, a political structure was set for the future that expelled other local Somali groups and individuals struggling for a different agenda than that of becoming war-lords. They were left to compete for junior positions within the humanitarian agencies operating in Somalia. Because UNOSOM focused on the personalized faction polities, there was not much room for alternative political forces. On the contrary, nonmilitant groups were largely ignored. If spoils politics is one of the troubling features of the Somali socio-political culture, then the continuance of humanitarian assistance in the present form is not contributing to a move in a different direction. Local security arrangements allowing for peaceful conflict resolution is a pre-condition for moving on towards rebuilding peaceful political structures in war-torn societies. But, as long as external humanitarian assistance uncritically fuels spoils politics, it will never do anything but help to keep Somalia caught up in its structures of violence.

In sum, the arguments presented suggest that, while significant achievements in terms of saving lives in Somalia were accomplished, the combined humanitarian assistance interventions also contributed to the evolution of political structures of violence (warlordism). Thus, a transformation of Somali politics and society that could establish a stable connection between society and political authorities was in fact impeded, particularly in southern and central Somalia. Instead, foreign assistance contributed to the emergence of a fragmented mosaic of local political institutions. This mosaic consists of a combination of traditional authorities, local governmental institutions functioning as interlocutors to the international donor community, as well as militarized faction leaders, coexisting in different combinations of relative strength.

Notes

1 The *Isaaq* clans from the former colony "British Somaliland" had been marginalized by the elite from the former "Italian Somaliland" since the two merged after their independence in 1961 (Marchal 1996).

2 This was one of the main elements of criticism that the UN Special Representative, Mohamed Sahnoun, launched against the UN system and which eventually led to his resignation (Sahnoun 1998). However, Sahnoun did facilitate a meeting on 12 October 1992, between the donors, UN agencies, ICRC and INGOs in Geneva, where a new 100-day plan for accelerated relief to Somalia was agreed in replacement of the former and less successful 90-day plan of April 1992 (United Nations 1996: 92–93).

3 According to ICRC this is still a problem in southern Somalia. Interviews in Hargeysa, May 1999, and with ICRC in Nairobi, October 1999.
4 Interview with Somali Relief and Rehabilitation Association (SORRA) Hargeysa, May 1999.
5 Interview with Islamic Relief Committee (IRC), Hargeysa, May 1999.
6 Interview with Rhoda Ibrahim, ICD, Hargeysa, May 1999.
7 Interview with Rhoda Ibrahim, ICD, Hargeysa, May 1999.
8 Interview with the Minister of Planning, Government of Somaliland, May 1999.
9 However, it is significant that the WFP Somalia today does not have an institutional memory that can explain how and why the changes in food aid delivery approaches took place (discussions with WFP staff in Nairobi, October 1999).
10 Interviews with WFP staff in Nairobi, October 1999.
11 According to several issues of the Integrated Regional Information Network newsletters 1999/2000.
12 Interview with SORRA, May 1999.
13 My own observations from southern Somalia in the fall of 1999.
14 Interview in Merca, October 1999.
15 Externality is a term borrowed from the discipline of economics and refers to the spill-over effect of an economic activity on an external activity not directly related to it. An externality is when the activity of one agent affects the options, and activities of another agent. In our context it is the spoils, such as the jobs humanitarian agencies provide, the cars, compounds, guards that can be hired, etc., that has an externality effect.
16 Interviews in Hiran region of Somalia, September 1999.
17 Interviews with Somali national UN staff in Somalia, October 1999.
18 Apparently it is not possible to retrieve meaningful figures from donors or implementing agencies. Even the Somali Aid Co-ordination Body (SACB) in Nairobi does not have any statistics over the aggregate funds spent on Somalia.
19 *Table 8.1* Estimated humanitarian assistance to Somalia compared with other major types of income[a]

	1992	1993	1994	1995	1996/97	1998	1999
Humanitarian assistance	410,666	215,382	55,569	60,037	109,165	56,000	50,316
Livestock[b]					140,000×2	70,000	80,000
Remittances[c]	300,000	300,000	300,000	300,000	300,000×2	300,000	300,000
GDP estimated[d]				1,000,000			

Sources: DHA (United Nations Department of Humanitarian Affairs) www.un.org/ Depts/dha; OCHA (Unied Nations Office for the Organization of Humanitarian Affairs) www.reliefweb.int/ocha_ol; UNDP 1998; Bradbury and Coultan 1998; Refugee Policy Group 1994.
Notes:
[a]Amounts are in thousands of US dollars.
[b]Livestock for 1998 and 1999 is an estimate based on figures from UNDP 1998.
[c]The figure for remittances is an average of the estimated suggestions found in the literature.
[d]GDP is based on an estimated GDP per capita between 176–200 US dollars.
The purpose of Table 8.1 is not to provide precise figures, but rather to give an impression of the magnitude of the assistance flow to Somalia. This should give an idea of the relative significance of the assistance in both socio-economical and political terms.

20　Interview with ACF, Nairobi, October 1999.
21　Interviews in Nairobi, September 1999.
22　Interview with IRC, May 1999.
23　Interview with UN staff in Baidoa, and local INGO staff in Merca, October 1999.
24　The ICRC did not have this problem because they could use the existing network of the Somali Red Crescent Society (SRCS).
25　This example is based on my own observation from southern Somalia in the fall of 1999. The anonymity is out of respect to my sources.
26　Interviews in Jowhar and Baidoa, October 1999.
27　The principle says that those Somalis who create peace in their area will benefit from assistance.

References

Abdillahi, M.S. (1998) "The Emergence of Local NGOs in the Recovery and Development Process of Somaliland (Northwest Somalia)," *Voices from Africa*, 8: 73–84.

Adam, H. (1992) "Somalia: Militarism, Warlordism and Democracy?," *Review of African Political Economy*, 54: 11–26.

African Rights (1992) *Operation Restore Hope: A Preliminary Assessment*, London: African Rights.

Allen, C. (1995) "Understanding African Politics," *Review of African Political Economy*, 65: 301–320.

—— (1999) "Warfare, Endemic Violence and State Collapse in Africa," *Review of African Political Economy*, 81: 367–384.

Anderson, M.B. (1999) *Do No Harm: How Aid Can Support Peace – or War*, Boulder: Lynne Rienner.

Augelli, E. and Murphy, C.N. (1995) "Lessons of Somalia for Future Multilateral Humanitarian Assistance Operations," *Global Governance*, 1: 339–365.

Bradbury, M. and Coultan, V. (1998) "Somalia: Inter-Agency Flood Response Operation Phase 1, July 1998," in valuation sponsored by the governments of Sweden, USA and UK, UNICEF.

Bryden, M. and Steiner, M. (1998) *Somalia between Peace and War, Somali Women on the Eve of the 21st Century*, UNIFEM: Nairobi.

Clarke, W. and Herbst, J. (eds) (1997) *Learning from Somalia – The Lessons of Armed Humanitarian Intervention*, Oxford: Westview.

Compagnon, D. (1998) "Somali Armed Units: The Interplay of Political Entrepreneurship and Clan-Based Factions," in Clapham, C. (ed.) *African Guerrillas*, Oxford: James Currey.

De Waal, A. (1997) *Famine Crimes: Politics and the Disaster Relief Industry in Africa*, London and Oxford: African Rights and James Currey.

Jean, F. (1996) "Aide humanitaire et économie de guerre," in F. Jean and J.-C. Rufin (eds) *Économie des guerres civiles*, Paris: Hachette.

Keen, D. (1998) "The Economic Functions of Violence in Civil Wars," *Adelphi Papers*, 320, Oxford: International Institute of Strategic Studies.

Lewis, I.M. (1961) *A Pastoral Democracy*, Oxford: Oxford University Press.

Marchal, R. (1996) *Final Report on the Post Civil War Somali Business Class*, Nairobi: EU Somalia Unit.

Maren, M. (1997) *The Road to Hell – The Ravaging Effects of Foreign Aid and International Charity*, New York: The Free Press.

Milas, S. (1997) *Causes and Consequences of the Somali Conflict*, Nairobi: UNICEF.

Natsios, A.S. (1997) "Humanitarian Relief Intervention in Somalia: The Economics of Chaos," in W. Clarke and J. Herbst (eds) *Learning from Somalia – The Lessons of Armed Humanitarian Intervention*, Oxford: Westview.

NDC (1994) *Humanitarian Aid to Somalia*, Evaluation Report, The Hague: Netherlands Development Co-operation.

Prendergast, J. (1997) *Crisis Response – Humanitarian Band-aids in Sudan and Somalia*, London and Chicago: Pluto Press.

Rawson, D. (1994) "U.S. Assistance and the Somali State," in A.I. Samatar (ed.) *The Somali Challenge: From Catastrophe to Renewal?*, Boulder: Lynne Rienner.

Refugee Policy Group (1994) *Hope Restored? Humanitarian Aid in Somalia 1990–1994*, Washington, DC: RPG.

Reno, W. (2000) "Shadow States and the Political Economy of Civil Wars," in M. Berdal and D.M. Malone (eds) *Greed and Grievance: Economic Agendas in Civil Wars*, Boulder and London: Lynne Rienner.

Sahnoun, M. (1998) *Somalia – The Missed Opportunities*, Washington DC: US Institute of Peace Press, (first 1994).

Thomson, A. (2000) *An Introduction to African Politics*, London: Routledge.

United Nations (1996), *The United Nations and Somalia 1992–1996*, New York: United Nations.

UNDP (1998) *Human Development Report Somalia*, ed. by K. Menkhaus and R. Marchal, Nairobi: UNDP Somalia.

Uvin, P. (1998) *Aiding Violence – The Development Enterprise in Rwanda*, West Hartford: Kumarian Press.

Yannis, A. (1999) "Humanitarian Politics in Collapsed States: A Critical Appraisal of the Role of International NGOs in the Somali Crisis", Geneva: mimeo.

9 Conclusions

The political economy of war-making and state-making in a globalizing world

Dietrich Jung

> Then leave Complaints: Fools only strive
> To make a Great and Honest Hive
> T' enjoy the World's Conveniencies,
> Be fam'd in War, yet live in Ease,
> Without great Vices, is a vain
> Eutopia seated in the Brain.
> Fraud, Luxury and Pride must live,
> While we the Benefits receive:
> Hunger's dreadful Plague, no doubt,
> Yet who digests or thrives without?
> (Bernard Mandeville)[1]

In sharp contrast to Kant's principle-guided liberalism, the *laissez-faire* moral of Bernard Mandeville's satire the *Fable of the Bees* discerns the dynamics of the rising modern society in its vices. His apologia of early capitalism reflects the social conditions of Great Britain after the "Glorious Revolution" of 1688, and it expresses the self-confidence of Britain's ascending bourgeoisie (Euchner 1980: 10). In his cynical analysis of bourgeois society, private vices create public benefits, and Mandeville declares the masses' poverty, misery and their daily struggle for survival to be necessary preconditions for the evolution of a prosperous society. Public welfare does not result from the virtuous social life of man, but ultimately from competitive strife, crime and war. In Mandeville's hive, the dividing lines between capitalist profit-seeking and crime are blurred beyond recognition. Based on his pronounced pessimism about human nature, Mandeville declares that evil is a driving force behind the flourishing of bourgeois society.

The "intermestic negotiations in south-eastern Europe," the "Balkan routes to state formation," or the deadly but profitable militia economies in war-torn Lebanon evoke a similar picture to Mandeville's account of early capitalism, but on a more global scale. Although embedded in the neoliberal schemes of a developed global capitalism, the political economy of contemporary intra-state war reminds us rather of the "original economic sin" which Marx discerned in the period of "primitive accumulation." Partly coinciding with Mandeville's historical background, this period was not characterized by the "idyllic" means of liberal economic appropriation such as formal property rights and contracted labor. Quite the contrary, the historical signature of this infancy of the capitalist mode of production had been drawn by conquest, enslavement, robbery and murder. Whether in the form of Spanish, Portuguese, Dutch, French and British colonialism, in the trade wars among European nations, or in the religious and civil wars that destroyed the social orders of Europe's traditional societies, physical force was the crucial means of primitive accumulation, or in the words of Karl Marx: "Force is the midwife of every old society pregnant with a new one. It is itself an economic power" (Marx 1867: 779).[2]

More recently, Charles Tilly (1990) analyzed European state formation also in the historical context of primitive accumulation. He explained this centuries-long process as a complex interplay between the accumulation and concentration of capital on the one hand, and of the means of coercion on the other. In this way, the use and control of physical force played a crucial role in the rise of modernity. Yet there was no evolutionary necessity behind the termination of primitive accumulation; and the rise of the legally based capitalist accumulation of the liberal market economy was inextricably bound to the differentiation between two distinct realms of politics and economy. Both Mandeville and Marx associated the emergence of a purely economic realm of violence-free competition with the rise of the modern state. In Mandeville's opinion, it was only the firm ordering hand of politics that was able to balance the evils of human nature and to integrate diverging interests in a stable nation-state (Euchner 1980: 45). In Marx's reading, however, the modern state was not so much a prudent and neutral organization balancing competing interests, but rather an instrument of the bourgeoisie "for the mutual guarantee of their property and interests" (Marx and Engels 1845–1846: 62).

Returning to the present, it is precisely this "traditional" logic of state formation that has been contested by recent studies on contemporary warfare. Without denying similarities between features of so-called "new wars" (Kaldor 1999) and Marx's period of primitive accumulation, Klaus Schlichte (Chapter 2) comes to the conclusion that the political economy of current intra-state war actually contradicts the traditional logic of European state formation. Contrary to Tilly's findings in "War Making and State Making as Organized Crime" (1985), in contemporary primitive accumulation the circularity of the competencies of territorial control and economic extraction does not lead to the same results as in Europe's past. To be sure, in current intra-state wars we can observe the emergence of similar kinds of protection rackets that Tilly put at the beginning of European state formation. Lebanese militias, Somali warlords, or the political entrepreneurs in the Balkans apply comparable methods of producing a threat and then charging for its reduction (cf. Tilly 1985: 171). From this perspective, current guerilla forces resemble their European predecessors in their attempts at "reaching an equilibrium between public acceptance and the fear they can instill through their ability to enforce their rules and inflict punishment" (Suárez 2000: 587). Yet does this analog relationship of threat imposition, protection and extraction eventually lead to the establishment of functioning, territorially integrated states?

According to Schlichte's analysis, there is no doubt: the internationaliz-ation of public functions and the accompanying informalization of both the political and economic structures of societies at war no longer result in the establishment of territorial states. Rather, Schlichte discerns the emer-gence of a complex "patchwork of appropriated competencies and vested interests," of various mixtures of local, "national" and international authorities that can hardly be called coherent forms of state authority. During the Lebanese war, according to Jürgen Endres's study, (Chapter 6) the authoritative functions of the Lebanese state were distributed among militia-ruled cantons, remaining national institutions, and foreign states with their respective Lebanese proxies. The 1990 Ta'if accord put an end to warfare, but it established a quasi-state deprived of the monopoly of physical force. This core institution of modern statehood so far has been in the hands of the Syrian regime. In Somalia, the various means of physical force have been entirely fragmentized and have come under the control of various local warlords. At the same time, state-related public services have been financed and distributed through international and transnational organizations. In this "glocal" structural setting, Somali warlords provide both security threats to the population and protection for foreign humani-tarian assistance that alleviates the war-inflicted plights of society. What is crucial here is that the interaction between international humanitarian aid and local warlordism has entered a vicious circle, reproducing structures of violence.

The contributions in this book all reveal a complex interplay among local, regional and international forces. In general terms, they confirm Susan Strange's contention "that state authority has leaked away, up-wards, sideways, and downwards" (Strange 1995: 56). However, while in the OECD world this "diffusion of authority away from the state" can still be associated with the substitution of military strife by economic competition, this book demonstrates that this move towards "perpetual peace" does not reflect the social reality in large parts of the world. On the contrary, the studies presented here show that the "commercialization of international relations" has also been accompanied by the resurrection of methods of primitive accumulation. Current war economies present combinations of primitive accumulation with more sophisticated modes of economic reproduction. The political economy of intra-state wars com-prises looting, pillaging and robbery at gunpoint, as well as the establishment of protection-rackets that temporarily assume state-like forms of extraction by levying tolls and taxes on the territories under their control. On the one hand, these war economies derive their revenues from a variety of local resources, for instance by monopolizing trade and production, exploiting natural resources or enforcing labor and slavery. On the other hand, war economies interrelate not only with illegal global markets, such as those involved in drugs and arms trade, but also very closely with formal international markets, and their financial means come to a substantial degree from humanitarian aid, foreign military assistance and political rents.

Alfredo Suárez, for instance, shows how the "insurrection economy" in Colombia is, with "regular expenses, coherent flows of income and systemized investments," closely tied to the formal economy. Thereby the formal and the illicit economy have established a relationship that is characterized by a combination of "predatory behavior with parasitic and symbiotic actions" (Suárez 2000: 577 and 584). The war entrepreneurs in Colombia, the former Yugoslavia, Lebanon, northern Iraq or Somalia are at the same time local, national and global economic players. In reality, the analytical distinction between formal and shadow economies is thus blurred. Given the absence of functioning governmental authority, economies under the condition of intra-state war are always shadow economies, in particular in the sense of being characterized by unrecorded economic activities (cf. Flemming *et al.* 2000). In this context, offshore financial centers provide nodal points between formal and shadow economies (Singh 2000: 105–119). Moreover, as Michael Robert Hickok's analysis shows in the example of northern Iraq in Chapter 4, international embargo policies distort regional and local economies, thereby engendering the spread of gray market activities and perpetuating them.[3]

Since September 11, 2001, we should be aware that the political economy of contemporary intra-state wars, this global mixture of peaceful trade with forceful economic appropriation of various kinds, will not remain without political repercussions in the OECD world. Economic globalization increasingly affects both the zone of peace and the zone of conflict. In particular the War on Drugs is a good example of how the decay of formerly functional socio-political institutions of OECD states becomes intertwined with the spread of armed conflicts within and between "developing states." Looked at from Hans T. van der Veen's perspective,[4] the mutually reinforcing internationalization of both anti-drug law enforcement and the drug industry becomes a cause of both the decline of Western liberal democratic institutions and the impediment of democratization in the Third World. In this context, drug trade indicates much more than only a "leading example of a global criminal network" (Duffield 1998: 72). Van der Veen in Chapter 5 presents the complex picture of a systemic relationship in which state agencies, various forms of organized crime, warlords, and individuals from the center and the periphery interact. Therefore his analysis exemplifies further that the contemporary political economy of war-making and state-making is reflected in both images of the defective state: on the one hand, in the gradual erosion of the democratic and distributive social institutions of Western welfare states and, on the other hand, in the derailed processes of state building in the Third World.

In the light of this brief summary of the major arguments in this book, there are three crucial concluding points to be made. The first one concerns the current state of the state. It seems obvious that physical force has again become an economic power, yet without any guarantee of playing the role of the "midwife" to old societies in the process of giving birth to modern democratic states. Second, to a certain extent warlords and mafia entrepreneurs epitomize this resurgence of the violent midwife, and they are a key to comprehending how the transformation from traditional political orders to legal rule has been obstructed in the context of globalization. In this setting, mafia structures seem to function as a crucial link between formal and informal sectors of global economic exchange. As in Mandeville's hive, mafia activities entirely blur the distinction between capitalist profit-seeking and crime. Mafia and warlord structures are therefore one essential factor of a political economy that is characterized by the diffusion of political authority away from the modern role model of the European nation-state.

Regarding these two aspects of the current political economy of state making, neither the lack of personal qualities of non-Western statesmen, nor the lack of time in fighting similar centuries-long wars as in the European example represent sound arguments to explain why Tilly's mechanism of war-making and state-making is difficult to apply to postcolonial state formation.[5] The answer is rather to be found in the entirely different socio-political and international context in which these new wars take place. In the same way as the public benefits of Mandeville's hive resulted from the selfish vices of its individuals, Tilly's paradox is based on the methodological assumption of viewing the rise of the democratic modern nation-state as the unintended outcome of intended social actions. This methodological paradigm also suits an explanation of the distortion between the global schemes of economic reconstruction and punishment and the local realities of the Balkans and northern Iraq. Yet Bosnia's "neoliberal clientism," northern Iraq's suspended reality or the contribution of humanitarian aid to the persistence of Somalia's structures of violence are not the result of a mismatch between the intentions and consequences of social action alone. To a high degree, these phenomena reflect a decisive change in the structural conditions under which current processes of state formation, as well as the wars related to them, are taking place.

Finally, we have to ask whether this decisive change in the relationship between war-making and state-making in a globalizing world is adequately captured by terms such as *new wars* or *intra-state wars*. It is certainly not surprising that the blurring of political authority and economic appropriation finds its equivalent in the blurring of the distinctions between war, organized crime and large-scale violations of human rights. This is due to the fact that our concepts of legitimate political authority, of formal economic exchange, and of forms of violence are essentially structured by the social institution of the modern state. More specifically, both the blurred pictures of political economy and of forms of violence are two sides of the defective state. But do these findings allow us to speak of "new" or "postmodern" wars? Is Mary Kaldor's central argument right "that, during the 1980s and 1990s, a new type of organized violence has developed" (Kaldor 1999: 1)?

At first sight, this book confirms Kaldor's analysis that current warfare has to be understood "in terms of global dislocation," as global processes that "are breaking up the cultural and socio-economic divisions that defined the patterns of politics which characterized the modern period" (Kaldor 1999: 70). Indeed, globalization has brought about a radical change in the fundamental political economy of the circularity of political control and economic extraction that once was at the heart of European state formation. However, while this new global context has a major impact on the possible results of current state formation, the war-prone nature of these processes is very much the same. To a large extent, the killing fields of Yugoslavia, Lebanon, northern Iraq, or Somalia resemble the cruel face that European state formation had shown during the period of primitive accumulation. As in the European example, in the so-called new wars we observe ongoing processes of the monopolization and feudalization of physical force, we notice the violent decay of previously functioning social orders, and we discern the emergence of particular war economies. The wars of a looming postmodern era are not so different from those of Europe's past. Bearing this in mind, the notion of new wars is somehow deceptive. It is not so much the character of current warfare itself, but the cognitive and normative categories of our perception that make the difference. What is crucial here is that these categories themselves have been molded by the formation of the modern democratic nation-state.

It is in this sense that Kaldor's differentiation between war, crime and human rights violations implicitly applies the abstract concept of modern statehood. The analysis of the political economy of intra-state wars presented here points at the ongoing centrality of the state as a concept in explaining, understanding and combating current forms of organized violence. Against a superficial reading, globalization and state formation are not an antithesis, but stand in close interaction. Whether or not it is true that the classical nation-state is a political formation in decline, in functional terms the modern state remains the analytical core element for a sound understanding of both war and peace. Downsizing the state is therefore a problem of globalization rather than a solution to its perils.

In conclusion, it is the task of contemporary peace research to examine the possibilities of peaceful interaction in an era in which national paths of political development are becoming seemingly obsolete. If we want to direct private vices and competitive strife in a way that creates benefits for a global public, we have to take seriously Mandeville's standpoint that this is only made possible by the firm ordering hand of politics. Should the old international political landscape, made up of territorially demarcated nation-states, disappear, then the future of a more peaceful world depends on new forms of political organization that can serve as functional equivalents to the nation-state. Yet these cosmopolitan schemes of global governance beyond the nation-state must comprise both the zone of peace and the zone of conflict. In order to create a prosperous global hive, we have to take the challenges of shadow globalization seriously and give up the notion of a divided world. This analysis of the political economy of intra-state war proves that the causes and impacts of current wars are not confined to the world of conflict, but that these wars take place in an emerging world society.[6] In this respect, the subtitle of this book is deceptive too: there is no such thing as intra-state war.

Notes

1 The citation is from Mandeville (1924: 36).
2 The translation is taken from the "Marx–Engels Online Library," to be found under: http://csf.colorado.edu/mirrors/marxists.org
3 For an intriguing article about this gray market linking the economies of Turkey, Iran and Iraq, see Bozarslan (1996).
4 Hans van der Veen in Chapter 5 supports the argument of Philip Cerny, who associates with globalization a process in which states lose the ability to perform key tasks on the one hand, but, on the other hand, enhance their coercive capabilities (Cerny 1999: 18–20).
5 For a brief critique of these "cheap" arguments, see Sørensen (2001: 343–345).
6 For a conceptualization of world society that is based on sociological theory, see Jung (2001).

References

Bozarslan, H. (1996) "Kurdistan: économie de guerre, économie dans la guerre," in F. Jean and J-C. Rufin (eds) *Économie des guerres civiles*, Paris: Hachette.
Cerny, P.G. (1999) "Globalization and the Erosion of Democracy," *European Journal of Political Research*, 36: 1–26.
Duffield, M. (1998) "Post-Modern Conflict: Warlords, Post-Adjustment States and Private Protection," *Civil Wars*, 1 (1): 65–102.
Euchner, W. (1980) "Versuch über Mandevilles Bienenfabel," in B. Mandeville, *Die Bienenfabel*, Frankfurt a.M.: Suhrkamp.
Flemming, M.H., Roman, J. and Farrell, G. (2000) "The Shadow Economy," *Journal of International Affairs*, 53 (2): 387–409.
Jung, D. (2001) "The Political Sociology of World Society," *European Journal of International Relations*, 7 (4): 443–474.

Kaldor, M. (1999) *New and Old Wars: Organized Violence in a Global Era*, Cambridge: Polity Press.

Mandeville, B. (1924) *The Fable of the Bees: or, Private Vices, Public Benefits*, first vol., Oxford (1957): Clarendon Press.

Marx, K. (1867) "Die sogenannte ursprüngliche Akkumulation," in K. Marx (1988) *Das Kapital. Kritik der politischen Ökonomie (Erster Band)*, Berlin: Dietz Verlag.

Marx, K. and Engels, F. (1845–46) "Die deutsche Ideologie I, Feuerbach," in K. Marx and F. Engels (1969) *Werke*, Bd 3, Berlin: Dietz Verlag.

Singh, K. (2000) *Taming Global Financial Flows*, London: Zed Books.

Sørensen, G. (2001) "War and State-Making: Why Doesn't It Work in the Third World?" *Security Dialogue*, 32 (3): 341–354.

Strange, S. (1995) "The Defective State," *Daedalus*, 124 (2): 55–74.

Suárez, A.R. (2000) "Parasites and Predators: Guerillas and the Insurrection Economy of Colombia," *Journal of International Affairs*, 53 (2): 577–601.

Tilly, C. (1985) "War Making and State Making as Organized Crime," in P. Evans, D. Rueschemeyer and T. Skocpol (eds), *Bringing the State Back In*, Cambridge: Cambridge University Press.

—— (1990) *Coercion, Capital and European States, AD 900–1900*, Cambridge: Basil Blackwell.

Index